AF600566

THE CATHOLIC UNIVERSITY OF AMERICA
CANON LAW STUDIES
NUMBER 81

THE ADMINISTRATION OF VACANT AND QUASI-VACANT DIOCESES IN THE UNITED STATES

HISTORICAL SYNOPSIS OF GENERAL LEGISLATION AND COMMENTARY

A DISSERTATION

SUBMITTED TO THE FACULTY OF CANON LAW OF THE CATHOLIC UNIVERSITY OE AMERICA IN PARTIAL FULFILLMENT OF THE REQUIREMENT FOR THE DEGREE OF DOCTOR OF CANON LAW

BY
LEO ARNOLD JAEGER, A.B., J.C.L.
Priest of the Archdiocese of Dubuque

THE CATHOLIC UNIVERSITY OF AMERICA
WASHINGTON, D. C.
1932

Nihil Obstat:

VALENTINUS T. SCHAAF, O.F.M., J.C.D.
Censor Deputatus
Washingtonii, D. C., die XVI Aprilis, 1932

Imprimatur:

FRANCISCUS J. L. BECKMAN, S.T.D.
Archiepiscopus Dubuquensis
Dubuquii, die XXIX Maii, 1932

To the

Most Reverend Francis Joseph Beckman, S.T.D.

Archbishop of Dubuque

in

Reverence and Gratitude

TABLE OF CONTENTS

PART II

The Present Discipline Governing the Administration of Vacant and Quasi-Vacant Sees in the United States

PRELIMINARY REMARKS

CHAPTER V

CHAPTER VI

PAGE

CHAPTER VII

CHAPTER VIII

CHAPTER IX

CHAPTER X

CHAPTER XI

PAGE

CHAPTER XII

CHAPTER XIII

CHAPTER XIV

FOREWORD

The purpose of this study is to present in a practical form the law of the Church with respect to the administration of vacant and quasi-vacant episcopal sees in the continental United States. This does not signify, however, that there is at present particular legislation governing the administration of such sees in this country. Since the promulgation of the present Code of Canon Law, all vacant and quasi-vacant dioceses in the Latin Church, whether these have cathedral Chapters, or whether the Chapters are supplied by the Board of Diocesan Consultors, are administered according to one and the same legal provision. This is the practical innovation enacted by the Code. Previous to the present law, the appointment of Administrators for vacant sees in the United States was governed by the particular legislation of the Second Plenary Council at Baltimore. The present Code, however, acknowledged the particular institution of the Board of Diocesan Consultors as a provision of universal law, insofar as the Board supplies the cathedral Chapter as the council of the bishop in all dioceses where the latter institution does not exist. Canon 427, furthermore, subjects the Board of Diocesan Consultors to all the legal norms which govern the cathedral Chapter with respect to the administration of a diocese, either during its occupancy, or during its vacancy or quasi-vacancy. This forms the basis for the present study. The fundamental reason, however, for limiting the scope of this treatise to the United States is to make the work more practical for the clergy of this country by applying the common law to the particular conditions now existing here.

The administration of vacant and quasi-vacant sees has ever been a matter of grave concern to the Church, especially from the fourth century onward. Canonists in the past, consequently, have gathered from scattered sources the legislation relative to this subject, and have produced more or less extensive works. These treatises applied the law with reference to the cathedral Chapter and the Vicar Capitular. Studies of this nature, however, did not appear in English with respect either to the common law of the Church, or to the particular discipline prevailing in the United States. There were, nevertheless, writings of limited scope available.

Since the promulgation of the Code canonists have done little more than propose the present law either by a periphrastic statement of the canons, or, at most, by annexing a limited commentary to the legal text. The chief reason, undoubtedly, why no extensive work has appeared thus far may be found in the fact that the systematic arrangement of the present Code has done away with many difficulties experienced by canonists in the past in determining the requirements of the law. Then, too, it might be observed that the present law has incorporated substantially former discipline into its legal provisions, thus making earlier commentaries useful in many respects. There are many instances, nevertheless, where the present law proposes wholesome changes from the former. In consequence of this fact the second part of this treatise, which forms the commentary on the present law, is the result of a comparative study and critical analysis of former and present legislation according to the norms of canonical interpretation found in the *ambitus* of the Code. The first part of the treatise comprises a historical conspectus of general legislation on the subject. Owing to the extensive proportions of this field of legal history, many details have been omitted. The salient features alone have been taken into account, and these reasonably lack a degree of perfection which is attainable only by consulting sources not available in this country. The underlying reason, however, for giving a conspectus of the general legislation is to supply the reader with a foundation which will serve as an aid to greater appreciation and understanding of the present law by presenting the stages of development and crystallization of past legislation which culminated in the dispositions of the Code.

The writer avails himself of this opportunity to express his sincere appreciation and gratitude to the members of the Faculty of Canon Law for their untiring and able assistance in the preparation of this dissertation; to the librarians of the University Library for their repeated acts of helpfulness and courtesy; and to the Reverends Francis A. Mullin and Raymond F. Murphy, for their liberal co-operation in the final preparation of this text.

PART I

HISTORICAL SYNOPSIS OF GENERAL LEGISLATION

CHAPTER I

Discipline During the First Three Centuries

In the early period of Christianity there was but one church in each episcopal city presided over by the bishop as the chief administrator of the assembly. The priests and deacons assisted the bishop not only by the performance of the particular duties attached to the individual offices received, but also, and very significantly, as the council of the bishop and the senate of the Church.[1] As time progressed, however, the ever-increasing number of faithful necessitated the dividing of the individual assemblies and the erecting of new churches.[2] The council of the bishop and the senate of the Church then included not only the priests and deacons who were attached to the episcopal church, but all within the episcopal city; these formed one administrative body with the bishop in the governance of the see.[3] The clergy who thus formed the council of the bishop are commonly known as the presbytery (*presbyterium*).[4]

Since it was the duty of the presbytery to offer counsel to the bishop in the governance of the church, it is but natural that the constant and intimate association with ecclesiastical administration broadened the experience of the clergy and deepened their knowledge with respect to the administrative functions

[1] St. Ignatius, *Epistles: to the Magnesians*, n. 6, *to the Trallians*, n. 3, *to the Ephesians*, n. 2, *to Polycarp*, n. 6—MPG, V, 667, 799, 646, 723; cf. Thomassin, *Vetus et Nova Disciplina*, I, III, c. 7, nn. 2, 4; Bouix, *De Capitulis*, p. 3; Schneider, *Die Entwicklung der Bischöflichen Domkapitel*, pp. 7, 12-18.

[2] Cf. Damasus, *Vita Sancti Marcelli*, 310—MPL, CXXVII, 1481-82; Sozomen, *Historia Ecclesiastica*, I, 6—MPG, LXVII, 871; Schneider, *op. cit.*, pp. 8-9; Baronius, *Annales Ecclesiastici*, II, 166.

[3] "Episcopus nullius causam audiat absque praesentia clericorum; alioquin irrita erit sententia episcopi, nisi clericorum praesentia firmetur";—c. 6, C. XVI, q. 7; cf. c. 7, C. XVI, q. 1; St. Ambrose, *De Officio*, II, 27—MPL, III, 139.

[4] Cf. Schneider, *op. cit.*, p. 5; Hinschius, *System des Katholischen Kirchenrechts*, II, 49-50.

annexed to the episcopal office. A natural consequence of this characteristic of the organization of the clergy was that those who, during the life-time of the bishop, participated in the administration of the church, continued in an administrative capacity and assumed the duty of ruling in the bishop's stead during his absence, or upon the death of the prelate.[5]

As early as the second century there is evidence which indicates that the presbytery administered the see during its vacancy. It so happened that Marcion, the son of the bishop of Sinope in Pontus, had fallen into grave sin and in consequence was excommunicated by his father. The unfortunate youth made several attempts to become reconciled and to be readmitted into union with the Church, but his attempts were futile because of his insincerity. Unable any longer to bear the derision of his fellow-country-men, Marcion, according to the testimony of St. Epiphanius, came to Rome after the death of Pope St. Hyginus (142) to present his cause to the presbytery of the Roman see. The presbytery, however, refused to lift the band of excommunication, since such action would have conflicted with the policy adopted by the bishop of Sinope.[6]

Although this testimony does not disclose clearly the discipline of the second century, still it demonstrates that the presbytery enjoyed, during the vacancy of the see, the power to receive the excommunicated back into the fold. In the third century, however, testimonies are more accurate and explicit in their description of the duty of the presbytery during the absence of the bishop, or after his death. It was during the strenuous days of the Decian persecution that Pope St. Fabian fell victim to the truculency of the pagans. As a consequence, the see of Rome remained vacant for nearly two years owing to the fact that the critical condition of the times caused the election of a successor to be deferred.[7] Co-

[5] Hinschius, *op. cit.*, 50; cf. Schneider, *op. cit.*, p. 18; Thomassin, *op. cit.*, I, III, c. VII, n. 13.

[6] St. Epiphanius, *Adversus Haereses, XLII,* 2—MPG, XLI, 695.

[7] ". . . post excessum nobilissimae memoriae viri Fabiani, nondum est episcopus propter rerum et temporum difficultates constitutus."—St. Cyprian, *Epistle* XXXI—MPL, IV, 312; cf. Baronius, *Annales,* III, 4-5.

incident with this circumstance, St. Cyprian, the bishop of Carthage, prudently chose to retire into voluntary exile, for to remain in Carthage during this time was to court death. Thus both sees were without a bishop. The administration of ecclesiastical affairs in both Rome and Carthage during this period of stress is aptly described in the epistles of St. Cyprian and in those of the Roman presbytery.

The Roman clergy had learnt from Crementius, a subdeacon, that the violence of the persecution in Africa had caused St. Cyprian to withdraw from Carthage. With their accustomed zeal for the faith, the Roman clergy undertook to remind the clergy of Carthage of their duty, and instructed them, furthermore, as to what action they should adopt with respect to the *lapsi* during the absence of St. Cyprian. The letter reads as follows:

> Since, moreover, it devolves upon us who appear to be placed on high, in the place of a shepherd, to keep watch over the flock; if we be found neglectful it will be said to us, as it was said to our predecessors also, who in such wise negligent had been placed in charge, that we have not sought for that which was lost, and have not corrected the wanderer. . . . We are unwilling, therefore, beloved brethren, that you should be found hirelings, but we desire you to be good shepherds, since you are aware that no slight danger threatens you if you do not exhort our brethren to stand steadfast in the faith. . . . Neither is it in words only that we exhort you to this; but you will be able to ascertain from very many who come to you from us, that, God blessing us, we both have done and still do all these things ourselves with all anxiety and worldly risk. . . . You see, then, brethren, that you also ought to do the like, so that even those who have fallen may amend their minds by your exhortation; and if they should be seized once more, may confess, and may so make amends for their previous sin. And there are other matters which are incumbent on you, which also we have here added, as that if any who may have fallen into this temptation begin to be taken with sickness, and repent of what they have done, and desire communion, it should in any wise be granted them. Or if you have widows or

> bedridden people who are unable to maintain themselves, or those who are in prisons or are excluded from their own dwellings, these ought in all cases to have some to minister to them. Moreover, catechumens who are seized with sickness ought not to be deceived, but help is to be afforded them. And, as matter of greatest importance, if the bodies of the martyrs and others be not buried, a considerable risk is incurred by those whose duty it is to do this office. By whomsoever of you, then, and on whatever occasion this duty may have been performed, we are sure that he is regarded as a good servant . . . [8]

The presbytery of the Roman church wrote a letter to St. Cyprian giving further testimony as to their conduct during the vacancy of the see.

> In respect, however, of Privatus of Lambesa, you have acted as you usually do, in desiring to inform us of the matter, as being an object of anxiety; for it becomes us all to watch for the body of the whole Church, whose members are scattered through every various province. But the deceitfulness of that crafty man could not be hid from us even before we had your letters; for previously, when from the company of that very wickedness a certain Futurus came, a standard-bearer of Privatus, and was desirous of fraudulently obtaining letter from us, we were neither ignorant who he was, nor did he get the letters which he wanted.[9]

While in exile St. Cyprian wrote the following to the presbytery of Carthage:

> . . . and as the condition of the place does not permit me to be with you now, I beg you, by your faith and your religion, to discharge there both your own office and mine, that there may be nothing wanting either to discipline or diligence. In respect of means, moreover, for meeting the expenses, whether for those who, having confessed their Lord with a glorious voice, have been put in prison, or for

[8] St. Cyprian, *Epistle* II, § 1—*Ante-Nicene Fathers,* V. p. 280; cf. MPL, IV, 224.

[9] St. Cyprian, *Epistle, XXX,* n. 4—MPL, IV, 506-7; translation taken from *Ante-Nicene Fathers,* V, 308.

> those who are labouring in poverty and want, and still stand fast in the Lord, I entreat that nothing be wanting, since the whole of the small sum which was collected there was distributed among the clergy for cases of that kind, that many might have means whence they could assist the necessities and burthens of individuals. I beg also that there may be no lack, on your parts, of wisdom and carefulness to preserve peace. . .[10]

Another letter of St. Cyprian to the presbytery of Carthage states:

> Relying, therefore, upon your love and your piety, which I have abundantly known, in this letter I both exhort and command you, that those of you whose presence there is least suspicious and least perilous, should in my stead discharge my duty in respect of doing those things which are required for the religious administration. In the meantime let the poor be taken care of as much and as well as possible; but especially those who have stood with unshaken faith and have not forsaken Christ's flock, that, by your diligence, means be supplied to them to enable them to bear their poverty, so that what the troublous time has not affected in respect of their faith, may not be accomplished by want in respect of their affections. Let a more earnest care, moreover, be bestowed upon the glorious confessors. And, although I know that very many of those have been maintained by the vow and by the love of the brethren, yet if there be any who are in want either of clothing or maintenance, let them be supplied with whatever things are necessary, as I formerly wrote to you ,while they were still kept in prison—only let them know from you and be instructed, and learn what, according to the authority of Scripture, the discipline of the Church requires of them, that they ought to be humble and modest and peaceable. . . [12]

These testimonies accurately depict an image of the ancient discipline of the Church before the fourth century with respect

[10] St. Cyprian, *Epistle,* IV, n. 1—MPL, IV, 230; translation, *op. cit.,* V, 282.

[11] St. Cyprian, *Epistle,* V, n. 2—MPL, IV, 232; translations, *loc. cit.*

to the administration of vacant sees, as well as of those sees which were deprived of the presence of the bishop, as in the case of St. Cyprian. It is evident from the letters that the Roman presbytery realized that theirs was the office of the deceased Pontiff, and that duty made it incumbent upon them to fulfill all obligations with care and diligence, not only over the see of Rome, but over the universal Church. They admonished the presbytery of Carthage as to their office and the necessity of performing all duties conscientiously. Their relations with the *lapsi,* as expressed in the epistles, clearly shows that the presbyteries enjoyed the power of removing ecclesiastical penalties.

The presbytery of Carthage likewise administered the see during the absence of St. Cyprian in such a fashion that they took the place of the bishop, and were exhorted to fulfill all duties with care and diligence. In a word, the presbyteries of both Rome and Carthage appear to have exercised administrative power in spiritual as well as temporal affairs. It may also be observed that nowhere in the epistles is reference made to any particular individual whose duty it was to exercise administration, but all matters were left to the charge of all the members of the presbytery.[13]

The available testimonies of the first three centuries disclose the discipline of the western Church only. The absence of evidence for the East, however, is not a decided disadvantage in determining the nature of the discipline existing there. Later testimonies, especially the letter of St. Cyril of Alexandria which he wrote to his priests and deacons during his absence from Alexandria while attending the Council of Ephesus,[14] are indicative of the fact that the same practice of administering vacant sees prevailed in both the East and the West. Thomassin[15] draws this conclusion from the evidence found in the letter written by the Fathers of the Council

[13] Cf. Thomassin, *Vetus et Nova,* I, III, c. 7, nn. 13-14; Schneider, *op. cit.,* pp. 18-19; Hinschius, *op. cit.,* II, 228; Maroto, *Institutiones,* I, n. 759.

[14] *Council of Ephesus,* act. I—Mansi, IV, 1243; cf. Schneider, *op. cit.,* p. 18.

[15] *Op. cit.,* I, III, c. 7, n. 14.

of Ephesus to the priests, economes and other clerics of Constantinople after the deposition of Nestorius, and the author maintains that the entire administration of the Church, both in spiritual and temporal affairs, was under the charge of the clergy.[16]

It is interesting to observe also that the presbytery, during the time they administered the vacant see, refrained from transacting certain negotiations of graver import; these matters they left for the consideration of the new incumbent to the episcopal throne.[17] This principle—"sede vacante nihil innovetur"—was later adopted as the universal law of the Church by the Decretals, and subsequently incorporated in the present Code of Canon Law.[18]

16 "Cognoscat reverentia vestra, blasphemum Nestorium propter impias suas praedicationes et contra ecclesiasticos canones contumaciam, hesterno die, qui fuit praesentis mensis Junii vigesimus secundus, a sancta synodo juxta ecclesiasticas sanctiones depositum et ab omni ecclesiastico gradu amotum fuisse. Proinde omnia, quae ad ecclesiam pertiment custodite, ut et rationem illi reddituri, qui Dei voluntate, piissimorumque imperatorum nostrorum nutu, ordinandus est Constantinopolitanae ecclesiae episcopus."—*Epistle from the Council of Ephesus to the Clergy of Constantinople*—Hardouin, I, 1434; cf. Mansi, IV, 1303.

17 "... ante constitutionem episcopi *nihil innovandum* putavimus sed lapsorum curam mediocriter temperandam esse credimus; ut interius, dum episcopus dari a Deo nobis sutinetur, in suspenso eorum qui moras possunt dilationis sustinere causa teneatur, eorum autem vitae suae finem urgens exitus dilationem non potest ferre."—St. Cyprian, *Epistle*, XXXI, n. 8—MPL, IV, 314-315.

18 Tit. IX, lib. III, Decretalium; Canon 436.

CHAPTER II

Discipline from the Fourth to the Thirteenth Century

Art. 1. *Fourth to the Eighth Century*

The presbyterial administration during the first three centuries of the Church adequately safeguarded the spiritual and temporal welfare of vacant episcopal sees. In the fourth and subsequent centuries, however, the Church in many regions was obliged to contend with, and counter-act many difficulties which arose and which proved detrimental to the interests of vacant sees in particular. The presbytery as such, however, was soon felt to be too unwieldy a governing body to cope with the distressing conditions,[1] and in consequence various sections of the Western Church sought for a method of administering vacant sees which would be more adaptable in checking the abuses and in protecting the interests, both spiritual and temporal, of the sees.

Among the several basic causes which motivated a departure from the former discipline, of particular significance was the attitude frequently adopted by the clergy, and even the laity, when a see became vacant. The legislation which was enacted by many councils[2] indicates that the clergy were wont often to

[1] Hinschius, *System des Katholischen Kirchenrechts,* II, 228; Wernz-Vidal, *Jus Canonicum,* II, n. 708.

[2] "Non licere Clericis post obitum sui episcopi res ad eum pertinentes diripere, sicut antiquis quoque est canonibus constitutum. Quod si hoc facere tentaverint, graduum suorum periculo subjacebunt."—Council of Chalcedon (451) can. XXII—Mansi, VI, 1229; cf. c. 43, C. XII, q. 2; "Si qua de rebus ecclesiae cum Episcopus non est, presbyteri vendiderint, placuit rescisson contractu ad jus ecclesiasticum revocari. In judicio autem erit Episcopi constitutum, si pretium debeat recipi, necne: propterea quod saepe contingit distractarum rerum reditus ampliorem summam pro accepto pretio reddi."—Council of Ancyre (314), can. XV—*Ibid.*, II, 532; cf. Council of Rheims (630), can. XVI—*op. cit.,* X, 596; Apostolic Canons XL—*op. cit.,* I, 55; c. 5, D. LXXX; Council of Valence (524), can. II-III—*Ibid.*, VII, 620-22; Council of Grangres (circa 324), can. VI, VIII—*op. cit.,* II, 1106-7; Council of Antioch (341), can. XXIV-XXV—c. 5, C. X, q. 1, c. 23, C. XII, q. 1.

plunder and even sell the possessions of a deceased bishop and of the vacant see as well. Heresies and schisms sprang up in the Church, placing the welfare of vacant sees in precarious circumstances, while the barbaric invasions caused frequent and prolonged periods of vacancy.[3]

§ 1. The Discipline in the Western Church

The African Church digressed from its former discipline during the fourth century. The chief reason for a change in practice was the violence which the Donatists displayed during this time. These heretics directed their efforts to gain possession of the vacant sees by electing one of their own as its bishop, and if it was foreseen that their aims would not be realized, they employed drastic measures to prevent the election of a Catholic bishop. Their activities effected such momentous consequences that at the beginning of the fifth century forty Catholic dioceses were without bishops[4] The African Church counteracted these difficulties by authorizing the metropolitan[5] to commission Interventors (*Interventores*), or, as they were sometimes called, Intercessors (*Intercessores*), to take charge of a vacant see.[6]

St. Augustine appears to be among the first to employ this means of providing for vacant sees,[7] and after his time the practice became general. According to the council of Marciana, which was held in 419,[8] it was the duty of the Interventor

[3] Cf. Victor of Utice, *De Persecutione Vandalorum*, II, 8—MPL, LVIII, 209.

[4] Cf. St. Augustine, *Breviculus, primae diei*, c. 14—MPL, XLIII, 620; Bingham, *Antiquities of the Christian Church*, bk. II, chap. XI, sec. 3; Hefele, *Conciliengeschichte*, I, 632-33; Brueck, *History of the Catholic Church*, I, 160-61.

[5] In Africa the office of metropolitan was held by the senior bishop. Cf. Bingham, *op. cit.*, bk. I, chap. XVI, sec. 4.

[6] Cf. Du Cange, *Glossarium*, v. *Interventores*, III, 1500; idem, *op. cit.*, v. *Intercessores*, III, 1483; Bingham, *op. cit.*, bk. IV, chap. II, sec. 7.

[7] ". . . ne schema fieret, quoque modo velle sopire, dedisse quemdam interventorem populo suae communionis apud Carthaginem constituto . . . " —St. Augustine, *Epistle*, XLIV, c. VIII, n. 8—MPL, XXXIII, 177; cf. Du Cange, *op. cit.*, III, 1500; Thomassin, *Vetus et Nova*, III, II, LI, n. 2.

[8] "Ut interventores episcopi conveniant plebes, quae episcopum non habent,

to procure the election of a new bishop, and if he neglected to accomplish the purpose of his appointment he was to be removed, and the see was to be left without a bishop until the people would come to reason and plead for a bishop. Since the election of a bishop was dependent upon the common choice of both the clergy and the laity,[9] it appears that the Interventors, while promoting the election of a worthy candidate, were often obliged to subdue dissensions which the Donatists had frequently caused by their strategies; in this they sometimes failed.

It seems that the Interventors soon began to take liberties and use their office as means to ingratiate themselves with the faithful and to promote their own cause rather than that of the Church. This they may have accomplished by keeping the see vacant longer than necessary, or, if the see were better than their own, by getting themselves elected to it. The abuse, however, was not long lived, for the Fifth Council of Carthage enacted legislation whereby an Interventor was ineligible for the see over which he presided and was to be given one year to bring about a successful election, and this under penalty of removal.[10]

Authors[11] conclude from the legislation of these councils that the Interventors in Africa were given the primary duty of procuring a canonical election of a successor to the see, and that during the time required for this, they were assisted by the presbytery in keeping disorders in check, in preserving peace and in safe-guarding the interests of the Church. The presbyteries, consequently, were not entirely excluded from participation in the duty of administering the vacant sees.[12]

ut episcopum accipiant. Quod si accipere neglexerint, remoto interventore, sic remaneant, quamdiu sibi episcopum quaerant."—Council of Marciana, can. un.—Mansi, IV, 439.

[9] Cf. Bingham, *op. cit.*, bk. IV, chap. II, sec. 7, 12, 14.

[10] V Council of Carthage (438), can. VIII—Mansi, III, 970; cf. c. 22, C. VII, q. 1; this canon is found in the Code of the African Church, 401—Hefele, *Conciliengeschichte*, II, 83.

[11] Hinschius, *op. cit.*, II, 229; Hermes, *De Capitulo sede vacante et impedita*, pp. 12-13; Zallwein, *Principia Juris Ecclesiasticae*, IV, 366.

[12] Cf. Maroto, *Institutiones*, II, n. 759.

It is the opinion of Hefele[13] that the Interventors were bishops who lived in the nearest neighboring sees. This appears convincing, since the function of the Interventor in Africa was relatively as limited as those duties attached to similar offices held by nearest neighboring bishops in other regions of the western Church.[13a]

The discipline prevailing on the continent of Europe during these centuries was very much akin to that of Africa. This similarity, however, which existed between the office of the Interventor and that of the Administrators in Europe, commonly known as Visitators,[14] did not amount to an identity of practice, nor did the Visitators of the various sections of Europe, such as France, Spain and Italy, at all times enjoy the same prerogatives and administrative powers. In France, for instance, Pope John II in the year 534 commanded archbishop Caesarius of Arles to appoint a Visitator to the see of Riez which was made vacant by the dethronement of Bishop Contumeliosus [15]; and this Visitator was given full administrative power, excepting that of ordaining clerics.[16]

The administrative powers of the Visitator of Arles bears a striking contrast to the function of the office of Visitators in France, especially after the middle of the fifth century. In 439 the bishops of south-eastern Gaul convened in synod at Riez and enacted legislation governing the administration of vacant sees. It was provided that in order to prevent uncanonical ordinations for the future, the bishop from the nearest diocese, and no other, shall be allowed to go into the

[13] *Op. cit.*, II, 83; cf. Thomassin, *op. cit.*, III, II, c. 51, n. 11.

[13a] Cf. Council of Riez (439), can. VI-VII—Mansi, V, 1093-94; Council of Lerida (524), can. XVI—*ibid.*, VIII, 614-615; c. 38, C. XII, q. 2.

[14] Cf. Du Cange, *op. cit.*, v. *Visitator*, VI, 1650-51; *Dictionary of Christian Antiquities*, 2009.

[15] "In cuius locum visitatorem constituite . . . "—Pope John II, *Epistle to Caesarius of Arles*—Mansi, VIII, 809.

[16] ". . . sed ne eius ecclesia destituta videatur, in ejus loco visitatorem dari, praesenti auctoritate decernimus, cui a se ita noverit omnis exhibenda, ut nihil de ordinibus clericorum, nihil de ecclesiastica facultate praesumat, sed ea quae ad sacrosancta mysteria pertinent, exequatur."—Pope John II, *Epistle to the Gallican bishops*—Mansi, VIII, 807; cf. Baronius, *Annales*, IX, 456; Hefele, *op. cit.*, II, 752-55; Hinschius, *op. cit.*, II, 229.

episcopal city after the death of a bishop, and his shall be the duty to superintend the burial and to guard against irregularities. After seven days he, too, must leave the city again, and no bishop is again to enter it, except at the command of the metropolitan.[17] The council at Orleans in 533 [18] ordered that the nearest neighboring bishop who acted as Visitator shall assemble the priests of the vacant see and immediately take an inventory (*descripta*) of the bishop's residence (*domus ecclesiae*). This accomplished, he was to place these temporalities into the custody of fit persons.

The office of the Visitator in France, therefore, was of brief duration. It was held in each case by the nearest neighboring bishop, who acted under the supervision of the metropolitan.[19] It appears evident that since the Visitator functioned for such a limited period of time, the greater part of the administrative governance of the see was left to the presbyteries.[20]

The discipline of the Iberian peninsula differs little from that of France. This is evident from the fact that the council of Valence, when formulating its legislation with respect to the office of the Administrator, makes explicit reference to the legislation enacted by the council of Riez.[21] The nearest neighboring bishop who served in the capacity of a Visitator was obliged to perform the same duties as was demanded of the Visitator in France, with the added provision that the clergy, under his supervision, were to take an inventory of all the temporalities within eight days from the time of the death of the bishop, and a memorandum of this inventory

[17] Council of Riez, can. VI-VII—Mansi, V, 1093-94; cf. Thomassin, *op. cit.*, II, II, c. 3, n. 6.

[18] Can. VI—Mansi, VIII, 836.

[19] Thomassin, *op. cit.*, II, II, c. 3, n. 6; cf. *Dictionary of Christian Antiquities*, 2023.

[20] Cf. Thomassin, *op. cit.*, II, III, c. 11, n. 9; Gregory of Tours, *Histor. Franc.*, lib. IV, c. 5—MPL, LXXI, 273; V Council of Paris (615), can. VII—Mansi, X, 541; II Council of Orleans (533), can. VI—Mansi, VIII, 836.

[21] "... Quod ut confidentius, justitia manente, servetur, secundum Regensis synodi constituto, episcopo a corpore recedente, vicinior illi accedat episcopus, qui ex more exequiis celebratis, statim ecclesiae ipsius curam districtissime gerat ..."—Council of Valence (524), can. II—Mansi, VIII, 621.

was to be forwarded to the metropolitan, who was then obliged to appoint a capable cleric to act as the procurator for the see.[22] It is interesting to observe that the Administrator in Spain was sometimes termed the *Commendator,* since, according to the council of Valence,[23] he was expressly requested to "commend" prayers to God for the departed soul of his fellow bishop. Hence both in France and in Spain the Administrators dealt principally with the task of caring for the temporal affairs of the deceased bishop and of the vacant see, thus leaving the presbytery to exercise the provisional governance of the see until a new bishop was elected.[24]

The Roman Pontiffs, as early as the fifth century, appointed Visitators to take charge of vacant sees. This is evident from the writings of Popes St. Gelasius,[25] John II,[26] St. Agapetus I,[27] and especially St. Gregory the Great.[28] The latter Pontiff made the office of the Visitator extremely popular, although the Visitators appointed by him functioned chiefly in the provinces of Italy and Sicily.[29]

St. Gregory commissioned Visitators to take charge not only of those sees made vacant by the death of the bishop, but also of those which were without episcopal supervision because the bishop was unable to perform the function of his office because of some impediment, such as ill-health and infirmity,[30]

[22] Council of Valence, *loc. cit.*; cf. council of Lerida (524), can. XVI—Mansi, VIII, 614-15; c. 38, C. XII, q. 2.

[23] Can. IV—Mansi, VIII, 622; cf. Thomassin, *op. cit.*, II, III, c. 9, n. 9.

[24] Cf. Maroto, *op. cit.*, II, n. 759.

[25] *Epistle to Bishop Celestine*—c. 3, D. XXIV.

[26] *Epistle to the Gallican bishops*—Mansi, VIII, 807; *to Caesarius of Arles*—*op. cit.*, 809.

[27] *Epistle to Caesarius of Arles*—Mansi, VIII, 856-7.

[28] St. Gregory, *bk.* II, *epist.* XXXVII—MPL, LXXVII, 575; *bk.* II, *epist.* L—*op. cit.*, 645-46; *bk.* III, *epist.* XXIV—*op. cit.*, 622-23; *bk.* VI, *epist.* XLI—*op. cit.*, 830.

[29] "Dagegen beziehen sich die von Gelasius I. und vor allem zahlreich von Gregor I. vorgenommenen Deputirungen nur auf italienische and sicilianische Bisthumer."—Hinschius, *op. cit.*, II, 229; cf. Phillips, *Kirchenrecht,* V, 429; Alteserra, *Opera Omnia,* IX, 58.

[30] St. Gregory, *bk.* III, *epist.* XXIV—MPL, LXXVII, 622-23; cf. c. 14, C. VII, q. 1.

imprisonment by the enemy,[31] or when a bishop had gone into solitude to perform penance.[32] The Visitators in these instances did not enjoy equal administrative power, for it appears that in each case their duties and obligation were outlined in the apostolic letters of appointment.

The appointment of Visitators for vacant sees was of greater frequency than the appointments just referred to. The epistles of Pope St. Gregory clearly demonstrate the Visitators, who were ordinarily the neighboring bishops, and who were commissioned to administer vacant sees, were given, as a general rule, the duty to keep the temporalities of the see intact, to move the clergy and the people to hold a speedy and economical election of new bishops, to direct the elections, to see to it that the clergy fulfilled their offices conscientiously, to exercise special vigilance over monasteries within the confines of the see, and, in a word, to take charge of the entire administration of the bishopric.[33] So also were the clergy and the faithful requested to extend to the Visitators the same obedience and respect which they gave their own bishops.[34]

Some authors [35] falsely concluded that the Visitators ap-

[31] St. Gregory, *bk.* II, *epist.* XXXVII—MPL, LXXVII, 575; cf. c. 42, C. VII, q. 1.

[32] St. Gregory, *bk.* III, *epist.* L—MPL, LXXVII, 645-46; *bk.* VI, *epist.* XLI—*op. cit.*, 830.

[33] "Quoniam Fuscus Capuanae ecclesiae episcopus, hic positus de hac luce migravit, cura nobis fuit destitutae ecclesiae visitationem fratri et coepiscopo nostro Gaudentio Nolanae civitatis episcopo solemniter delegare: cui dedimus in mandatis, ut nihil de provectionibus Clericorum, reditu, ornatu ministeriisque a quoquam usurpari patiatur. Cujus vos assiduis adhortationibus convenit obedire: persistere, moresque vestros sub digna ecclesiastici regiminis disciplina componere. Nec quisquam vestrum ejus audeat praeceptionibus obviare, sed omni tam ecclesiastica observatione, quam etiam ecclesiae vestrae custodia, ejus provisionibus obedientiam exhibere, quatenus dum ejus regimini vestra fuerit obedientia commodata, et ecclesiae vestrae in nullo negligatur utilitas, et ejus sit cura propensior."—St. Gregory, *bk.* V, *epist.* XIV —MPL, LXXVII, 734; cf. *bk.* XIII, *epist.* XIII—*op. cit.*, 1268; *bk.* V, *epist.* XIII—*op. cit.*, 734; et al.

[34] Cf. St. Gregory, *bk.* III, *epist.* XXV—MPL, LXXVII, 623.

[35] "Wenn in frueherer Zeit eine Dioecese durch den Tod oder die Absetzung ihres Oberhirten erledigt worden war und die Wiederbesetzung derselben nicht sogleich bewerkstelligt werden konnte, so war es gebraeuchlich sie

pointed by St. Gregory ordinarily enjoyed the faculty of ordaining clerics. It is true that some were permitted to do so,[36] but it is clear from the epistles of St. Gregory that this faculty to ordain demanded a special mandate to that effect, and that such was given only when extraordinary circumstances necessitated such action.[37]

It is not evident from the epistles of Pope St. Gregory whether the Visitators were always remunerated for the services rendered to the vacant sees. There are, however, several instances recorded where the Visitators were expressly authorized to receive some remuneration, if not a salary, to defray the expenses incurred by them.[38]

Such, then, was the discipline governing the administration of vacant episcopal sees during the fifth and sixth centuries in the provinces of Italy and Sicily. For the most part it appears that the presbyteries were excluded from direct participation in the administrative government, although in some cases, especially when the faculties of the Visitator were very

durch den Bischof einer anderen Kirche verwalten zu lassen. Ein solcher hiess dann Episcopus Visitator; er hatte sich eifrig der Dioecese anzunehmen, *durfte Cleriker fuer dieselbe ordiniren* und hatte insbesondere dafuer zu sorgen, dass die Wahl des neuen Bischofs moeglichst bald und in gehoeriger Ordnung vollzogen wurde."—Phillips, *Kirchenrecht,* V, 458; "Ejusdem Visitatores erat clericos ordinare . . . ex eisdem Gregorii I epistolis."—Alteserra, *op. cit.,* IX, 59.

[36] Cf. St. Gregory, *bk.* I, *epist.* XV—MPL, LXXVII, 460-61; *bk.* III, *epist.* XXIV—*op. cit.,* 622-23; *bk.* III, *epist.* XXV—*op. cit.,* 623; *bk.* V, *epist.* XLIV—*op. cit.,* 774-75; c. 5, C. XXI, q. 1.

[37] "Pervenit ad nos quod Populensis ecclesia ita sit Sacerdotis officio destituta, ut nec poenitentia decedentibus ibidem, nec baptisma possit praestari infantibus. Hujus igitar tam piae rei tamque necessariae mole permoti, jubemus dilectioni tuae, ut hujus praeceptionis auctoritate commonitus, memoratae Ecclesiae Visitator accedas, ut unum Cardinalem illic presbyterum et duos debeas diacones ordinare. In parochiis vero praefatae ecclesiae tres similiter presbyteros: quos tamen dignos ad tale officium veneratione vitae et morum gravitate praevideris et quibus in nullo obvient constituta canonicae disciplinae, ut sanctae cum digna cautela provideatur ecclesiae."—St. Gregory, *bk.* I, *epist.* XV—MPL, LXXVII, 460-61; cf. *bk.* I, *epist.* LXXVIII—*op. cit.,* 531-32; *bk.* III, *epist.* LXIV—*op. cit.,* 661-62.

[38] St. Gregory, *bk.* III, *epist.* XXXV—MPL, LXXVII, 631-32; *bk.* V, *epist.* XII—*op. cit.,* 753; cf. Thomassin, *op. cit.,* II, III, c. 10, n. 3.

limited,[39] it can rightly be presumed that the presbyteries enjoyed a good part of the spiritual administration. Hinschius writes with great truth, however,[40] when stating that the administration by the presbytery became less popular in proportion to the increasing number of disorders that arose. These disorders were present even in Merovingian times, when the encroachments of the kings in assuming the right to fill vacant sees resulted in the hindering of orderly government during vacancy. Then, too, it must be remembered that during these belligerent ages of the Merovingians, the expense of maintaining an army and of carrying on incessant excursions, often drained the royal treasury. The all-powerful mayors of the royal palace, when confronted by this crisis, upon repeated occasions found confiscation of diocesan and monastic wealth a convenient means of re-imbursing their deflated coffers.[41]

§ 2. Oriental Discipline

It has been previously observed that the governance of vacant episcopal sees in the Eastern Church during the first three centuries was under the control of the presbytery. During the fourth century, however, a practice arose in some sections whereby the problem of administering vacant sees was entirely evaded. Epiphanius [42] states that no delay was made in electing a successor to a deceased bishop, but that one was presently chosen in order to avoid any possible discord among the factions who participated in the election. Liberatus [43] describes the custom which prevailed in Alexandria. The successor of the deceased bishop, the writer narrates, held a vigil over the body of his predecessor, placing his right hand upon the head of the corpse. Then, after burying

[39] Cf. John the Deacon, *Vita Sancti Gregorii*, lib. III, c. 22—MPL, LXXV, 143.

[40] *System*, II, 231.

[41] Funk, *Lehrbuch der Kirchengeschichte*, I, 399-400; Schneider, *Die Entwicklung der Bischoflichen Domkapitel*, p. 53.

[42] *Ad Haereses*, LXIX, n. 11—MPG, XLII, 220.

[43] *Breviarium*, c. 20—MPL, LXVIII, 1036.

him with his own hands, he placed upon his own shoulders the pallium of St. Mark.[44] Proclus, the bishop of Constantinople, according to the testimony of Socrates,[45] was consecrated and installed at the command of Theodosius, the emperor, before Maximian, the former bishop, was buried. The same writer mentions also that St. Cyril of Alexandria was in possession of the see before three days had elapsed after the death of Theophilus.[46] This custom, apparently, eliminated much disorder and abuse, yet the testimonies as such would not warrant the conclusion that this was more than a local and ephemeral practice.

In the beginning of the fifth century the Church in the East experienced also the distressing abuses perpetrated by the plunderers of ecclesiastical property during the vacancy of the sees.[47] The Fourth Council at Chalcedon, however, took action to eradicate these ills by formulating legislation which effected the governance of the sees when vacancies arose. The metropolitans under whose direction vacant sees were placed[48] were obliged, under pain of ecclesiastical penalty, to consecrate the succeeding bishop within three months from the time the see became vacant.[49] This was the first step taken to prevent long period of vacancy. The same council decreed, furthermore, that the cleric, known as the Econome (*oeconomus*),[50] who had charge of the temporalities of the see during its occupancy, should continue to administer the same when the see became vacant, and until the new bishop assumed possession of the see.[51]

44 Eusebius cites the tradition that St. Mark founded the Church in Alexandria: *Historia Ecclesiastica,* II, 16—MPG, XX, 174.

45 *Historia Ecclesiastica, lib.* VII, c. 40—MPG, LXVII, 830.

46 *Op. cit.,* lib. VII, c. 7—MPG, LXVII, 749.

47 Cf. IV Council of Chalcedon, can. XXII—Mansi, VI, 1229; cf. c. 43, C. XII, q. 2.

48 Thomassin, *op. cit.,* II, II, c. 9, n. 8; ibidem, *op. cit.,* III, II, c. 51, n. 11.

49 IV Council of Chalcedon (451), can. XXV—*Mansi,* VI, 1230; cf. c. 2, D. LXXV.

50 Canon XXVI of this council placed the demand upon every bishop to appoint such an official:—Mansi, VI, 1230; cf. c. 21, C. XVI, q. 7; Schneider, *op. cit.,* p. 51.

51 IV Council of Chalcedon, can. XXV—*loc. cit.*

The discipline in the Eastern Church, therefore, differed greatly from that of the Western after the fifth century, insofar as the office of the Interventor, or Visitator, had never been adopted.[52] The legal enactments of the council at Chalcedon did not represent a radical innovation, however, in the practice of the Eastern Church, for St. John Chrysostom, in the beginning of the same century, intimates in a letter to Pope Innocent I,[53] that the archdeacon of the cathedral Church generally took charge of the administration of the temporal affairs of the Church when the see became vacant. However, the decree of the council at Chalcedon had placed the norm for the discipline, which became imperative and general in the Eastern Church.

Art. 2. *Eighth to the Thirteenth Century*

Thus far it has been observed that the presbytery administered vacant episcopal sees during the first three centuries. After that time the administrative power of the presbytery was either wholly or in part supplied by the services of Interventors, Visitators and Commendators because of the difficulties of the times. The office of the Visitator in Italy, insofar as it quite frequently encompassed all administrative power in both spiritual and temporal affairs, had reached a significantly high point of development during the reign of Pope St. Gregory the Great. During the period extending from the eighth to the thirteenth century, however, the office of the Visitator declined, and in proportion to this decline, the basis of the discipline found in the Decretals gradually took formation.[54] The decline of the office of the Visitator, however, did not consist in an immediate cessation of the practice of appointing these ecclesiastics as administrators of vacant sees, for there is evidence to the effect that Visitators were commissioned as late as the eleventh century; although throughout this time the appointments became less and less frequent. The

[52] Cf. Thomassin, *op. cit.*, III, II, c. 51, n. 9.

[53] Baronius, *Annales*, VI, 407; cf. Thomassin, *op. cit.*, III, II, c. 51, n. 11.

[54] Wernz, *Jus Decretalium,* II, n. 795; cf. Thomassin, *op. cit.*, I, III, c. 9; Maroto, *Institutiones Juris Canonici,* II, n. 758.

decline in question is evidenced, rather, by a decided limitation of the powers attached to this office.

The principal cause which contributed to the subsequent relinquishment of the office of the Visitator as the ordinary, or generally adopted, practice of administering vacant sees, is found in the development and eventually accepted institution of community life among the diocesan clergy in the Cathedral Chapters. As early as the fifth century the clergy of the episcopal city lived in community with the bishop. St. Ambrose [55] writes that community life among secular clergy was introduced into the Western Church by St. Eusebius of Vercelli in the fourth century. St. Augustine was attracted by this method of clerical life, and having established it in his own episcopal city, promoted by his example this practice in other African sees.[56] The practice of common life of the clergy of the episcopal city gradually spread in Italy, Spain, Gaul and Britain.[57]

About the middle of the eighth century, however, St. Chrodegang, bishop of Metz (766), established greater uniformity in this type of clerical life and added new impetus to its general spread, especially in the Frankish kingdom.[58] The Saint, following the example of St. Augustine, assembled his cathedral clergy in a common dwelling and subjected them to rules and ascetic norms accommodated from the rule of St. Benedict.[59] The clergy remained under the supervision of

[55] *Epistle* LXIII, n. 66—MPL, XVI, 1207.

[56] Cf. St. Augustine, *Confessions,* VIII, c. VI, n. 15—MPL, XXXII, 755; Possidius, *Vita Sancti Augustini,* c. V, XI—MPL, XXXII, 37, 42; St. Augustine, *Sermon,* n. 353, c. IV—MPL, XXXIX, 1572-73; idem, *De Moribus Eccl. Cathol.,* I, c. XXXI, n. 67— MPL, XXXII, 1338; Thomassin, *Vetus et Nova,* I, III, c. 4, nn. 1-2; Theiner, *Histoire des Institutions d'Education Ecclésiastique,* p. 107.

[57] Cf. II Council of Toledo (531), can. I—Mansi, VIII, 785; cf. c. 5, D. XXVIII; IV Council of Toledo (633), can. XXIII—*op. cit.,* X, 628, cf. c. 1, C. XII, q. 1; Council of Auvergne (541), can. XV—*op. cit.,* VIII, 862; III Council of Orleans (538), can. XI—*op. cit.,* IX, 15, Venerable Bede, *Histor. Eccl. Gent. Engl.,* lib. I, c. XXVII—MPL, XCV, 562; Flodoard; *Hist. Rhem.,* lib. IV, c. XI—MPL, CXXXV, 113-15; Thomassin, *op. cit.,* I, III, c. 8; Hinschius, *op. cit.,* II, 231; Schneider, *op. cit.,* pp. 24-29.

[58] Cf. Schneider, *op. cit.,* pp. 30-41.

[59] Cf. *Regulae Chrodegangi*—Mansi, XIV, 313; Schneider, *loc. cit.*

the bishop, were distinct from the regulars, and were known as Canons.[60] The Frankish kings, Pepin and Charlemagne, took an active interest in the establishment and spread of community life, even to the extent that a general admonition was given that all ecclesiastics should be either regulars or canons.[61] Many councils, especially the one held at Aix-la-Chapelle (817),[62] imposed the same discipline on the clergy of other churches, but these formed distinct groups from the cathedral clergy, and became the collegiate chapters.[63] The practice had spread rapidly throughout the Frankish kingdom, Germany and Italy, and in the beginning of the tenth and eleventh centuries, community life of the cathedral clergy was adopted in very many churches.[64] It was this institution of the church, therefore, which grew more and more influential in the administration of vacant episcopal sees, gradually supplying entirely the office of the Visitator.

In the ninth and subsequent centuries, however, there are evidences of Visitators who were appointed by the Roman Pontiffs,[65] but the evidence is clear in the fact that these appointments were made only in particular cases, e.g., when a diocese had been vacant for an extraordinary long time, or when a bishop for reason of ill health, etc., was hindered from

[60] Cf. Council of Auvergne (541), can. X—Mansi, VIII, 862; *Karoli Magni Capitularia,* c. 71— *Monumenta Germaniae Historica, Capitularia Regum Francorum,* I, 64-65.

[61] "Ut illi clerici qui se fingunt habitu vel nomine monachos esse, et non sunt, omnimodis videtur corrigendos at que emendandos esse, ut vel veri monachi sint, vel veri canonici sint."—*Karoli Magni Capitularia* (789), c. 76—*loc. cit.;* "Qui se voto monachiae vitae constrinxerunt, monachice et regulariter vivant. Similiter qui ad clericatum accedunt, quod nos nominamus canonicam vitam, volumus, ut illi canonice secundum suam regulam vivant et episcopus eorum reget vitam."—*op cit.,* c. 72—*loc cit.;* cf. Schneider, *op. cit.,* pp. 32-33.

[62] Mansi, XIV, 149.

[63] Cf. Hinschius, *op. cit.,* II, 52-53; Schneider, *op. cit.,* pp. 33-35; Hefele, *op. cit.,* III, 664-65.

[64] Schneider, *op. cit.,* pp. 44-48; Hinschius, *op. cit.,* II, 56-58.

[65] Pope Nicholas (858-67)—c. 4, C. VII, q. 1; Adrian II (867-72), *Epistle* XVI—MPL, CXXII, 1280-81; John VIII (872-82), *Epistle* XXXVI—MPL, CXXVI, 690; cf. Thomassin, *op. cit.,* II, III, c. 19, n. 4, et, III, II, c. 53, n. 2; Du Cange, *Glossarium,* v. *Visitator,* VI, 1650.

functioning in office. In the diocese of Strassburg, however, it appears that Visitators were not appointed even by the Roman Pontiffs, but that the archdeacons were given the duty of administering the see when it became vacant.[66]

In France during these centuries the appointment of Visitators appears to have been the general practice. The *chorepiscopi,* who became very numerous in the kingdom during the eighth and early ninth century, and later in Germany, Austria, England and Ireland,[67] were often appointed to serve in the capacity of Visitator to administer vacant sees.[68] These clerics, who were distinct from the *chorepiscopi* of earlier times in the East,[69] possessed the true episcopal character,[70] and were introduced into the Western Church to meet the needs of the flourishing conditions; they exercised their episcopal power by assisting the bishops in evangelizing the remote regions of the dioceses.[71]

The *chorepiscopi,* however, do not appear to be the ordinary administrators of vacant sees in the ninth century especially in France. Hincmar, archbishop of Rheims, expressly claims in his epistle to the bishop of Laon, that it is the right of the metropolitan to appoint Visitators to govern vacant dioceses.[72] The metropolitans, however, made these appointments only with the consent of the king, as is clearly indicated in the epistles of the archbishop referred to.[73] The Visitators in

[66] Cf. Thomassin, *op. cit.*, I, II, c. 19, 20; Alzog, *Universal Church History,* II, 352.

[67] Phillips, *op. cit.*, II, 106; Maroto, *op. cit.*, II, n. 760.

[68] "... et quod terrena potestas hac materia saepe offenderet, ut videlicet episcopo quolibet defuncto per chorepiscopum solis pontificibus debitum ministerium perageretur, et res ac facultates ecclesiae secularium usibus expenderentur, sicut et in nostra iam secundo actum fuisset."—Flodoard, *Histor. Rhem.*, lib. III, c. 10—MPL, CXXXV, 151; cf. Hinschius, *op. cit.*, II, 164; Maroto, *op. cit.*, II, n. 760; Chelodi, *Jus de Personis,* n. 187.

[69] Zaplotnik, *De Vicariis Foraneis,* p. 18.

[70] Gottlob, *Das abenländische Chorepiskopat,* pp. 27, 30, 34, 59, 60, etc.; cf. Hinschius, *op. cit.*, II, 136; Maroto, *op. cit.*, II, n. 760.

[71] Sagmüller, *Die Entwicklung des Archispresbyterats und Dekanats,* 53; cf. Hinschius, *loc. cit.;* Hrabanus Maurus, *De Clericorum Institutione,* lib. I, c. V—MPL, CVII, 301.

[72] Thomassin, *op. cit.*, II, II, c. 21, n. 9.

[73] "Officio Visitatoris, consensu domini nostri Ludovici regis, nostrae

these instances were generally the neighboring bishops, and were accompanied by a civil officer or count, known as the *comes;* the duty of the latter was confined to a particular care for the temporal needs of the see. The chief duty of the Visitators, however, appears to center about the promotion and direction of a canonical election of a new bishop.[74]

An interesting description of the provisions which were made for the administration of vacant sees is found in the Capitularies of Charles the Bald.[75] Prior to his leaving on an expedition into Italy, the king sat in conference with the bishops of France and discussed matters of ecclesiastical discipline. The question arose as to what should be done if, during the absence of Charles the Bald, an archdiocese, or diocese should become vacant. The arrangements made were that if an archbishopric became vacant before the king returned, the neighboring bishop who was nearest to the metropolitan see, in company with the count (*comes*), should provide for the see until notice of the archbishop's death had reached the king. If, on the other hand, a bishopric became vacant, the archbishop should, according to the sacred canons, appoint a Visitator, who, with the count (*comes*), should protect the see from harm until the notice of the death of the bishop had reached Charles.

The epistles of Archbishop Hincmar and the Capitularies of the Frankish kings disclose to some extent the discipline governing the administration of vacant sees in France during

humilitatis metropolitana delegatione suscepto, ad eamdem ecclesiam quantocius studeas properare."—Hincmar, *Epistle* XLIX—MPL, CXXVI, 269; ". . . pro visitatione Morinensis ecclesiae post obitum Hunfridi episcopi, juxta dispositionem regis." — idem, *Epistle to Bishop Ragenel* — Flodoard, *Histor. Rem.*, lib. III, c. 23—MPL, CXXXV, 227.

[74] "Dignetur mihi dominatio vestra litteris suis significare, quem vultis de coepiscopis nostris, ut ei ex more litteras canonicas dirigam, et Visitatoris officio fungens, in eadem ecclesia electionem canonicam faciat: et aut per se, aut per litteras suas, vicario suo deferente, eamdem electionem cum decreto canonico singulorum manibus roborato ad me referat, ut per me ipsa electio ad dominationis vestrae discretionem perveniat."—Hincmar, *Epistle to Charles the Bald*—MPL, CXXVI, 268; *cf.* Thomassin, *op. cit.*, III, II, c. 54, n. 7.

[75] *Monumenta Germaniae Historica, Capitularia Regum Francorum* (877), I, 538-39.

the ninth century. It is also interesting to note that in those instances where the bishop, because of ill health, was unable to care for the diocese, economes, according to the practice of Pope St. Gregory the Great, were appointed to supply the incapacity of the prelate.[76]

These testimonies *per se*, however, do not describe the nature of the administrative powers enjoyed by the Visitators, but merely refer to the manner of appointment and the particular duty with respect to the election of a new bishop. Whether or not the Visitators and the count confined themselves merely to these limited duties, while the clergy of the cathedral Church, or the cathedral Chapter, administered the spiritual affairs, cannot be determined from the evidence at hand.[77] It appears, however, that the duty of administering the spiritual affairs of a vacant see gradually became attached to the office of the cathedral Chapter, while the Visitators had only to do with the process of electing a bishop and of administering the temporalities. This conclusion may readily be drawn from an old formulary of the tenth century relating to the election of a bishop,[78] wherein it is stated that the bishop who had been in charge of the funeral of a deceased prelate should be the Visitator of the vacant see, and take charge of the property in or belonging to the Church; the appointment to be made by the metropolitan.

The Council at Rome in 1080 [79] speaks of Visitators whom

[76] "Unde secundum quod in decretalibus epistolis Beati Gregori exemplo reperimus, statuimus illi oeconomum persuadere, qui ei suffragium et ecclesiae sibi commissae constudiam debitam et canonicam exhiberet, donec annuente Domino isdem frater venerabilis a sua infirmitate optabiliter convalesceret."—*Monumenta Germaniae Historica, Capitularia Regum Francorum* (853), I, 421.

[77] Thomassin (*op. cit.*, I, III, c. 9, n. 12) concludes from these testimonies and that which Flodoard (*Histor. Rhem.*, lib. III, c. XI—MPL, CXXXV, 155) records, that the cathedral Chapter in France already in the ninth century administered the spiritual affairs of vacant sees. These testimonies point, indeed, to such a conclusion, but certainly do not furnish direct and objective proof.

[78] This formulary is quoted by Du Cange (*Glossarium*, v. *Visitator*, VI, 1650-51) from the *Spicilegium Acheriense*, t. VIII, p. 154.

[79] "Quoties defuncto pastore alicujus ecclesiae alius est ei canonicae subrogandus, instantia visitatoris episcopi, qui ei ab apostolica vel metropoli-

the Apostolic See or the metropolitan appoint, and whose duties appear to be confined solely to the supervision of the election of a new bishop. The appointment of Visitator, however, in the eleventh century seems no longer to have been a general practice, for St. Peter Damian, when writing to the clergy of a vacant cathedral Church,[80] clearly testifies that the administration of both the temporal and the spiritual affairs of the diocese were in the custody of the cathedral clergy, and he advises them, furthermore, not to proceed with the election of a new bishop until the king has arrived.

By the close of the eleventh century the office of the Visitator seems to have ceased entirely as the ordinary manner of providing even for the election of a new bishop, although Visitators were commissioned in extraordinary instances. The Council of Nimes in 1096[81] directs the cathedral clergy to elect two of the more capable persons of the same see to administer the temporal affairs of the deceased bishop, and to safeguard faithfully all that pertains to the diocese. Pope Innocent II (1130-1143), furthermore, in the Council of the Lateran (1139),[82] extends to the cathedral Chapters the right to hold episcopal elections. After this time Visitators were appointed only in extraordinary cases by the Roman Pontiffs, and the duties attached to these commissions were not the same as those incumbent upon Visitators of previous centuries; the Visitator now held an office more in accord with that of the present day Administrator Apostolic.[83]

tana sede directus est, clerus et populus remota omni saeculari ambitione, timore atque gratia, Apostolicae sedis vel metropolitani sui consensu, pastorem sibi secundum Deum eligat. Quod si corruptus aliquo vitio aliter agere presumperit, electionis perperam factae omni fructu carebit et de caetero nullam electionis potestatem habebit."—can. VI—Mansi, XX, 533.

80 Lib. V, *epistle* 10—MPL, CXLIV, 353.

81 "Quotiens aliquis ecclesiae antistes ex hac vita migraverit, duae de melioribus eiusdem ecclesiae personae eligantur quae res episcopi defuncti, sicut ipse disposuerat, fideliter tractent et quae ad episcopatum pertinent, successuro pastori conservent."—can. V—Mansi, XX, 235; cf. Council of Rheims (1131), can. VII—Mansi, XXI, 465; II Council of Lateran (1139), can. IV—Mansi, XXI, 533; cf. c. 47, C. XII, q. 2.

82 Can. XXVIII—Mansi, XXI, 533; cf. c. 35, D. LXIII.

83 Maroto, *op. cit.*, II, n. 755.

CHAPTER III

Discipline During the Period of the Decretals

Art. 1. *Administration by the Cathedral Chapter*

The common law of the Church, emanating from the Decretals of the thirteenth and subsequent centuries prior to the Council of Trent, laid the substantial basis for the present discipline governing the administration of vacant episcopal sees. Pope Gregory IX, in 1227, commissioned his scholarly chaplain and confessor, St. Raymond of Pennafort, to make a compilation of all ecclesiastical laws. Upon the completion of this work, the pontiff promulgated it as authentic and exclusive, having the effect of universal law for the whole of the Latin Church.[1] This collection was followed by that of Popes Boniface VIII and Clement V, which, together with the constitutions of the popes of succeeding centuries, developed a definite course of action for the cathedral Chapter during the vacancy of a see.

According to the decretal of Pope Gregory IX,[2] an episcopal see became vacant when the bond of the mystical marriage between the bishop and his diocese was severed. It was clearly defined that this spiritual bond was broken only by the death, transfer, deposition or resignation of the bishop accepted by the Roman pontiff. Pope Boniface VIII added an equivalent cause when decreeing [3] that when a bishop is held captive by pagans or schismatics, the diocese is regarded as "quasi-vacant" and is then to be administered by the cathedral Chapter in the same manner as it would be were the bishop dead. This is the only occasion, other than true vacancy, when the cathedral Chapter was given administrative control over the

1 Bulla, *Rex Pacificus,* 15 Sept. 1234—*Magnum Bullarium Romanum,* III, 485.

2 C. 2, X, *de translatione,* I, 7.

3 C. 3, *de supplenda negligentia,* 1, 8, in VI°.

diocese. Thus, when a bishop, through perpetual or incurable infirmity, insanity, or senility, became unable to perform the functions of his office, the episcopal jurisdiction did not pass to the Chapter, but the disposition for the governance of the see was left to the Supreme pontiff; the afflicted bishop, however, was authorized by the decree to appoint one or two members of the Chapter to act as his coadjutors, but if this arrangement was not made, or did not prove satisfactory, the only course of action which remained was to refer the situation to the Holy See.[4]

§ 1. The Jurisdiction of the Cathedral Chapter during Quasi-vacancy and Vacancy of the Episcopal See

When the diocese became vacant the cathedral Chapter immediately came into control of the governance of the see, and enjoyed ordinary episcopal jurisdiction. This power of the Chapter was unquestionably acknowledged by Pope Gregory IX, who, in a decree [5] declared that it was the right of the cathedral Chapter during the vacancy of a see to confirm the elections performed in monasteries. Since the power to confirm such election was inherent in the ordinary jurisdiction of a bishop, the law directly acknowledged the fact that the Chapter possessed the same jurisdiction of the bishop during vacancy.[6]

A repeated recognition of this power of the cathedral Chapter during vacancy of see is found in the decretal of Pope Boniface VIIII,[7] wherein the pontiff declared expressly that, in view of the ordinary jurisdiction of the bishop which devolves upon the Chapter when a diocese becomes vacant, the Chapter possesses the faculty of absolving from those censures, either *a jure* or *ab homine,* which can be absolved by the bishop himself.[8] Likewise in another decree the same pontiff

[4] C. un., *de clerico aegrotante*, III, 5, in VI°.

[5] C. 14, X, *de maioritate et obedientia,* I, 33.

[6] ". . . patet . . . manifeste quod, vacante ecclesia, potestas sive jurisdictio episcopi devolvitur ad capitulum."—glossa ad c. 14, X, *de maioritate et obedientia,* I, 33.

[7] C. un., *de maioritate et obedientia,* I, 17, in VI°.

[8] Cf. glossa ad c. un., *de maioritate e tobedientia,* I, 17, in VI°.

re-iterates that a Visitator could be appointed only by the sovereign pontiff to take charge of a vacant see, unless the cathedral Chapter would neglect the administration of the spiritual and temporal affairs of the see, or did so with neglect.[9]

There is a third decree of the same pontiff which undeniably demonstrates that the cathedral Chapter enjoyed ordinary episcopal jurisdiction. It was declared [10] that when a bishop was taken captive by pagans or schismatics it was the duty of the cathedral Chapter, and not of the archbishop, to take charge of the spiritual and temporal affairs of the see until the bishop was released, or until the Holy See, after being informed of the circumstances, would make other provisions.

1. Powers of Ordinary Episcopal Jurisdiction in General

The ordinary jurisdiction of the bishop which devolved upon the cathedral Chapter when the diocese became vacant or quasi-vacant, according to the common opinion of canonists,[11] comprised in general terms all that common law of the Church included in the ordinary jurisdiction of the bishop, with the exception, however, of certain restrictions expressly stated in the common law, or by papal constitution. All those rights, consequently, which the bishop exercised by way of special privilege, or as a delegate of the Holy See, and all those privileges or delegations which were attached to the person or dignity of the bishop, did not fall within the scope of the cathedral Chapter's power during vacancy or quasi-vacancy. All delegated power, however, which either common law or papal constitution permanently affixed to the episcopal

[9] C. 4, *de supplenda negligentia*, I, 8, in VI°; the Visitator spoken of in this decretal is the fore-runner of the present Administrator Apostolic. cf. Maroto, *Institutiones*, II, n. 755.

[10] C. 3, *de supplenda negligentia*, I, 8, in VI°.

[11] Cf. Reiffenstuel, *Jus Canonicum Universum*, lib. III, tit. IX, nn. 25 ss; Schmalzgrueber, *Jus Ecclesiasticum Universum*, lib. III, tit. IX, nn. 1 ss; Garcia, *De Beneficiis*, P.V, c. VII, nn. 1 ss; Barbosa, *Jus Ecclesiasticum Universum*, lib. I, c. XXXII, n. 61; Gutierrez, *Questiones Canonicae*, lib. I, c. XI, n. 10; Scarfantoni, *Animadversiones ad Lucubrationes Canonicales*, P. II, lib. IV, tit. VII, n. 2; et al.

office, devolved upon the Chapter.[12] Those acts which demanded episcopal character for their performance, could not be performed by the Chapter, since the power of orders did not pass to them, yet they were privileged to commission another who possessed the episcopal character to perform such function, provided, however, that special laws did not prohibit this in particular instances.[13] Finally, all those rights which were attached to the episcopal office by way of an established custom formed also a part of the ordinary jurisdiction of the Chapter during vacancy.[14]

II. Rights of the Cathedral Chapter in Particular

The general principles of the ordinary episcopal jurisdiction enjoyed by the cathedral Chapter during vacancy or quasi-vacancy form the basis of their rights in particular matters. They consequently possess true legislative power and could make laws which retained effect even after the new bishop had taken possession of the see; this power of jurisdiction, however, was circumscribed for no laws could be passed which would result in a change of the status of the diocese or prove prejudicial to the rights of the succeeding bishop.[15] Just as the Chapter was empowered to make laws, they likewise could dispense from laws in all cases in which the bishop himself, by force of his ordinary jurisdiction, could dispense.[16]

[12] Cf. Scarfantoni, *op. cit.*, P. II, lib. IV, tit. VII, n. 2; Barbosa, *De Canonicis et Dignitatibus*, c. XLII, n. 107; Bouix, *De Capitulis*, p. 557.

[13] Cf. Leurenius, *Forum Beneficiale*, t. IV, tract. III, q. 466; Pellegrinus, *Praxis Vicariorum*, p. I, sect. IV, subsect. 2, n. 6; Reiffenstuel, *op. cit.*, t. III, tit. IX, n. 72; Schmier, *Jurisprudentia Canonico-civilis*, t. II, lib. III, tract. I, p. I, c. IV, sect. 2, n. 96.

[14] "Capitulum succedit in jurisdictione, quam episcopus de consuetudine quia eadem ratio debet esse in additamento, quae in principali."—Abbas Panormitanus, *Super Libros Decretalium*, v. *Cum olim, de majorit. et. obed.;* Leurenius, *op. cit.*, t. IV, tract. III, q. 460; Bouix, *De Capitulis*, p. 557.

[15] Cf. Reiffenstuel, *op. cit.*, t. III, tit. IX, n. 66; Schmalzgrueber, *op. cit.*, t. III, tit. IX, n. 30; Leurenius, *op. cit.*, t. IV, tract. III, q. 470; Fagnanus, *Commentaria*, lib. III, c. I, n. 14; c. 1, X, *ne sede vacante aliquid innovetur*, III, 9; c. ult., X, *ne sede vacante aliquid innovetur*, III, 9.

[16] Cf. Reiffenstuel, *op. cit.*, t. III, tit. IX, nn. 49-53; Schmalzgrueber, *op. cit.*, t. III, tit IX, n. 31; Leurenius, *op. cit.*, t. IV, tract. III, q. 479.

The Chapter not only possessed the power, but had the obligation to exercise vigilance over the clergy and the laity and, if it was found necessary to make canonical visitations or to convoke synods in order to curb sinful practices or to punish culprits, they were at liberty to do so.[17] They also had the power to judge all causes pertaining to the ecclesiastical forum, provided these causes fell within the competence of the episcopal court. The power to judge implied also the power to inflict punishments, even of suspension, excommunication, interdiction, deprivation, and deposition of clerics guilty of crime.[18]

The ordinary episcopal jurisdiction possessed by the Chapter included also the power to absolve any subject of the bishop, in both the internal and external forum, from all sins and censures, either *a jure* or *ab homine,* from which the bishop himself could absolve.[19] The Chapter was also permitted to grant dimissorial letters to their subjects at any time during the period of vacancy,[20] and could grant indulgences in the same manner as the bishop himself.[21]

§ 2. Prohibitions in General and in Particular

The ordinary episcopal jurisdiction of the cathedral Chapter [22] did not comprise, however, the plentitude of the powers of the bishop. The preceptive rubric *ne sede vacante aliquid innovetur* found in the third book, ninth title, of the Decretals,

[17] Cf. glossa ad c. 1, *de haereticis,* V, 3, in Clem.; Alteserra, *Opera Omnia,* I, 225.

[18] Cf. Schmalzgrueber, *op. cit.,* t. III, IX, nn. 30-31; Leurenius, *op. cit.,* t. IV, tract. III, q 472; Barbosa, *De Canonicis et Dignitatibus,* c. XLII, n. 72; Pellegrinus, *op. cit.,* p. I, sect. IV, subject. 2, n. 46.

[19] Cf. c. un., *de maioritate et obedientia,* I, 17, in VI°; Leurenius, *op. cit.,* t. IV, tract. III, qq. 476-77; Schmalzgrueber, *op. cit.,* t. III, tit. IX, n. 31; Reiffenstuel, *op. cit.,* t. III, tit. IX, n. 62.

[20] C. 3, *de temporibus ordinationem,* I, 9, in VI°.

[21] Cf. Barbosa, *op. cit.,* lib. I, c. XXXII, n. 91; Pellegrinus, *op. cit.,* p. I, sect. IV, subsect. 2, n. 38.

[22] Reiffenstuel *(op. cit.,* t. III, tit. IX, n. 23.) refers to some of the older canonists who made a distinction between the necessary and the voluntary jurisdiction of the bishop, and held that the voluntary jurisdiction did not devolve upon the cathedral Chapter.

placed certain restrictions upon the powers of the cathedral Chapter during the vacancy of the see; these restrictions still remain in force according to the dispositions of the present Code of Canon Law.[23]

Pope Gregory IX made the general prohibition that during vacancy of see no innovation should be made, since the diocese lacked its legitimate defender and protector.[24] This general restriction of the power of the Chapter took into its scope all those acts which contained a true innovation or change in the status of the vacant see.[25] In view of this fact, consequently, the cathedral Chapter was forbidden to donate or alienate the goods of the vacant see, or of the *mensa episcopalis,* or to convert the revenues of the latter to their own uses.[26] The Chapter was also forbidden to appear in court without permission of the Apostolic See, in defense of the rights or property of the Church or of the *mensa episcopalis,* and if the former bishop had already begun such action, the Chapter could not continue the process; the chief reason for this provision was that the diocese, during the time of vacancy, does not enjoy the protection of its proper "defender," the bishop.[27]

All administrative power with respect to benefices was for the most part excluded from the powers of the cathedral Chapter during vacancy or quasi-vacancy. The Chapter was forbidden to suppress or unite benefices, and, according to the more common opinion, to dismember or divide them.[28] The

23 Canon 436.

24 "Attendentes, igitur, quod episcopali sede vacante, non debet aliquid innovari, cum non sit, qui episcopale jus treatur."—c. 1, X, *ne sede vacante aliquid innovetur,* III, 9; cf. c. ult., X, *ne sede vacante aliquid innovetur,* III, 9.

25 Cf. Schmalzgrueber, *op. cit.,* lib. III, tit. IX, nn. 1-4.

26 C. I, X, *ne sede vacante aliquid innovetur,* III, 9; c. ult., *ibid.;* c. 42, *de electione et electi potestate,* I, 6, in VI°; cf. c. 38, C. XII, q. 2; c. 42, C. XII, q. 2; Schmalzgrueber, *op. cit.,* lib. III, tit. IX, nn. 48 ss.

27 Cf. C. 1, 4, 15, X, *de praescriptionibus,* II, 26; Reiffenstuel, *op. cit.,* lib. III, tit. IX, n. 74; Fagnanus, *op. cit.,* lib. III, c. I, nn. 14, 22; Schmalzgrueber, *op. cit.,* lib. III, tit. IX, n. 53; Leurenius, *op. cit.,* t. IV, tract. III, q. 500.

28 Barbosa, *De Canonicis et Dignitatibus,* c. XLII, n. 99; Hermes, *De Capitulo sede vacante et impedita,* p. 75.

Chapter was also forbidden to confer benefices, since such collation formed a part of the income (*fructus*) and the rights attached to the episcopal office, and consequently was reserved to the succeeding bishop.[29] Hence, during the entire period of vacancy, the Chapter was not permitted to confer benefices of free appointment reserved to the bishop, or even those which the bishop, with the consent or advice of the Chapter, was free to bestow.[30] Nor could the Chapter present or elect candidates to benefices when it was the prerogative of the bishop to present or elect.[31] The law provided, however, that the Chapter could institute those candidates who were presented to a benefice in those instances where it was the right of the bishop to do so.[32] So also could the Chapter confirm those elected,[33] and bestow those benefices which, during the occupancy of the see, could be conferred either by the bishop or by the cathedral Chapter.[34] In all instances, however, when a benefice which was reserved to the succeeding bishop or to the Holy See became vacant, the Chapter, in order to safeguard the welfare of souls and the interests of the Church, had not only the right but also the duty to appoint a capable vicar or administrator over the benefice as soon as certain notification of the fact of vacancy was received; they were also to assign a portion of the income of the benefice for the support of such an individual. The vicar or administrator remained in control of the benefice until the succeeding bishop had made other provisions for the benefice.[35]

29 "Capitulum non potest conferre beneficia, quae pertinent ad episcopum vacante ecclesia, quia omnes fructus et jura episcopatus debent fideliter custodiri et reservari successori . . . sed collatio beneficiorum inter bona episcopalia et fructus computatur, et magnum fieret praejudicium episcopo successori per talem collationem."—glossa ad. c. 14, X, *de maioritate et obedientia,* I, 33.

30 C. un., *ne sede vacante aliquid innovetur,* III, 8, in VI°.

31 Cf. Reiffenstuel, *op. cit.,* lib. III, tit. V, n. 181.

32 C. I, *de institutionibus,* III, 6, in VI°.

33 C. 14, X, *de maioritate et obedientia,* I, 33.

34 C. un., *ne sede vacante aliquid innovetur,* III, 8, in VI°.

35 Cf. Reiffenstuel, *op. cit.,* lib. III, tit. V, n. 183; Garcia, *De Beneficiis Ecclesiasticis,* p. V, c. VII, n. 53; Schmalzgrueber, *op. cit.,* lib. III, tit. IX, n. 17.

ART. 2. *The Method Employed by the Chapter in Administering Vacant Sees*

A familiarity with the method employed by the cathedral Chapter in exercising its jurisdiction during the vacancy of a see is essential to an understanding of certain practices which continued for some time after the dispositions enacted by the Council of Trent had taken effect; some of these practices either militated against, or were contrary to the spirit of the Tridentine legislation. The law of the decretals did not prescribe a particular norm according to which the Chapter was to use its power. In consequence of this freedom of choice, negatively granted the Chapter, since the law was silent in the matter, gave rise to a diversity of practice. The Chapter administered a vacant see either collectively,[37] or by commissioning the individual members of the Chapter to take turns in governing the diocese for a limited period of time.[38]

The more common practice adopted by the cathedral Chapters, however, was very much in accordance with a practice which existed already in the eleventh and twelfth centuries.[39] The Chapters, accordingly, appointed one or two vicars for a limited period of time or for the whole period of vacancy to administer the diocese in their name and according to the dispositions of their mandates of commission.[40] The office of

[37] "Potest etiam colligere, quod ipsum collegium per se potest exercere hanc jurisdictionem . . . cum capitulum succedit in jurisdictione sede vacante . . ."—Abbas Panormitanus, *Super Libros Decretalium,* v. *Irrefragabili, de jud. ord.*

[38] Cf. Benedict XIV, *De Synodo Dioecesana,* lib. II, c. IX, n. 1; Barbosa, *Jus Ecclesiasticum,* lib. I, c. XXXII, n. 29; Leurenius, *op. cit.,* t. IV, tract. III, q. 467.

[39] Cf. St. Peter Damian, lib. V, *Epistle,* 10—MPL, CXLIV, 353; Council of Nimes (1096), can. V—Mansi, XX, 935; II Council of the Lateran (1139), can. XXVIII—*Ibid.,* XXI, 533.

[40] ". . . ex quo infertur, quod cum capitulum succedit in jurisdictione sede vacante, non tenetur, si non vult, constituere vicarium, sed potest per se jurisdictionem exercere, est tamen utile . . . ut capitulum committat uni vel duobus, sed non est necessarium."—Abbas Panorimitanus, *Super Libros Decretalium, loc. cit.;* cf. Benedict XIV, *op. cit.,* lib. II, c. IX, n. 2; Alteserra, *Opera Omnia,* IX, 58-59; Council of Toledo (1347), can. III—Mansi, XXVI, 126; Thomassin, *Vetus et Nova,* I, III, c. IX, n. 13; Pius IX, const., *Romanus Pontifex,* 28 Aug. 1873—*Fontes* n. 565.

the vicars or delegates of the Chapter was identical with that of the vicar-general of the bishop.[41] A natural consequence of this identity of office was that the vicars of the Chapter were freely appointed and removed from office by the Chapter, bound by the same limitations attached to the office of the vicar-general, needed the same faculties and qualities, and enjoyed the same power and privileges as the vicars-general of the bishop.[42] It may safely be said also that the vicar of the Chapter, like the vicar-general, had at least to be a cleric, twenty-five years of age, and qualified with sufficient knowledge to fulfill the duties of his office.[43] There was no necessity, however, that the vicar be a member of the Chapter; it appears that frequently he was not a cathedral canon.[44]

As a general rule the power of jurisdiction enjoyed by the vicar of the Chapter was less extensive than the jurisdiction possessed by the Chapter during vacancy. This appears evident from the fact that the vicar of the Chapter needed a special mandate to proceed with certain acts which fell within the scope of the ordinary jurisdiction of the bishop.[45] Although the vicar of the Chapter possessed ordinary jurisdiction, there-

41 "Numquid autem vicarius generalis episcopi vel capituli sede vacante habeant hanc potestatem procedendi super crimine haeresis . . ."—John of Imola, *In Clementinas*, v. *Multorum querela, de haereticis;* "Sed quid de officiali quem dat capitulum episcopali sede vacante? Licet ille dici non possit officialis episcopi, qui non est . . . credo tamen haec constitutio etiam illum intendit includere, cum fit officialis jurisdictionis episcopalis."—glossa ad c. 2, *de rescriptis,* I, 2, in Clem.

42 Cf. Rebuff, *Praxis Beneficiorum,* tit. *Forma vicariatus archiepiscoporum et aliorum collatorum,* n. 203.

43 Cf. Rebuff, *op. cit.*, nn. 29, 35.

44 "Quaero an si capitulum sede vacante facit aliquem de canonicis officialem possit ei determinare salaria de bonis praelaturae vacantis. Conclude quo sic, quia non debet iste officialis suis stipendiis militare."—John of Imola, *In Clementinas*, v. *Statutum, de elect.*

45 "Numquid autem vicarius generalis episcopi vel capituli sede vacante habeant hanc potestatem procedendi super crimine haeresis, dicit Lapus quod non, quid requiritur speciale mandatum et in hoc erit tunc delegatus, licet in aliis sit ordinarius, et ideo si in hoc crimine appelletur a vicario habente speciale mandatum, appellabitur ad delegantem episcopum vel capitulum sede vacante."—John of Imola, *In Clementinas*, v. *Multorum querela, de haereticis.*

fore, this was not as extensive in scope as the ordinary episcopal jurisdiction, for the Chapter was permitted to reserve to itself a certain portion of this power. It was precisely this characteristic of pre-Tridentine practice which gave rise to difficulties and misunderstanding with respect to the interpretation of the law enacted by the Council of Trent.

The law of the decretals governing the administration of vacant episcopal sees as well as those which were quasi-vacant, is but a mute witness to the great solicitude which the Church has ever shown throughout the vicissitude of the preceding centuries for the temporal as well as the spiritual interests of dioceses which happened to be in the abnormal condition of quasi-vacancy or vacancy. The discipline, however, had not as yet arrived at the highest stage of development and efficiency and was still in need of some adjustments. The Fathers of the Council of Trent concerned themselves with the matter and there resulted legislation complementary to that of the Decretals, which has retained its force even in the present discipline of the Church.

CHAPTER IV

Discipline from the Council of Trent to the Present Code of Canon Law

Art. 1. *The Cathedral Chapter and the Vicar Capitular*

The Fathers of the Council of Trent readily perceived from the experiences of previous centuries that the discipline governing the administration of vacant episcopal sees was seriously in need of reform. The administration by the cathedral Chapter, as a body or through the appointed vicars whom the Chapter was at liberty to appoint and remove from office at will, or whose power it was free to limit, was productive of grave inconveniences, discords and a general lack of uniformity in practice.[1] The Council of Trent took measures, therefore, to eradicate these ills and formulated the following decree:

> When a see is vacant, the Chapter in those places where the duty of receiving the fruits devolves upon it, shall appoint one or more faithful and diligent stewards (*oeconomi*) to take care of the property and revenues of the church, of which they shall afterwards give an account to him whom it may regard. It shall also be absolutely bound, within eight days after the decease of the bishop, to appoint an official, or vicar, or to confirm the one who fills that office; who shall at least be a doctor or a licentiate of Canon Law, or otherwise as competent a person as can be produced: if anything be done contrary hereto, the appointment aforesaid shall devolve on the metropolitan. And if the church be itself the metropolitan, or exempted, and the chapter shall be, as has been said above, negligent, then shall the oldest of the suffragan bishops in that metropolitan church, and the nearest bishop in regard to that church that is exempted, have power to appoint a competent steward and vicar. And

[1] Cf. Quaranta, *Summa Bullarii earumque summorum pontificium*, v. *Capitulum sede vacante*, p. 180; Benedict XIV, *De Synodo Dioecesana*, lib. II, c. IX, n. 4; Bouix, *De Capitulis*, p. 487.

> the bishop who is promoted to the said vacant church shall demand, from the steward, vicar and all other officers and administrators, who during the vacancy of see, were, by the chapter, or others, appointed in his room—even though they shall belong to the chapter itself—an account of those things which concern him, of their functions, jurisdiction, administration, or of any other their charge whatsoever; and shall have power to punish those to who have been guilty of any delinquency in their office of administration, even though the officers aforesaid, having given in their accounts, may have ordained a quittance or discharge from the chapter, or those deputed thereby. The chapter shall also be bound to render an account to the said bishop of any papers belonging to the church if any such have come into the possession thereof.[2]

It is evident from this decree that the Council had made the law of the Church more exacting with respect to the administration of the temporalities of the vacant dioceses by demanding that the custody of these affairs be placed in the charge of qualified persons. The new obligation incumbent upon the Chapter, furthermore, demanding that it elect a vicar within eight days from the time the see became vacant, and that this individual take the place of the Chapter in administering the vacant see, is an expression of the mind of the Fathers of the Council that the unity of governance and the uniformity of official acts can be efficiently attained only by placing the administration of the diocese in the charge of one, rather than of many, for just as a diocese is given but one bishop, so also ought the see during vacancy have but one administrator.[3] The law of the Council of Trent, consequently, did not place restrictions upon the jurisdiction itself which the Chapter receives when a diocese becomes vacant, but merely limited the time during which the Chapter may exercise governance.

[2] Waterworth, *The Decrees of the Council of Trent*, pp. 223-24; cf. Council of Trent, sess. XXIV, *de ref.*, c. 16—*Canones et Decreta*, p. 196.

[3] S.C.C., *Ruthenensis*. 4 Sept. 1871, decret.—*Archiv Für Katholisches Kirchenrecht*, XXVII (1872), p. XIV.

A comparative analysis of this legislation and that contained in the present Code of Canon law [4] will disclose the fact that no substantial change has taken place in this discipline. Yet centuries of practice and numerous decrees and decisions of the Sacred Congregations were required to bring all to a common understanding of the true interpretation of the decree and the intention of the Fathers of the Council when formulating this provision.[5] The present article will be given to a consideration of the general trend of the discipline from the time of the Council of Trent to the present Code of Canon law, as it is portrayed by the teaching of canonists and the pronouncements of the Sacred Congregations. The first matter to be discussed is naturally the nature and effects of vacancy and quasi-vacancy of a diocese, for this is the basis or starting point of the administrative office of the Chapter and the Vicar Capitular. This consideration shall be followed by references to the election or appointment of the Vicar Capitular, the qualifications demanded by law for his licet and valid appointment, his powers of jurisdiction, removal from office, and lastly, the cessation of the office and the rendering of an account of the administration to the new bishop.

§ 1. The Nature and Effects of Vacancy and Quasi-vacancy

A see becomes vacant, according to the law of the Decretals,[6] when the bond of the mystical marriage which exists between the bishop and his diocese is dissolved. The causes contributing to this dissolution are the natural death, transfer, resignation accepted by the Roman pontiff, and the deposition of the bishop. Canonists [7] added the notorious heresy of the bishop as the

[4] Cf. Canons 432-34.

[5] Since much of the legislation and many of the opinions of older canonists will necessarily be used in the interpretation of the present law of the Code, according to the provision of canon 6, numbers 2 and 3, a goodly share of the minor phases of the discipline will be eliminated in this chapter of the historical synopsis.

[6] C. 2, X, *de translatione*, I, 7.

[7] Leurenius, *Forum Beneficiale*, t. IV, tract. III, q. 454; *Fagnanus, Commentaria*, lib. V, c. IX, n. 35; Bouix, *De Capitulis*, p. 484.

fifth cause, although vacancy in this instance became effective only when the bishop received certain notification of the fact that the sentence had been imposed upon him. In all cases of vacancy the Chapter was not permitted to exercise jurisdiction until they had certain knowledge of the fact that the see was actually vacant.[8]

Vacancy arising from the transfer of a bishop was subject, however, to special provisions. When a bishop, who was aware of the fact that he was to be transferred and was willing that this take place, was transferred to another see, his former diocese became vacant the moment his transfer was announced in public consistory. But before he received certain notification of the fact from the secretary of the Sacred Consistorial Congregation, or from other authentic sources, he retained his jurisdiction, except with respect to the power of conferring ecclesiastical offices and benefices. When he received authentic notification of his transfer, he lost all power of jurisdiction. The governance of the diocese passed immediately to the cathedral Chapter, and their obligation to appoint a Vicar Capitular began from this moment.[9] But if the Holy See transferred a bishop who was unaware of the transfer, or unwilling that this be done, the diocese was not regarded as vacant until the bishop had consented to the transfer, unless the Roman pontiff had expressly stated otherwise. Hence, in this case the bishop retained his power of jurisdiction, even with respect to conferring benefices, until he accepted the notice of his transfer and had given consent to the action taken by the Apostolic See. And if the Roman pontiff expressly stated that the transfer would be effective without his consent, this jurisdiction was supplied until he received certain notification of the pontifical acts.[10]

It has already been observed that in only one instance did a

[8] S. C. EE. et RR., *Neritonen,* 24 Maii, 1651—Ferraris, *Prompta Bibliotheca,* v. *Capitulum,* art. III, n. 37.

[9] Urban VIII, breve, *Nobis super,* 20 Martii 1625—*Bullarium Romanum,* XIII, 304-305; cf. S.C. EE. et RR., 14 Dec. 1624—*Fontes,* n. 1720; Benedict XIV, *De Synodo Dioecesana,* lib. XIII, c. XVI, n. 10; Wernz, *Jus Decretalium,* II, n. 527 (p. 267).

[10] *Ibidem.*

diocese become legally vacant, or quasi-vacant. This occurred when a bishop was made captive, or reduced to slavery by pagans or schismatics. In such instances the administration of both the temporal and spiritual affairs of the see devolved upon the Chapter until the bishop was released, or the Apostolic See made other provisions.[11]

This decree of Pope Boniface VIII was interpreted by the Sacred Congregation of the Council to the effect that when a bishop was thus held in captivity, his jurisdiction was not suspended, and the see, consequently, was not quasi-vacant, when he was able to communicate even by letter with his diocese.[12]

Canonists [13] held as a common opinion, therefore, that when a bishop was held in captivity by pagans or schismatics and was unable to communicate with his diocese, his jurisdiction and that of his vicar-general was suspended, and therefore, he was also unable to appoint a vicar to govern the see in his stead. For this reason, consequently, the law prescribed that the governance of the diocese devolved upon the cathedral Chapter.

The decree of Pope Boniface VIII referred only to captivity by pagans and schismatics. Some Chapters in the nineteenth century assimilated exile, deportation, or imprisonment by civil governments, and upon this basis assumed the governance of the diocese and proceeded to elect a Vicar Capitular. Thus, in the year 1837, when Archbishop August of Cologne was imprisoned by the Prussian government, the Chapter elected a Vicar Capitular, but Pope Gregory XVI pronounced the election invalid, since this action encroached upon the prerogatives of the vicar-general.[14] The Sacred Congregation of Bishops and Regulars, a few years later, reproved several Chapters in Sicily for similar infringements on the rights of

[11] C. 3, *de supplenda negligentia,* I, 8, in VI°; cf. Benedict XIV, *op. cit.,* lib. XIII, c. XVI, n. 11.

[12] S.C.C., *Hiberniae,* 7 Aug. 1683—*Fontes,* n. 2873.

[13] Reiffenstuel, *Jus Can. Univ.* lib. I, tit. XXVIII, n. 106; Pellegrinus, *Praxis Vicariorum,* p. I, sect. II, subsect. 6, n. 16; Barbosa, *De Officio et Potestate Episcopi,* p. III, alleg. 54.

[14] Gregory XVI, *brevia in causa Colonensi,* 9 Maii 1838—Bizzarri, *Collectanea,* p. 608.

the bishops and vicars-general when the prelates were expelled by civil power.[15] In more recent times, when the revolution in Mexico had driven bishops out of the country, or kept them out of their dioceses, or imprisoned them or obliged them to flee or conceal themselves, some Chapters assumed the prerogative of electing Vicars Capitular, thus depriving the vicars-general of the right to exercise their jurisdiction. The situation was referred to the Holy See, and the Sacred Consistorial Congregation, acting in the name of Pope Benedict XV, declared that there was in those cases no legitimate cause for electing Vicars Capitular and that the election already held was null and void.[16]

The "Schema" submitted to the Vatican Council [17] proposed to prescribe that when a bishop was hindered from governing his see by captivity, relegation, or exile, the vicar-general or anyone delegated by the bishop should assume the governance of the see until the Holy See shall provide otherwise. If there were no vicar-general or delegate of the bishop at hand, of if these were themselves hindered from acting, a Vicar Capitular should then be appointed, and the situation referred to the Holy See. This arrangement, proposed to the Vatican Council, although never promulgated, was adopted by the present Code of Canon law.[18]

In all other instances, when a bishop was hindered from governing his see, the administration did not pass to the Chapter, but immediate recourse had to be made to the Holy See. Thus, when a bishop was sojourning in remote regions, and his vicar-general had died or was not present, the administration of the diocese did not devolve upon the Chapter, but the matter had to be referred immediately to the supreme authority.[19] Neither did the Chapter receive govern-

[15] E.C. EE. et R.R., 3 May, 1862—*Ibid.*, pp. 153-54.

[16] S.C.Consist., declar., Mexicana, 6 Dec. 1914—AAS, VI (1914), 698, cf. *Fontes*, n. 2089.

[17] Cf. Martin, *Collectio Omnium Concilii Vaticani*, p. 134.

[18] Canon 429.

[19] S.C. EE. et RR., *Messanen*, 11 Jan. 1616—*Fontes*, n. 1671; c. un., *de clerico aegrotante*, III, 5, in VI^{0}; cf. Leurenius, *Forum Beneficiale*, t. IV, tract. III, q. 454; Fagnanus, *Commentaria*, lib. III, c. V, nn. 13 ss;

ance of the diocese when the bishop was unable to fulfill the duties of his office because of infirmity, old-age, insanity, or when he had incurred a censure which deprived both himself and his vicar-general of the right to exercise jurisdiction.[20]

§ 2. The Election or Appointment of the Vicar Capitular

According to the new provisions enacted by the Council of Trent [21] the cathedral Chapter was permitted to administer the see for eight days only from the time it was known that the see was vacant. During this time the administrative power resided with the Chapter as a body, and previous to the appointment of a Vicar Capitular they were permitted to exercise this power either corporately or by delegating one or the other Canon to administer the see in their name, just as they had done before the Council of Trent.[22]

"When a see is vacant," the law of Trent states, "the Chapter, in those places where the duty of receiving the fruits devolves upon it, shall appoint one or more stewards *(oeconomi)* to take care of the property and revenues of the church . . . It shall also appoint an official, or vicar, or to confirm the one who fills that office . . . " [23]

This prescription of the Council, it will readily be perceived, made it incumbent upon the Chapter to fulfill two obligations which did not exist in the time of the Decretals. The first of these duties—the appointment of competent Economes—was necessary, however, only when the Chapter had charge of the

Ferraris, *Prompta Bibliotheca,* v. *Capitulum,* art. III, n. 36; Monacelli, *Formularium Legale Practicum,* t. I, tit. I, form. I, n. 2; a contrary view, however, was held by Barbosa *(De Officio et Potestate Episcopi,* p. III, alleg. 523) and Pellegrinus *(Praxis Vicariorum,* p. I, sect. IV, subsect. 5, n. 1.).

20 Cf. c. un. *de clerico aegrotante,* III, 5, in VI°; Leurenius, *loc. cit.*

21 Sess. XXIV, *de ref.* c. 16—*Canones et Decreta,* p. 196.

22 S.C.C., *declar.,* 19 Sept. 1620—Pellegrinus, *Praxis Vicariorum,* p. I, sect. IV, subsect. 1, n. 5; cf. Barbosa, *Jus Ecclesiasticum,* lib. I, c. XXXII, nn. 29, 31; Leurenius, *op. cit.,* t. IV, tract. III, q. 545; Ferraris, *op. cit.,* v. *Capitulum,* art. III, nn. 10, 30.

23 Sess. XXIV, *de ref,* c. 16—*Canones et Decreta,* p. 196.

diocesan revenues, nor was there an obligation on the part of the Chapter to appoint these officials within the period of eight days from the time of vacancy; but if this duty were neglected entirely the competent superior (metropolitan or senior suffragan bishop) had to make the appointment.[24] In those countries, therefore, such as France, where the *mensa episcopalis* consisted in a governmental pension, the Economes were not appointed.[25]

The Chapter, however, was strictly bound to elect a Vicar Capitular within eight days from the time they received certain notification of the fact of the vacancy of the see.[26] And if the Chapter neglected to accomplish this duty, or otherwise performed an invalid election, the right of appointing the Vicar devolved upon the metropolitan, or, as the case might be, the senior suffragan bishop. But the Council did not prescribe the precise form of election to be employed by the Chapter—a fact which gave rise to diversity of opinion. Some canonists [27] held that this election, in order to be valid, had to be performed by secret ballot; they held thus by way of analogy with the elections of bishop and of prelates and superiors in religious orders, and argue also from a decision of the Sacred Congregation of Bishops and Regulars.[28] Other canonists [29] held the commonly accepted opinion that a secret ballot was not necessary for the validity of this election since the Council of Trent did not prescribe any special form for the election of the Vicar Capitular, and furthermore, because the Council meant this to be a simple appointment rather than an election proper. This latter intention appears quite evident from the

[24] Cf. Schmalzgrueber, *Jus Eccl. Univ.*, t. III, tit. IX, n. 8.

[25] Bouix, *De Capitulis*, p. 488.

[26] Cf. Benedict XIV, *op. cit.*, lib. II, c. IX, n. 2.

[27] Pellegrinus, *op. cit.*, p. I, sect IV, subsect. I, n. 8; Monacelli, *op. cit.*, t. I, tit. I, form. 2, n. 10; Ferraris, *op. cit.*, v. *Vicarius Capitularius*, art. I, n. 15.

[28] S.C. EE. et RR., *Siculana*, 18 Nov. 1625—*Fontes*, n. 1723; cf. c. 42, X, *de electione et electi potestate*, I, 6; Council of Trent, sess. XXV, *de regularibus et monialibus*, c. 6—*Canones et Decreta*, p. 212.

[29] Scarfantoni, *Animadversiones*, p. II, lib. III, tit. 7, nn. 22ss; Schmalzgrueber, *op. cit.*, t. I, tit. XXVIII, n. 29; Garcia, *De Benificiis*, p. V, c. VII, n. 22; Bouix, *op. cit.*, p. 537.

phrase in the Tridentine canon, "or to confirm the one who fills that office" which has reference to a simple confirmation of the vicar-general as Vicar Capitular.

The Council prescribed, however, that the appointment of the Vicar Capitular should be made *a capitulo* which signifies that the right and the duty did not reside in any particular individual of the Chapter, but in the Chapter collectively.[30] Since the election or appointment was to be performed collectively, therefore, its validity required all that was necessary for capitular acts. Hence, it was incumbent upon the first dignity, or the one authorized by law, custom or particular statute, to notify all the members of the Chapter that the election was to take place, expressly stating the exact place, day and hour of the conclave.[31] Those members present formed the exclusive electoral body, while written votes sent in by absent members of the Chapter were of no juridical effect.[32] There was one exception, however, with respect to absent members of the Chapter. Those who were hindered from attending the election by some publicly known impediment, or if the impediment were occult and duly proven by oath, could submit their vote by proxy. Here again a distinction was made. If the proxy was a member of the Chapter, the vote had to be counted, whereas if another, not a member, acted as proxy the Chapter was free to accept or to refuse it.[33]

The Vicar Capitular was validly elected only by a majority of the votes of those present and voting. It mattered not at all if this majority was attained and dependent upon the vote which a member cast in his own favor, nor would the election be invalid if only one member of the Chapter voted in case the others had either died or had become disqualified.[34]

30 S.C. EE. et RR., *Siculana,* 18 Nov. 1625—*Fontes,* n. 1723; cf. Pignatelli, *Consultationes Canonicae,* t. I, consult. XXVIII, n. 7.

31 Schmalzgrueber, *op. cit.,* lib. I, tit. VI, n. 25; Monacelli, *op. cit.,* p. I, tit. I, form. 2, nn. 7-9.

32 Cf. S. Rota, decis., *Leodien.,* 10 Dec. 1498—Monacelli, *op. cit.,* p. II, decis. 39, in append.; cf. Pignatelli, *op. cit.,* t. I, consult. XXIII, nn. 7, 8; Bouix, *op. cit.,* pp. 534-44.

33 Schmalzgrueber, *op. cit.,* lib. I, tit. VI, n. 27; Monacelli, *op. cit.,* t. I, tit. I, form. 2, n. 8.

34 S.C.C., *Turritana,* 21 Nov. 1722—*Fontes,* n. 3248; *Laquedoniensi,* 16

1. The Number of Vicars Capitular Permitted by the Council of Trent

The Council of Trent did not expressly prohibit the Chapter from electing more than one Vicar Capitular, although it is to be inferred from the decree itself, [35] that the Fathers of the Council had intended that but one Vicar should be elected. Garcia [36] construed the decree as permitting the Chapter to elect more than one vicar, but the decrees and decisions of the Sacred Congregations soon threw light upon the correct interpretation of the law.

In the year 1592 the Sacred Congregation of the Council issued the following significant decree: "Congregatio Concilii censuit, ex decreto Concilii cap. 16 sess. XXIV a capitulo sede vacante, unum tantum vicarium esse eligendum. Caeterum non esse eo decreto sublatam consuetudinem duos aut plures eligendi, praesertim immemorabilem." [37] This decree was followed by many others [38] in which the same doctrine was re-iterated. Although these pronouncements clearly state that the law of the Council of Trent does not abrogate custom legitimately prescribed and especially the immemorable custom of having more than one Vicar, the Holy See nevertheless desired, especially as time went on, that even immemorial customs should cease in this regard and that only one Vicar Capitular should be elected. This intention of the Church is clearly expressed in a rescript of the Prefect of the Sacred Congregation of the Council in the year 1871.[39] In this

Mart. 1912—AAS. IV (1912), 404; cf. Leurenius, *op. cit.*, t. IV, tract. III, q. 551; Reiffenstuel, *op. cit.*, lib. I, tit. VI, nn. 138 ss; Scarfantoni, *Animadversiones*, p. II, lib. III, tit. VII, nn. 23-24.

35 Sess. XXIV, *de ref.* c. 16—*Canones et Decreta*, p. 196.

36 *De Beneficiis*, p. V, c. VII, n. 36.

37 S.C.C., *Panormitana*, 21 Apr. 1592—*Fontes*, n. 2242; cf. Fagnanus, *Commentaria*, lib. I, c. IX, n. 68.

38 S.C.C., *Tirosonen.*, 13 Jul. 1669 ad 3—*Fontes*, n. 2814; S.C. EE. et RR., *Cassanen.*, 6 Aug. 1596—*Fontes*, n. 1557; *Bobien.*, 12 Mart. 1607—*op. cit.*, n. 1642; *Potentina*, 30 Aug. 1641—Bizzarri, *Collectanea*, p. 610; Ferraris, *op. cit.*, v. *Capitulum*, art. III, n. 40.

39 S.C.C., *Ruthenensis*, 4 Sept. 1871—*Archiv für Katholisches Kirchenrecht*, XXVII (1872), p. XIV; cf. Bonal *Institutiones Canonicae*, I, 656,

particular document it is stated that diocese should have but one Vicar Capitular just as it has but one bishop, for this is most conducive to unity of governance, and uniformity of official action, which is a preventive of discord and dispute. The rescript continues to state that in dioceses which are exceptionally large, nothing prevents the Vicar Capitular from appointing "pro-vicars" who shall assist him and function in the pastoral ministry under his power and direction.

The decrees cited necessarily affected the common opinion among canonists that nothing in the law disturbed an immemorable custom of appointing *in solidum* several Vicars Capitular. Controversy among authors, however, did not cease here, for the phrase "Caeterum non esse eo decreto sublatam consuetudinem duos aut plures eligendi, *praesertim immemorabilem*" contained in the decree of 1592, proved to be the point of much discussion. Canonists took opposite views on the question as to whether or not custom other than immemorable, although legitimately prescribed, was sufficient in the eyes of the law to privilege the Chapters to elect more than one Vicar. The legitimately established custom in France, however, of appointing several Vicars *in solidum* was tolerated by the Holy See.[40] These customs were recognized or tolerated by the Church until the promulgation of the present Code of Canon law, whereby all custom contrary to the election of one Vicar Capitular was abrogated.[41]

II. The Devolution of the Right to Elect the Vicar Capitular

The primary purpose of the law of the Council of Trent was that the Chapter should administer the see for no more than eight days from the time knowledge of vacancy was received.

[40] A good statement of this question may be found in the following works: Bouix, *De Capitulis*, pp. 489-504; Bonal, *Institutiones Canonicae*, I, 652-656; Hermes, *De Capitulo sede vacante et impedita*, pp. 88-109; De Angelis, *Praelectiones*, lib. I, tit. XXVIII, n. 18; Fagnanus, *Commentaria*, lib. I, c. IX, n. 68; Leurenius, *Forum Beneficiale*, t. IV, tract. III, q. 547; Monacelli, *Formularium*, t. I, tit. I, form. 2, n. 13; Vecchiotti, *Institutiones Canonicae*, I, pp. 318-319; Giraldi, *Expositio Juris Pontifici*, p. 127.

[41] Canon 433 § 1.

Within this period of eight days the law made it the absolute duty of the Chapter "to appoint an official, or vicar, or to confirm the one who fills that office; who shall at least be a doctor or a licentiate of Canon Law, or otherwise as competent a person as can be produced; if anything be done contrary hereto, the appointment aforesaid shall devolve on the metropolitan. And if the church be itself the metropolitan, or exempted, and the Chapter shall be, as has been said above, negligent, then shall the oldest of the suffragan bishops in that metropolitan church, and the nearest bishop in regard to that church which is exempt, have power to appoint a competent steward, and vicar." [42]

This disposition of the Council governing the devolution of the right to appoint a Vicar Capitular afforded ground for discord of opinions among canonists as to the correct application of the law in particular instances. Since the law required that the election be held within eight days, the first question to arise was whether or not an election performed by the Chapter after the period of eight days had elapsed and before the metropolitan made the appointment, was invalid by force of the law. Some canonists [43] held that such an election was valid, for the law of devolution is penal and applies only to true canonical elections; and that since the election of the Vicar Capitular was merely an appointment, the right of appointing on the part of the Chapter did not cease at the end of the prescribed eight days, but resided cumulatively with the Chapter and the metropolitan. The more common opinion, however, was that the right of the Chapter to hold the election was forfeited at the close of the eighth day, if it had neglected to make the appointment before this time, and that an election performed after the right was forfeited was invalid, unless the metropolitan either expressly or tacitly approved of the action of the Chapter.[44]

[42] Sess. XXIV, *de ref.*, c. 16—*Canones et Decreta*, p. 196.

[43] Barbosa, *De Officio et Potestate Episcopi*, p. III, alleg. XLIV, n. 164; Garcia, *De Beneficiis*, p. V, c. VII, n. 7.

[44] Pellegrinus, *Praxis Vicariorum*, p. I, sect. IV, subsect. I, n. 29; Bonal, *Institutiones*, I, 650; Pignatellus, *Consultationes*, t. VIII, consult, XXXIV, n. 8.

Little difficulty, therefore, was had in regard to the devolution of the right of the Chapter to hold the election if it neglected to do so within the prescribed period of time. The bone of contention, however, centered about an invalid election held by the Chapter during the eight days. The election of the Vicar Capitular could be invalid on either of two grounds; because it was done in violation of chapter sixteen, session twenty-four on reformation of the Council of Trent, or because it was not performed as a collegiate, or chapter act. In the latter instance the invalidity of the election was decided by the judge superior to the Chapter in question. Hence, the metropolitan gave the decision when the questionable election was performed by the Chapter of a suffragan see, and the Sacred Congregation of the Council in case of a metropolitan or exempt Chapter, and if the election was found to be invalid, the original Chapter was permitted to repeat their act eight days from the time they received the decision of the judge.[45]. If, on the other hand, the question of the invalidity of the election resulted from a violation of the law of the Council of Trent, the matter was decided by the metropolitan or the senior suffragan bishop, as the case might be. In the instance where the election was invalid because the Chapter held it after the period of eight days, all canonists agreed that the metropolitan or senior suffragan bishop could proceed immediately with the appointment of the Vicar. But if the election was invalid because the Vicar did not possess the qualification demanded by the law, e.g., doctor or licentiate in Canon Law, the question arose among scholars as to whether or not the metropolitan or senior suffragan bishop was permitted to proceed with the appointment of another Vicar immediately after pronouncing the election invalid, or whether he was obliged to inform the Chapter of the invalidity and then give them eight days time to repeat the election. Some canonists [46] held that in both cases where the Chapter neglected to appoint a

[45] Hermes, *De Capitulo sede vacante et impedita*, p. 136; Bouix, *op. cit.*, p. 530.

[46] Monacelli, *Formularium*, p. I, tit. I, form. 2, n. 5; Barbosa, *Jus Eccl. Univ.*, lib. I, c. VII, n. 102; Guaranta, *Summa Bullarii*, v. *Archiepiscopi auctoritas*, n. 35.

Vicar within eight days, or when they elected on not a doctor or licentiate or otherwise fit, the right of electing devolved upon the metropolitan or senior suffragan bishop and he could proceed immediately with the appointment of a new Vicar. The more common opinion, however, appears to draw its strongest argument from a decree of the Sacred Congregation of the Council, [47] and provides that in case the Chapter invalidly elected a Vicar Capitular because the latter did not possess the qualifications demanded by the Council of Trent, the metropolitan or senior suffragan bishop was to give the Chapter another period of eight days to repeat the election; and it was only after the lapse of this time that the right of electing passed to the metropolitan or senior suffragan bishop.

When the right of electing the Vicar had once lawfully devolved upon the metropolitan or senior suffragan bishop, and either of these appointed a Vicar, any appeal advanced by the Chapter against this appointment had to be submitted to the Holy See and had only devolutive effect. If, on the other hand, the Vicar appointed by the metropolitan or suffragan bishop died, or relinquished his office, the right of electing another passed to the original Chapter as in the first instance.[48]

Since the devolution of the right to elect a Vicar Capitular was nothing more than the right to supply that which was lacking in the first election, the metropolitan or senior suffragan bishop was obliged to comply with all other regulations incumbent upon the Chapter in their election of the Vicar.[49] Hence, the metropolitan or the senior suffragan had to make the appointment within eight days and choose as Vicar only those possessing the required qualifications. If this appointment was

[47] S.C.C., *Mazariensi*, 19, Dec. 1569: "Archiepiscopus constituere debet capitulo octo dierum spatium ad eligendum vicarium doctorem, casu quo elegisset non doctorem, et eo non electo, omnis electionis potestas ad archiepiscopum transfertur."—Richter, *Canones et Decreta*, p. 373, n. 4; cf. Richter, *op. cit.*, p. 374, n. 9; Pignatelli, *op. cit.*, t. VIII, consult. XXXIV, n. 8; Bouix, *op. cit.*, p. 532.

[48] Barbosa, *De Jure Ecclesiastico*, t. I, c. VII, n. 102; Monacelli, *op. cit.*, p. I, tit. I, form. 2, n. 6, Bouix, *op. cit.*, p. 533.

[49] Cf. Hermes, *op. cit.*, p. 142.

neglected, the Vicar Capitular was then to be appointed by the Apostolic See.[50]

§ 3. The Qualifications of the Vicar Capitular

The Council of Trent prescribed [51] that the Chapter elect as Vicar Capitular one "who shall at least be a doctor or a licentiate of Canon law, or otherwise as competent a person as can be produced." This gave rise to many questions and diverse opinions among canonists as to whether the Chapter was obliged to elect a doctor of Canon law, and if it were necessary that a member of the Chapter be elected, and in either instance would the validity of the election be dependent upon such choice. Owing to the fact that the present Code of Canon law requires only for the liceity of the election that the Vicar capitular be a doctor of theology or Canon law,[52] the controversies in the past in this regard are more of historical rather than of juridical value. For this reason a brief statement of the principal elements of the discipline will be regarded as sufficient.

I. The Necessity of Electing a Doctor or Licentiate of Canon Law

Canonists took opposite views in the interpretation of the phrase "a doctor or a licentiate of Canon law, *or otherwise as competent a person as can be produced.*" The fact that the Sacred Congregation of the Council had ratified in certain instances [53] the elections of Vicars Capitular who were not doctors even though there were available doctors, had given rise to an opinion that the Chapter was at liberty to elect whomsoever they desired as long as the candidate was otherwise competent. Contrary and more numerous opinions however, of

[50] Pellegrinus, *op. cit.,* p. I, sect. IV, subsect. I, n. 29; Monacelli, *op. cit.,* p. 11, tit. XVI, form. 8.

[51] Sess. XXIV, *de ref.,* c. 16—*Canones et Decreta,* p. 196.

[52] Canon 434 § 2.

[53] S.C.C., *Carniolen,* 22 Sept. 1714—*Fontes,* n. 3138; *Leopolien,* 14 Jan. 1736—*op. cit.,* n. 3453; *Tiburtin,* 14 Apr. 1764—Richter, *op. cit.,* p. 373, n. 8; cf. Nazarena, 11 Sept. 1717—*op. cit.,* p. 373, n. 7; *Acernan,* 16 Dec. 1708—*op. cit.,* n. 6.

the Sacred Congregations of the Council and of Bishops and Regulars [54] established the general rule that when there were competent doctors at hand the validity of the election was dependent upon the election of one of them if the vicar-general were the one elected.[55]

The discipline prevailing previous to the promulgation of the present Code of Canon law, consequently, demanded the doctorate in Canon law for validity of the election. Hence, if there were no doctors among the cathedral Canons, the Chapter was regularly obliged to elect a capable doctor who was not a Canon.[56] The law, however, did not over-emphasize the necessity of the doctorate to an unreasonable extent, for it was permitted that the Chapter elect one not a doctor, but who possessed knowledge, prudence and probity of life, when an available doctor was incompetent.[57] The whole question of this requirement of law was the subject of much discussion among canonists chiefly because the Sacred Congregation of the Council had given decisions in particular instances which seemed to conflict with the general norm of action.[58] The commonly accepted regulations in effect previous to the present Code may be expressed as follows. It was necessary for the validity of the election that the Vicar Capitular be a doctor of Canon law, where there was a number of doctors in the cathedral chapter. If there were, indeed, doctors in the Chapter but all, or all except one, were incompetent for the office of the Vicar, then one not a doctor but a more capable administrator could be elected. In the latter instance, the vicar-general

[54] S.C.C., *Mazariensi,* 19 Dec. 1569—Richter, *op. cit.,* p. 373, n. 4; *Triventina,* 15 Dec. 1586—*loc. cit.; Camplensi,* 11 Maii 1624—*Fontes,* n. 2450; *Cortonensi,* 9 Maii 1637—*Fontes,* n. 2588; *Salernitana,* 9 Dec. 1662—*Fontes,* n. 2781; cf. Bizzarri, *Collectanea,* p. 610; *Thesaurus Resolutionum,* XXXVII, 238.

[55] Leurenius, *op. cit.,* t. IV, tract. III, q. 557; Monacelli, *op. cit.,* t. I, tit. I. form. 2, n. 12; Pignatelli, *op. cit.,* t. III, Consult. XXXIV; Bouix, *op. cit.,* pp. 512-514.

[56] S.C.C., *Tricaricen,* 8 Maii 1592—Richter, *op. cit.,* p. 373, n. 4.

[57] S.C.C., *Carniolen.,* 22 Sept. 1714—*Fontes,* n. 3138.

[58] A statement of this question may be found in the following works: Hermes, *De Capitulo sede vacante et impedita,* pp. 110-123; Bouix, *op. cit.,* pp. 512-520.

was presumed to be the most capable administrator, and it was he whom the Chapter was to elect, although this was not of strict obligation.

It was necessary, however, that the candidate be a doctor or licentiate of Canon law. Degrees of theology, civil law, or any other department of study were expressly proclaimed as insufficient to meet the requirements of the law.[59] The doctorate or licentiate of Canon law, furthermore, had to be a degree conferred by a public university after the individual had completed the prescribed course of study.[60] All honorary titles, therefore, did not suffice; nor was a degree obtained from a university which was not under the direct supervision of the Holy See adequate to satisfy the prescriptions of the law.[61]

II. The Necessity of Electing a Member of the Cathedral Chapter

The decree of the Council of Trent [62] did not make it incumbent upon the cathedral Chapter to elect as Vicar Capitular one who was a member of the Chapter. The Council simply stated the obligation of electing "a doctor or licentiate of Canon law, or otherwise as competent a person as can be produced." In the year 1643 the Sacred Congregation of the Council,[63] however, interpreted the Tridentine decree to the effect that one who was not a cathedral Canon could be elected Vicar Capitular, but if there were qualified and competent candidates in the Chapter, "istum ceteris paribus esse praeferendum." The term "ceteris paribus," according to the same decree, signified that it was sufficient for the Vicar to possess the qualities demanded by the Council of Trent, i.e., the doctorate or licentiate of Canon law, or otherwise fit.

Canonists took opposite views on the real meaning of the phrase "istum ceteris paribus esse praeferendum." Some regarded this as a mere exhortation, while others understood

59 S.C.C., *Astensi*, 11 Jul. 1626—*Fontes*, n. 2469; *Oriolensi*, 24 Mart. 1627—*Fontes*, n. 2479; cf. *Thesaurus Resolutionum*, XXXVII, 238.

60 S.C.C., *Montis Regalis*, 19 Jan. 1664—*Fontes*, n. 2789.

61 Leurenius, *op. cit.*, t. IV, tract. III, q. 557; Bouix, *op. cit.*, p. 517.

62 Sess. XXIV, *de ref.*, c. 16—*Canones et Decreta*, p. 196.

63 *Neritonen.*, 24 Jul. 1643—*Fontes*, n. 2646.

it as a requirement for the validity of the election. Thus, when there was a choice between a cathedral Canon and an extern, both of whom were doctors or licentiates of Canon law, or otherwise competent, some canonists [64] held that in this instance the election of the extern would be invalid. Hermes [65] and others whom he cites maintain that such an election would not be vitiated. Opposite views were likewise taken in regard to the election of an extern who was better qualified than a sufficiently qualified cathedral Canon. Certain canonists regarded such an election as invalid, [66] but the more common opinion appears to be in favor of its validity. [67]

III. Other Necessary Qualifications of the Vicar Capitular

Insofar as the office of the Vicar Capitular is an ecclesiastical office the strict sense of the term, it was required that the incumbent possess qualifications other than those specified expressly by the Council of Trent for the Vicar Capitular. No one, consequently, who was excommunicated, interdicted or suspended and who was thereby deprived of the right of exercising jurisdiction could be appointed to the office of Vicar Capitular. It was further demanded that the Vicar Capitular be a cleric, of legitimate birth and at least twenty-five years of age. [68]

It was the common opinion of canonists [69] that a pastor, or one having care of souls, who did not reside in the episcopal city could not be elected Vicar Capitular. This opinion was based upon certain decisions of the Sacred Congregation of

[64] Pignatelli, *op. cit.*, t. VII, consult. IV, n. 1; Garcia, *De Beneficiis*, p. V, c. VII, n. 12; Leurenius, *op. cit.*, t. IV, tract. III, q. 556; Bouix, *op. cit.*, p. 523.

[65] *Op. cit.*, p. 523.

[66] Cf. footnote 64 supra.

[67] Cf. S.C.C., *Tiburtin.*, 14 Apr. 1764—Richter, *op. cit.*, p. 373, n. 8; De Angelis, *Praelectiones Juris Canonici*, lib. I, tit. XXVIII, n. 19; Wernz, *Jus Decretalium*, II, n. 795.

[68] Bouix, *op. cit.*, p. 528; Barbosa, *De Jure Ecclesiastico*, t. I, c. XXXII,

[68] Bouix, *op. cit.*, p. 528; Barbosa (*De Jure Ecclesiastico*, t. I, c. XXXII, n. 54), held that a cleric who was twenty-three years of age could be validly elected.

[69] Leurenius, *op. cit.*, t. IV, tract, III, q. 558; Pignatellus, *op. cit.*, t. VII, consult. IV, n. 6; Bouix, *op. cit.*, p. 525; Wernz, *Jus Decretalium*, II, n. 795.

Bishops and Regulars.[70] These decisions stated that since a pastor living in the episcopal city would not violate the law of residence attached to both the office of the pastor and that of the Vicar Capitular, and furthermore, since it was not altogether impossible for one and the same individual to perform the duties of both offices, the law did not prohibit such a pastor from being elected Vicar Capitular. Bouix [71] summarized the common teaching of canonists in the following manner. If a pastor who lives outside the episcopal city is elected Vicar Capitular, the election is null and void. The election of a pastor living in the episcopal city is valid as long as he is absolutely capable of fulfilling the duties of both offices. Regularly the election of a pastor living in the episcopal city is illicit, for ordinarily it is more probable that he cannot satisfy the obligations of both offices.

The Constitution of Pope Pius IX [72] renewed the common law of the Church when forbidding anyone who was nominated, presented, or elected for a bishopric to administer the see even in the capacity of a Vicar Capitular before exhibiting to the Chapter or authorized individuals the papal bulls of his appointment.[73] The same constitution provided that those who violated this law incurred excommunication *ipso facto* reserved to the Holy See. But, if during the term of office a Vicar Capitular were presented to the vacant see by civil authority, it was the opinion of Hermes [74] that his office of Vicar Capitular ceased immediately. Other canonists [75] however, held the opposite view.

[70] S.C. EE. et RR., 19 Junii 1603, et *Sutrina,* 16 Julii 1610—Pignatelli, *loc. cit.*

[71] *Op. cit.*, p. 528.

[72] *Romanus Pontifex,* 28 Aug. 1873—*Fontes,* n. 565.

[73] Cf. C. 1, *de electione et electi potestate,* I, 3, in Extravag. Comm.

[74] *Op. cit.*, p. 133.

[75] De Angelis, *Praelectiones,* lib. I, tit. V, VI, n. 13; Bonal, *Institutiones,* I, 662-63.

§ 4. The Power of Jurisdiction of the Vicar Capitular and His Removal from Office

Although the decree of the Council of Trent [76] did not expressly speak of the power of the Vicar Capitular, or of the fact that when once duly appointed to office he should retain it through the period of vacancy, the intention of the Fathers of the Council may easily be adduced from the text of the law. The very fact that the decree made it imperative for the Chapter to elect a Vicar Capitular within eight days was sufficient to indicate that the Council desired to change the former discipline whereby the Chapter was free to appoint, or not to appoint a Vicar, or to limit his powers or term of office, or to remove him from office at will. So also was it intended that the whole jurisdiction of the Chapter should pass to the Vicar Capitular, and that he be independent of the Chapter, for the law expressly states that when the diocese ceases to be vacant the Vicar Capitular is obliged to render an account of his administration to the new bishop and not to the Chapter.

But after the Council of Trent a contrary practice prevailed for some time. The influence of ante-Tridentine discipline and the similarity between the office of the vicar-general and that of the Vicar Capitular was undoubtedly the underlying motive which leads Chapters to limit the powers of the Vicar Capitular, or to make appointments for a limited period of time. There were many canonists [77] too, who vindicated this right of the Chapter.

In the year 1632 the Sacred Congregation of the Council [78] declared that the Vicar Capitular needed a special mandate

[76] Sess. XXIV, *de ref.*, c. 16—*Canones et Decreta*, p. 196.

[77] Pignatelli, *Consultationes*, t. IX, consult. CLIX, n. 4; Barbosa, *De Canonicis et Dignitatibus*, c. XLII, n. 21; Quaranta, *Summa Bullarii*, v. *Capitulum sede vacante*, p. 183 ss; Garcia, *De Beneficiis*, p. V, c. VII, n. 25; Scarfantoni, *Animadversiones*, lib. IV, tit. VII, n. 61.

[78] " . . . Episcopos . . . non posse absolvere, nec dispensare in casu haeresis, neque in aliis nova lege post Concilium Sedi Apostolicae reservatis. Verum in his casibus, in quibus Episcopis talis facultas non est adempta, eam utique transferri in Vicarium Capitularem sede episcopali vacante, *dummodo talis facultas specialiter per Capitalum eidem Vicario tributa fuerit.*"—S.C.C., *Camenecen.*, 3 Dec. 1632—*Fontes*, n. 2548.

from the Chapter to absolve or dispense in certain reserved cases when it was within the power of the bishop to do so. This declaration of the Sacred Congregation was contrary to the doctrine that the entire jurisdiction of the Chapter passed to the Vicar Capitular, and consequently led to difficulties. There were indeed several earlier decisions of the same Congregation and also that of the Bishops and Regulars which stated that all the jurisdiction of the deceased bishop devolved upon the Vicar Capitular when he was duly appointed.[79] But it seems that the decision of 1632 injected some doubt into the discipline in this regard, for even in the year 1835 a cathedral Chapter contended that the Vicar Capitular needed a special mandate to absolve from cases reserved to the bishop.[80] Pope Pius IX, however, brought all discussion in the matter to a close in his Constitution *Romanus Pontifex* August 28, 1873,[81] wherein the independence of the Vicar Capitular was unmistakably established, and the nature and extent of his jurisdiction clearly described. Subsequent decrees and decisions of the Sacred Congregation of the Holy Office[82] explained more extensively the power of the Vicar Capitular with reference to the habitual faculties delegated to ordinaries by the Holy See.

In the year 1651 the Sacred Congregation of the Council decided that it was the right of the Chapter and not of the Vicar Capitular to select those who had proven to be best qualified in a *concursus* for appointment to a parish, since the Congregation recognized the fact that the Chapter had reserved this right to themselves.[83] The disposition of this decision was unanimously retracted by subsequent decisions of the Sacred

79 S.C.C., *Derthonen,* 21 Dec. 1591—*Fontes,* n. 2238; S.C. EE. et RR., *Reatina,* 21 Nov. 1603—*Fontes,* n. 1624.

80 S.C.C., *Ardien.,* 30 Maii 1835—*Thesaurus Resolutionum,* XCV, 213.

81 *Fontes,* n. 565.

82 Cf. S.C. de Offic., *litt. encyl.,* 20 Febr. 1888, n. 3—*Collectanea S.C. Prop. Fide,* n. 1985; decr., 20 Apr. 1898—*op. cit.,* 1996; 24 Nov., 1807—*op. cit.,* n. 1985; 5 Sept. 1900—*Fontes,* n. 1247.

83 S.C.C., 18 Nov. 1651—Richter, *op. cit.,* p. 374, n. 11; cf. Scarfantoni, *Animadversiones,* lib. IV, tit. VII, n. 61.

Congregations [84] and the Chapter was explicitly forbidden to restrict or reserve to themselves any part of the jurisdiction of the Vicar Capitular. Pope Pius IX, in his Constitution already referred to, gave his Apostolic approval to these decisions and stated that all reservations made by the Chapter at the time of the election are to be regarded as non-existent and absolutely invalid.

Just as the Chapter was wont to limit the power of the Vicar Capitular, so, too, it followed the practice of appointing a Vicar for a limited period of time, and claimed the right to remove him from office at will. Quaranta [85] states that the Chapter may appoint the Vicar for a limited period of time, after which his jurisdiction ceases. He quotes as his authority a decision of the Sacred Congregation of the Council on July 26, 1589. Scarfantoni [86] quotes a decision made by the same Congregation (January 16, 1644) wherein it is said that the Chapter was permitted to remove at will the Vicar Capitular elected by them, provided that they elect another within eight days. These decisions, however, were contrary to all others [87] which strictly forbade the Chapter to elect a Vicar Capitular for a limited period of time or to remove him without the authority of the Holy See.

The same prohibition extended, also, to the Vicars Capitular appointed by the metropolitan or senior suffragan bishop. Barbosa [88] however, maintained that the metropolitan could remove at will the Vicar appointed by him, and cited a decision of the Sacred Congregation of the Council (September 29,

[84] S.C.C., *Elven.*, 1 Dec. 1736—*Fontes*, n. 3465; *Ardien*, 30 Maii 1835—Richter, *op. cit.*, p. 374, n. 12; S.C. EE. et RR., *Caientana*, 20 Oct. 1587—*Fontes*, n. 1415; *Reatina*, 21 Nov. 1603—*op. cit.*, n. 1624; *Tropien*, 6 Martii 1681—*op. cit.*, n. 1810; *Capuana*, 30 Aug. 1686—*op. cit.*, n. 1814; cf. Benedict XIV, *De Synodo Dioecesana*, lib. IV, c. VIII, n. 10.

[85] *Summa Bullarii*, c. *Capitulum sede vacante*, n. 9.

[86] *Animadversiones*, lib. IV, tit. VII, n. 17.

[87] Cf. S.C. EE. et RR., *Neapolitana*, 1 Sept. 1603—*Fontes*, n. 1622; *Potentina*, 30 Aug. 1641—*op. cit.*, n. 1784; *Potentina*, 7 Maii 1604, et, 3 Maii 1647—Bizzarri, *Collectanea*, p. 608; S.C.C., *Elven.*, 1 Dec. 1736—*Fontes*, n. 3465.

[88] *De Canonicis et Dignitatibus*, c. XLII, n. 48.

1625) as authority for his statement. In the year 1725 a metropolitan acted on the basis of this decision, but the secretary of the Sacred Congregation maintained that this decision could not be found in the "register" of the Sacred Congregation.[89]

The law of the Church with respect to the removal of the Vicar Capitular from office, or his appointment for a limited period of time, received due consideration in the Constitution of Pope Pius IX.[90] The final word was then stated in this regard, and it was to be understood definitely and finally that the Vicar Capitular was to be elected for the whole period of vacancy, and that the Apostolic See alone was competent to remove him from office.[91]

It may be well to summarize here the principal legislation enacted from the time of the Council of Trent to the present discipline, insofar as it affected the jurisdiction of the Vicar Capitular and his rights *utilia et honorifica.* All that was stated, however, with respect to the rights and prohibitions of the cathedral Chapter[92] applies also to the Vicar Capitular. The following, therefore, are post-Tridentine modifications:

a. The Vicar Capitular was forbidden to grant dismissorial letters during the first year of vacancy, except in the case of the *arctati.*[93] If, however, the bishop *in mortis articulo* had given any of his subjects permission to be promoted to orders, the Chapter or the Vicar Capitular could permit these to be ordained within the first year of vacancy.[94]

b. The Vicar Capitular was permitted to visit the diocese only after one year had elapsed from the time that the Ordinary made his last visitation.[95] He was entitled to be

[89] S.C.C., *Civitatensi,* 9 Junii 1725—*Fontes,* n. 3298.

[90] *Romanus Pontifex,* 28 Aug. 1873—*Fontes,* n. 565.

[91] This norm has been incorporated in the present law of the Church. Cf. Canons 437, 443.

[92] Cf. pp. 28-33.

[93] Council of Trent, sess. VII, *de ref.,* c. 10—*Canones et Decreta,* p. 47; sess. XXIII, *de ref.,* c. 10—*op. cit.,* p. 159.

[94] S.C.C., *Mexicana,* 24 Apr. 1700—*Fontes,* n. 2978.

[95] S.C.C., 13 Sept. 1781—Fontes, n. 3232; cf. Benedict XIV, *op. cit.,* lib. II, c. IX, n. 6.

remunerated for expenses incurred and was to proceed with the visitation according to the ritual prescribed by Pope Gregory XVI.[96]

c. The Vicar Capitular was forbidden to give permission for the erection of a new monastery of Regulars if such institution had not already existed in the diocese,[97] or to erect, or give consent for the erection or aggregation of religious congregations.[98]

d. The Vicar Capitular was obliged to reserve for the future bishop all revenues, such as the cathedraticum *(ex jurisdictione)* and the chancery fees *(ex sigillo)*, which during the occupancy of see belonged to the bishop. He was permitted, however, to deduct from this amount a reasonable salary and other expenses.[99] Any pecuniary fines which accrued from ecclesiastical penalties inflicted during the period of vacancy were to be converted to pious places and causes and were not to be appropriated by the Chapter or the Vicar Capitular to their own uses.[100]

e. The Vicar Capitular was always conceded the same privileges of honor which were given the vicar-general. According to the motu proprio *Inter Multiplices* February 21, 1905,[101] the Vicar Capitular enjoys the privileges and insignia of a Titular Prothonotary Apostolic during his tenure of office.

96 Benedict XIV, *op. cit.*, lib. X, c. X, n. 6; S.R.C., decret., 8 Nov. 1843—Gardellini, *Decreta Authentica,* VIII, n. 4826

97 S.C. EE. et RR., resolut., 19 Febr. 1633—Bizzarri, *Collectanea*, p. 608; cf. Vermeersch, *De Religiosis,* I², n. 104; Ferraris, *op. cit.*, V. *Vicarius Capitularis,* art. II, n. 66.

98 S.C. Indulg., resp., 15 Nov. 1878—*Decreta Authentica*, n. 438; cf. ASS, XI, 353.

99 S.C.C. *Agrigentina,* 17 Nov. 1594—*Fontes,* n. 2275; *Nullius,* II Jul. 1626—*op. cit.*, n. 2470; *Goan,* 6 Mart. 1847—Richter, *Canones et Decreta,* p. 374, n. 19; decret., 8 Febr. 1913—AAS, XI (1915), 45-47.

100 S.C.C., *Mazarien.*, 6 Dec. 1642—*Fontes,* n. 2639; *Elnen.*, 28 Mart. 1648—*op. cit.*, n. 2681.

101 Nn. 62, 64, 66-68, 70, 76—*Fontes,* n. 665, pp. 644-45; cf. *American Ecclesiastical Review,* XXXII (1905), 625-26.

§5. The Cessation of the Office of the Vicar Capitular and the Rendering of Account

The office of the Vicar Capitular expires when the new bishop who is legitimately promoted to the see presents the apostolic letters of his promotion to the cathedral Chapter; and if the diocese has no chapter, the presentation is made to the one who, according to the sacred canons or by a special disposition of the Holy See, administers the diocese, or to him who was authorized to appoint the Vicar Capitular.[102]

The office of the Vicar ceases also by his death or by his resignation. The resignation must be made according to law and made public, but it is not necessary that the Chapter accept it in order that it become effective.[103] So also does the Vicar lose his office when he is removed by the Sacred Congregation of the Council or the Congregation of Bishops and Regulars. The metropolitan or the Chapter, however, cannot remove the Vicar from office, even though either of them had made the appointment.[104] The Vicar Capitular, however, does not lose his office by being elected or nominated to the vacant see which he is administering.[105]

If the Vicar Capitular loses his office before the vacant see is provided with a new bishop the cathedral, or, if there is no Chapter, others who are duly authorized to make such appointments, must appoint another Vicar within eight days unless the Sacred Congregation of Bishops and Regulars provides for the diocese in some other manner, e.g., by appointing an Administrator apostolic.[106] But one who is already elected bishop to the see by the Chapter, or nominated or presented by lay authority, may not be elected as its Vicar Capitular. And if the Chapter, or any other attempts to make such an appointment, the act is null and void, and the individual appointed

102 C. 1, *de electione et electi potestate,* I, 3, in Extravag. Comm.; Pius IX, const., *Romanus Pontifex,* 28 Aug. 1973—*Fontes,* n. 565; Benedict XIV, *op. cit.,* lib. II, c. V, nn. 6-7.

103 Wernz, *Jus Decretalium,* II, n. 795, (p. 611).

104 Benedict XIV, *op. cit.,* lib. II, c. IX, n. 4.

105 De Angelis, *Praelectiones Juris Canonici,* lib. I, tit. VI, n. 13.

106 Cf. Wernz, *op. cit.,* p. 612.

ipso facto is deprived of his election or nomination to the see, and incurs excommunication reserved specially to the Holy See.[107]

It has already been observed in the statement of the decree of the Council of Trent that the bishop who is promoted to a vacant see must demand an account of the administration, not only of the Vicar Capitular, but from all who in any way participated in the administration during the period of vacancy. This, then, is the final obligation incumbent upon the Vicar Capitular, and if he is found guilty of any delinquency, he is liable to punishment to be inflicted by the new bishop.[108]

ART. 2. *The Administration of Dioceses Without Cathedral Chapters*

The legislation enacted in the period of the Decretals and by the Council of Trent governing the administration of vacant and quasi-vacant sees made no explicit reference to the election of a Vicar Capitular, or of the provision for the administration of those dioceses which were without cathedral Chapters. The law governing the devolution of the right of electing the Vicar Capitular, however, served as a means whereby Vicars Capitular were appointed for dioceses without Chapters. According to the decisions of the Sacred Congregation of the Council[109] the metropolitan must appoint the Vicar Capitular for suffragan sees which are without cathedral Chapters. And if a suffragan see became vacant during the vacancy of the metropolitan see, the right of appointing the Vicar does not pass to the senior suffragan bishop, but to the cathedral Chapter of the metropolitan see. This provision served as the norm governing the devolution of the right of electing the Vicar up to the present Code of Canon law.

[107] Pius IX, const., *Romanus Pontifex*, 28 Aug. 1873—*Fontes*, n. 565.

[108] Council of Trent, sess. XXIV, *de ref.*, c. 16—*Canones et Decreta*, p. 196; cf. Bouix, *op. cit.*, pp. 592-93.

[109] S.C.C., decis., 28 Aug. 1683, et decis., 14 Apr. 1685—Richter, *op. cit.*, p. 375; n. 24; cf. Benedict XIV, *op. cit.*, lib. II, c. IX, n. 2.

§ 1. The Constitution *Quam ex sublimi* January 26, 1753

Pope Benedict XIV had readily perceived that the common law of the Church in regard to the administration of vacant sees was not sufficiently extensive and adaptable to meet the needs of sees in many regions of the Church, especially with respect to the missionary fields far distant from the Eternal City. There were vicariates and prefectures Apostolic in India, America and other sections of the Church which generally were without cathedral Chapters because of the primitive stage of development of the Church in those parts. Then, too, there were many countries such as Ireland, Albania, Macedonia, Servia, Bulgaria, Persia, Mesopotamia, and sections in the proximity of the Aegean Sea, where there were many dioceses without cathedral Chapters.[110]

Moved by a desire to meet the needs of the situation in all parts of the world, the Pope promulgated his Constitution *Quam ex sublimi* on January 26, 1753. By this Constitution [111] the common law of the Church enacted by the Council of Trent was made more extensive in scope, and admirably adjusted to the conditions of the ever-expanding missionary fields of the world. The Constitution was, for the most part, a repetition of the Constitution *Ex sublimi* issued by the same pontiff a few years previously for the Church in India.[112] The substance of the Constitution was later incorporated in the "Schema" submitted to the Vatican Council [113] and finally adopted by the present Code of Canon law.[114]

The Constitution made the following provisions:

a. All vicars Apostolic who had no co-adjutors with the right to succession, nor vicars-general, either secular or religious, were obliged to appoint as vicars-general capable secular or religious priests. When the vicar Apostolic was taken by

[110] Cf. Benedict XIV, const., *Quam ex sublimi,* 26 Jan. 1753 § 3—*Fontes,* n. 436.

[111] *Fontes,* n. 436.

[112] 29 Jan. 1753—*Fontes,* n. 423.

[113] Cf. Martin, *Collectio Omnium Concilii Vaticani,* pp. 135-36.

[114] Cf. Canon 309.

death, the vicar-general, as a delegate of the Apostolic See, assumed the governance of the vicariate Apostolic and continued in this office until a new vicar Apostolic, appointed by the Holy See, took possession of the vicariate. The faculties enjoyed by the vicar-general during vacancy included all that common law attached to the office of the Vicar Capitular. The vicar-general, furthermore, possessed and could exercise all to be retained, even though ecclesiastics other than cathedral exception of those acts which demanded episcopal consecration. In urgent cases, however, the vicar-general was permitted to consecrate chalices, patens, and portable altars with the sacred oils blessed by a bishop. This law applied also to those vicars Apostolic who did not possess the episcopal character.

b. The third paragraph of this Constitution applied to other countries referred to previously, where cathedral Chapters did not exist universally. In those dioceses which had Chapters, the custom in vogue with respect to the election of the Vicar Capitular was to be retained, even though ecclesiastics other than cathedral Canons participated in the election. In the dioceses without Chapters the prevailing custom was to be followed, whether or not this consisted in a practice of electing the Vicar Capitular by the pastors only, or by all ecclesiastics in the diocese. The prescriptions of the Council of Trent, however, were to be followed as closely as possible.

c. The fourth paragraph applied to all residential Ordinaries who had neither cathedral Chapters, nor pastors in the cathedral city or diocese, but simple priests dispersed throughout the see. In these instances the vicar-general of the bishop *ipso facto* became the Vicar Capitular as soon as the residental Ordinary died. The vicar-general enjoyed the same rights which the Vicar Capitular possessed according to common law, and retained office until the new Ordinary took possession of the see.

§ 2. The Discipline Prevailing in the United States

Within the present limits of the continental United States, the question of administering vacant sees can scarcely be said to have come into prominence before the nineteenth century.

Previous to this time the territory which now comprises the continental United States was divided into portions and placed under the jurisdiction of various vicariates Apostolic. Thus the territory of New France in America was at first under the jurisdiction of the archbishop of Rouen, France, and later under Bishop Laval, vicar Apostolic of Quebec, Canada. The thirteen colonies which comprised the English missions were subject to the vicariate Apostolic of the London District, while the Spanish missions of the south and west formed a part of the Cuban and Mexican dioceses.[115]

But after the Sacred Congregation of the Propaganda erected the see of Baltimore, placing Bishop Carroll over it as its first Bishop, the formation and erection of other dioceses and vicariates Apostolic successively followed. It was only after this time, that the problem of providing for the administration of vacant sees had to be taken into consideration. When the metropolitan or suffragan bishops had co-adjutors bishop who enjoyed the right to succession, the situation solved itself. But in those dioceses which were less fortunate, some provision had to be sought for the governance of the vacant see.

It appears that the Constitution of Pope Benedict XIV served as a norm for the discipline in the United States. Although there is little testimony to be found before the year 1866 which might throw light upon the discipline prevailing in this country before the Second Plenary Council at Baltimore, there is sufficient at hand to indicate that the vicar-general assumed the governance of the diocese when it became vacant by the death or transfer of the bishop.[116]

On the twentieth of July, 1801, Bishop Luis Penalvery y Cardenas of New Orleans was promoted to the metropolitan see of Guatemala. Before taking up his duties, he appointed

[115] Cf. Shea, *History of the Catholic Church in the United States*, I, 226, 259, 300, 366;IV, 300; *The Life and Times of Archbishop Carroll*, pp. 50, 543, 570.

[116] Guilday (*A History of the Councils of Baltimore*, pp. 108-9) mentions certain duties incumbent upon the vicar-general after the death of a bishop which seems to imply that the administration of the vacant diocese was in the hands of the vicar-general.

Canon Hassett and Reverend Patrick Walsh, who were his vicars-general, to administer the see until a new bishop took possession of it.[117] The same is true of Bishop Francis Garcia Diego, the first bishop of the diocese of the two Californias. Before death he appointed his vicar-general, the Very Reverend Joseph M. Gonzales Rubio, to act as the Administrator of the see when it became vacant.[118]

At the Second Plenary Council at Baltimore, 1866, under the presidency of Archbishop Spalding, who acted in the capacity of Apostolic Delegate, definite legislation was formulated for the United States with respect to the appointment and the jurisdiction of Administrators of vacant sees. The Council decreed that "each bishop can communicate the faculties he has received from the Holy See to worthy priests that have labored in the diocese; especially should he do so at the approach of death, so that during the vacancy of the see there will be some one to take the place of the departed bishop, until the Apostolic See, having been duly informed at the earliest convenience, should provide for the diocese in some other way." [119] "But if at the demise of the archbishop or bishop," the Council continued, "there is no priest to whom the aforesaid faculties were properly communicated; or also should the see become vacant in any other manner than by the death of its prelate, then the metropolitan, or, in his default of taking the matter in hand, as also when the metropolitan see itself becomes vacant, the senior suffragan bishop, will designate some worthy priest who will administer the diocese . . . until the Holy See, on receiving the necessary intelligence of the fact shall dispose otherwise."[120]

In the United States, therefore, the bishops appointed Ad-

[117] Guilday, *The Life and Times of John Carroll*, II, 703; Shea, *The Life and Times of Archbishop Carroll*, p. 581.

[118] Shea, *The History of the Catholic Church in the United States*, IV, 355.

[119] Smith, *Notes on the Second Plenary Council at Baltimore*, pp. 61-62; cf. II Plenary Council at Baltimore, tit. III, c. II, n. 96—*Acta et Decreta*, p. 67.

[120] Smith, *loc. cit.*; II Plenary Council at Baltimore, tit. III, c. II, n. 97 —*op. cit.*, p. 68.

ministrators before their death. The appointment could be made at any time, and could likewise be freely revoked by the bishop himself. Whether the appointment had to be made according to a special form is a matter of question. Baart [121] was of the opinion that the appointment had to be made in writing in order to be valid, and that no priest of the diocese needed to recognize an oral appointment. When a metropolitan or suffragan appointed an Administrator for a see other than their own, the appointment was only tentative and entirely dependent upon the provision which the Holy See would make after being informed of the situation.

The jurisdiction of the Administrator comprised all that common law attributed to the Vicar Capitular. The ordinary faculties of the bishop could be delegated to the Administrator by the bishop who was empowered to make the appointment.[122] All faculties, however, which required for their exercise the use of the Holy Oils or the episcopal character could not be delegated.[123] It is interesting to note also that the Council petitioned the Holy See to grant the metropolitans and bishops the privilege of delegating to the Administrator the extraordinary faculties enjoyed by them,[124] but the Holy See remained silent in the matter. The same petition was repeated in the Tenth Provincial Council at Baltimore, 1869, and was granted, but only to the province of Baltimore.[125]

The Administrator was also bound to the same restrictions which circumscribed the powers of the Vicar Capitular. He consequently could not change the status of the diocese by in-

121 *Legal Formulary,* pp. 34-35.

122 These faculties may be found in Smith, *Notes on the Second Plenary Council at Baltimore,* pp. 463-468.

123 *Facultates Ordinariae,* form. I, n. 28—Smith, *op. cit.,* p. 468.

124 II Plenary Council at Baltimore, tit. III, c. II, n. 98—*Acta et Decreta,* p. 68; *Facultates extraordinariae,* form. I, C,D,E,—Smith, *op. cit.,* pp. 469-75.

125 "Sanctitas Sua, licet ea super re nil pro nunc decernendum expresserit, coluit tamen, ut si quam interim *ex tuae provincae dioecesibus* vacare contigerit, administrator, sede vacante, donetur facultatibus extraordinariis contentis sub formulis C.D.E., exceptis iis, quae characterem episcopalem requirunt."—*Acta et Decreta Conciliorum Recentiorum.* III, 599; cf. *Concilii Provincialis Baltimorensis* X—*Acta et Decreta,* p. 76.

novation, could not incardinate or excardinate priests, appoint pastors (except provisionally), and was strictly forbidden to incur debts for which the see would be liable, or to alienate any property of the Church. He was also obliged to give an account of the administration to the incoming bishop.[126] The Third Plenary Council at Baltimore added the special prescription that the Administrator was bound to obtain the consent of the Board of Diocesan Consultors in all instances indicated in the law, where such consent had to be obtained by the bishop.[127]

The particular legislation enacted by the Second Plenary Council at Baltimore continued to direct the practice of appointing Administrators for vacant sees in the United States up to the promulgation of the present Code of Canon Law. The provisions of canon 427 now serve as a uniform norm governing the administration of quasi-vacant and vacant episcopal sees in all dioceses throughout the Church of the Latin Rite where the cathedral Chapters have not as yet been instituted or revived.

The particular institution of the Board of Diocesan Consultors, which now forms the fundamental basis for the legislation of the Code with respect to the administering of vacant and quasi-vacant sees in the United States, as well as in all dioceses where this institution now exists, owes its origin to the Church in this country. Shortly after the beginning of the nineteenth century there was a trace of the early institution of Diocesan Consultors; two or more priests of the diocese were appointed to assist the bishop in the governance of the see, thereby substituting for the cathedral Chapter in this respect.[128] The First Plenary Council at Baltimore urged the bishop of this country to establish this institution in their dioceses.[129] The practice was recommended also by the Fathers

126 II Plenary Council at Baltimore, tit. III, c. II, n. 99—*Acta et Decreta*, p. 68; cf. Wernz, *Jus Decretalium*, II, n. 795.

127 III Plenary Council at Baltimore, tit. II, c. II, n. 22—*Acta et Decreta*, p. 16.

128 Cf. Klekotka, *Diocesan Consultors*, p. 18.

129 I Plenary Council at Baltimore, n. 6—*Acta et Decreta Conciliorum Recentiorum*, III, 146.

of the Second Plenary Council at Baltimore,[130] and the system of appointing Diocesan Consultors was adopted universally in this country. But the lack of definite legislation caused the institution to be little more than nominal.[131]

When the archbishops of the United States met in Rome in 1883 to prepare for the Third Plenary Council at Baltimore, the Holy See, desirous of bringing the organization of the Church in America more and more in conformity with common law, proposed that cathedral Chapters be established in this country. The prelates, however, considered that the time had not as yet come for such measures, and the Sacred Congregation of the Propaganda then proposed that the appointment of Consultors be resorted to until conditions would permit the erection of Chapters. As a consequence of this proposal, the Fathers of the Third Plenary Council decreed that in every diocese a certain number of priests must be appointed as Consultors to act as the regular advisers of the bishops until circumstances would make it possible to replace their services by Canons as common law demanded.[132] At the same time, to give efficacy to their enactment, they defined the rights and duties of the consultors, their mode of appointment, their number, qualifications, and term of office.[133] This legislation served as a pattern for subsequent practices adopted in Australia and Latin America,[134] and this particular institution was finally recognized by the present Code of Canon law.[135]

The common law of the Church makes it now incumbent upon all bishops in whose dioceses it has not yet been possible to institute cathedral Chapters, or to revive former ones, to appoint at least six, or, even in dioceses with few priests, at least four priests who are commendable for piety, good charac-

130 II Plenary Council at Baltimore, tit. II, c. V—*Acta et Decreta*, pp. 53-58.

131 Cf. Smith, *Notes on the Second Plenary Council at Baltimore*, p. 66.

132 III Plenary Council at Baltimore, tit II, c. II, n. 17—*Acta et Decreta*, p. 14.

133 Idem, c. II—*op. cit.*, pp. 14-16.

134 Cf. Klekotka, *op. cit.*, pp. 23-24.

135 Canons 423-428.

ter, knowledge and prudence, to serve as Diocesan Consultors.[136] The office of the Consultors lasts for three years, and if the triennial term expires during the vacancy of the bishopric, the term is prorogued until the new bishop takes possession of the see.[137] The purpose of the institution and the duties attached to the office of the Consultors is contained in canon 427 where it is stated that the Board of Diocesan Consultors takes the place of the cathedral Chapters as the council of the bishop. Whatever part the canons of the Code give the cathedral Chapter in the government of the diocese either during the reign of the bishop or during a vacancy is to be also the part of the Board of Consultors.

This canon of the Code was a decided innovation in the common law of the Church. Since the canon does not explicitly mention the right of the Board of Diocesan Consultors to elect Administrators for vacant sees, a doubt remained in the minds of some prelates and canonists in this country as to whether canon 427 had abrogated the dispositions of the Second Plenary Council at Baltimore with respect to the appointment of the Administrator. The question was proposed to the Holy See, and the Pontifical Commission for the Authentic Interpretation of the Code answered in the affirmative.[138]

136 Canons 423-425.

137 Canon 426 §§ 1, 4.

138 24 Nov. 1918—AAS, XI (1919), 75; cf. *Irish Ecclesiastical Record,* 5s, XIII, 337-338.

PART II

THE PRESENT DISCIPLINE GOVERNING THE ADMINISTRATION OF VACANT AND QUASI-VACANT SEES IN THE UNITED STATES

PRELIMINARY REMARKS

The scope of the present study is limited to a consideration of the discipline of the Church with reference to the administration of vacant and quasi-vacant episcopal sees in the United States. This does not signify, however, that there is extant at present any particular legislation peculiar to this country. The legal provisions found in canon 427 are indicative of that fact that according to the present common law of the Church all dioceses, whether they have cathedral Chapters, or whether this institution as the senate or council of the bishop is supplied by that of the Board of Diocesan Consultors, are governed by one and the same norm as far as the administration of vacant and quasi- vacant sees is concerned.[1] The desired aim of this treatise, therefore, is to arrive at a practical application of the common law to the present conditions and organization of the Church in the United States.

Since canon 427 explicitly specifies that whatever the canons attribute to the cathedral Chapter as the council of the bishop in relation to the government of the diocese, either during the occupancy or during the vacancy or quasi-vacancy of the see, applies also to the Board of Diocesan Consultors, the term "Board of Diocesan Consultors" will be substituted throughout this study for the term cathedral Chapter. The Board of Diocesan Consultors, however, must not be confused with the Parish Priest Consultors referred to in canons 385-390, for the latter institution is an entirely distinct canonical provision.

The present discipline of the Church concerning vacant and quasi-vacant sees is based substantially upon the law of the decretals and the decree of the Council of Trent already referred to in the Historical Synopsis. With but few exceptions the former and present law bear a striking identity, and it is only in particular instances that the new Code of Canon Law has departed from previous practice by introducing innovations. The canons in Book II, Part I, Chapter VII, *De sede impedita*

[1] Canons 427 et 423; 429-444.

aut vacante ac de Vicario Capitulari, will frequently be found subject, therefore, to the interpretive rules of the *ambitus* of the Code.[2] It is only by a critical analysis of the text and context of these canons that one can determine whether they restate wholly or in part any of former legislation, and in view of this fact they will be subject either wholly or partially to the interpretation approved prior to the present Code. The norm of such interpretation is stated in the second section of canon 6, where it is specified that in such instances the opinion of approved authors must be accepted. Among the approved authors, canonists[3] regard the members of the various Sacred Congregations as particularly reliable and worthy of consideration as prudent and recognized canonists. The phrase *ex veteris juris auctoritate* in the second paragraph of canon 6 encompasses not only the law of the decretals and of the Council of Trent, but the various pronouncements of the Roman Pontiffs as well, and the decrees and decisions of the Sacred Congregations whose competence extended to all matters with reference to the administration of quasi-vacant and vacant episcopal sees.[4]

The decree of the Council of Trent instituting the office of the Vicar Capitular implicitly included all that was contained in the law of the Decretals with reference to the nature, causes and effects of vacant and quasi-vacant sees, and the administrative office of the cathedral Chapter upon such occasions. For this reason the interpretations placed upon the decree of the Council of Trent by the various Sacred Congregations, necessarily involved the interpretation of relative legislation found in the decretals. The Sacred Congregation of the Council at first interpreted the law of the Council of Trent with reference to the discipline in question, and was later assisted by the Sacred Congregation of Bishops and Regulars. The decisions of these Congregations, especially the former, which held a

[2] Canon 6 §§ 2-4.

[3] Van Hove, *De Legibus Ecclesiasticis,* p. 69; Vermeersch-Creusen, *Epitome,* I, 49.

[4] Prümmer, *Manuale Juris Canonici,* pp. 22-23.

status relative to the decrees of the Council of Trent similar to that which the Pontifical Commission holds with reference to the new Code, must be regarded as authoritative declarations of the meaning of the provisions of the Council. A careful distinction must be preserved, however, between responses authentically interpreting the law itself, and those which apply it to certain peculiar and mutable circumstances.[5]

A word may be inserted here with reference to the term "Vicar Capitular". This term has enjoyed usage in ecclesiastical legislation since the Council of Trent, at which time this office was instituted. The incumbent of this office is called the Capitular since he is chosen by the Chapter (*capitulum*) and administers the see in their place. Strangely enough, the present law applies the same name to the individual who is elected by the Board of Diocesan Consultors, who are not termed a *capitulum* but rather a *coetus.*[6] The presence of the name Vicar Capitular in canon 426 § 5 may possibly be due to the fact that the schema of the new Code referred to the Board of Diocesan Consultors as the *Capitulum consultorum dioecesanorum,* and, whereas the term *capitulum* was changed to *coetus* for the authentic edition of the Code, the name Vicar Capitular was retained. Blat [7] concludes from this that even though the cleric be elected by the Diocesan Consultors, he is nevertheless called the Vicar Capitular. This appears to be the intention of the legislator, for, with the exception of the Vicar Capitular appointed by the metropolitan or senior suffragan bishop in view of devolutive right, the Code is consistent in terming as administrators all who receive the office of administering sees from authorities other than the cathedral Chapter or the Board of Diocesan Consultors.[8]

In the United States it has ever been the custom of terming as Administrator the individual who was duly appointed to

[5] *Periodica,* XVII (1928), 136-38.

[6] Cf. Canons 426 § 5, 427.

[7] *Commentarium Textus Codicis Juris Canonici,* II, 403.

[8] Cf. Canons 431 § 2, 309, §4, 312-318.

administer a vacant see.[9] Since the promulgation of the present Code the nomenclature has been retained. It is no more than the vernacular expression of the canonical term "Vicar Capitular", and consequently may legitimately be applied to the individual elected by the Board of Diocesan Consultors to administer a vacant or quasi-vacant episcopal see. Just as the term " Board of Diocesan Consultors," therefore, will substitute that of the " cathedral Chapter " in this treatise, so also will the term " Administrator " be employed instead of " Vicar Capitular." The Administrator referred to in this study, however, must not be confused with the Administrator Apostolic. The latter, according to canon 312, is a prelate appointed by the Sovereign Pontiff, for special and grave reasons, to rule in his name a canonically erected diocese. The canonical provisions relative to this office are contained in canons 312-318.

Reference may also be made here with respect to the terms diocese or see, and bishop. According to canon 215 § 2, in law the term "diocese" comprises also an abbey or prelature *nullius;* and the name "bishop" refers also to an abbot or prelate *nullius* unless the nature of the matter or context require a different interpretation. In the United States there are no prelatures *nullius* and only one abbey *nullius,* which is situated at Belmont, North Carolina.

The canonical discussion of the administration of vacant and quasi-vacant episcopal sees will be divided for the most part according to the sequence of the canons, with the exception, however, that quasi-vacancy shall be discussed after, rather than before, vacancy proper. The nature, causes and effects of vacancy will first be established according to the present discipline. This forms the basis upon which rests the entire structure of the legislation governing the administration of such sees. This will be followed by the office of the Board

[9] Cf. Shea, *The Life and Times of Archbishop Carroll,* p. 581; *The History of the Catholic Church in the United States,* IV, 355; The Second Plenary Council at Baltimore, tit. III, c. II, nn. 96-99—*Actat et Decreta,* pp. 67-68; Smith, *Notes on the Second Plenary Council,* pp. 61-62; Baart, *Legal Formulary,* pp. 33-35; Smith, *Elements of Ecclesiastical Law,* pp. 364-367.

of Diocesan Consultors during the vacancy of the see. The subsequent chapters will be given to a consideration of the appointment of the Administrator, his qualifications, particular duties and independence; the nature and extent of the jurisdiction attached to the administrative office; the rights, honorary and useful, of the Administrator; the cessation of the administrative office and the final account of the administration to be given the incoming bishop.

CHAPTER V

The Nature, Causes and Effects of Vacancy

An episcopal see becomes vacant when the incumbent ceases to hold title to office, or to be the bishop of the diocese. The modes by which this may occur, and the exact time when vacancy actually takes place, are determined by canon 430. A statement of the law will be found helpful in arriving at an understanding of the present discipline.

Canon 430 § 1. Sedes episcopalis vacat Episcopi morte, renuntiatione a Romano Pontifice acceptata, translatione ac privatione Episcopo intimata.

§ 2. Nihilominus, excepta collatione beneficiorum aut officiorum ecclesiasticorum, omnia vim habent quae gesta sunt a Vicario Generali, usque dum hic certam de obitu Episcopi notitiam acceperit, vel ab Episcopo aut Vicario Generali, usque dum certa de memoratis actibus pontificiis notitia ad eosdem pervenerit.

An episcopal see becomes vacant, therefore, in the same four ways as any other irremovable ecclesiastical office.[1] And since the episcopacy, in common with all other offices in the Church, is a true ecclesiastical office, the general norms of canons 184-195 governing the loss of these will find their proportionate application here. The following paragraphs will be given to an individual consideration of each cause and its effects.

Art. 1. *Vacancy by the Death of the Bishop*

The death of the bishop is the usual manner by which a see becomes vacant. Insofar as death is a dissolution of all existing ties between the bishop and his office, vacancy becomes immediately effective. The ordinary effect following from vacancy is that the jurisdiction of the vicar-general ceases. But this gen-

[1] Cf. Canon 183 § 1.

eral prescription of canon 371 is offset by the disposition of canon 430 § 2, whereby common lay prorogues the jurisdiction of the vicar-general in all matters excepting the appointments to ecclesiastical office and benefices, until he has received certain notification of the fact that the see is actually vacant. Hence, even if several days or weeks had elapsed since the actual death of the bishop, as long as the vicar-general remains ignorant or uncertain of the fact, his official acts retain their validity. Augustine defines the nature of certainty demanded by law for the vicar-general, and his interpretation has been adopted by other canonists.[2] "Certainty, we know, may be either physical or moral," writes Augustine,[3] "according as it it derived from the bodily senses or based on reasons which leave no room for reasonable doubt. Besides, there is juridical certainty, obtained by means prescribed in law; for instance, peremptory admonition, official summons, or a document. The last-named kind of certainty is not required for the death notice of a bishop, because the text demands only certain notice, and 'one who is already certain need not be further informed.'[4] Moreover, the case does not fall under any heading of law requiring certainty. Hence if the vicar-general receives notice through trustworthy witnesses, or by letter from one who is in a position to know and willing to tell the truth, he may be said to have certainty. But he is not obliged to believe the newspapers, as they sometimes report people dead when they are still among the living. Of course, the surest way of notifying the vicar-general is through the episcopal chancery (with the diocesan, not episcopal seal)."

Art. 2. *Vacancy by Resignation of the Bishop*

Resignation in general entails the loss of one's proper ecclesiastical office resulting from an act freely performed, motivated

[2] Coronata, *Institutiones,* I, 531, footnote 4; Klekotka, *Diocesan Consultors,* p. 159.

[3] *Commentary,* II, 476.

[4] "Eum qui certus est, certiorari ulterius non debet."—Reg. 31, R.J., in VI°.

by a reasonable and just cause, and accepted in due form by a competent ecclesiastical superior.[5] A bishop validly resigns, therefore, only when he is in full possession of his mental faculties and capable of performing an human act. He must act freely, furthermore, unhampered by unjust and grave fear, substantial error, or deceit, and the resignation must be disassociated entirely from any simoniacal agreement connected with the negotiation.[6] The resignation must be submitted to the Roman Pontiff, and as soon as he accepts it, the diocese becomes vacant.[7] Some canonists[8] maintain, however, that vacancy does not arise until the resigning bishop receives authentic notification from the Sacred Consistorial Congregation to the effect that his resignation has been accepted. According to this opinion the term "intimata" in canon 430 § 1 modifies not only "privatione," but also "renuntiatione a Romano Pontifice acceptata."[9] Coronata[10] holds the former opinion and argues that the see becomes vacant the moment the resignation is accepted by the Roman Pontiff, for the second paragraph of canon 430 seems to indicate that vacancy is not dependent upon the notification, since the law specifies that with the exception of appointing to offices and benefices, all official acts of the bishop himself, and of his vicar-general, are valid until certain notification of the pontifical acts is received. This opinion is accepted by the majority of canonists[11] and appears to express the true significance of canon 430. The only difference in the effect between the two opinions is that, according

[5] Cf. Canons 184-186.

[6] Canones cit.; cf. Blat, *Commentarium*, II, 401; De Meester, *Compendium*, II, n. 788 (pp. 228-229).

[7] Canon 430 § 1; De Meester, *op. cit.*, n. 788 (p. 229); Wernz-Vidal, *Jus Canonicum*, II, n. 707 (p. 757); Sipos, *Juris Canonici*, p. 285; Ayrinhac, *Constitutions of the Church*, p. 270; Coronata, *Institutiones*, I, 531; Cocchi, *Commentarium*, II, 337-338; et al.

[8] Vermeersch-Creusen, *Epitome*, I, n. 478 (p. 305); Augustine, *op. cit.*, II, 478.

[9] Cf. Canon 190.

[10] *Op. cit.*, 531, footnote 3.

[11] Cf. Footnote 7 supra.

to one, the resigning bishop and his vicar-general cannot validly confer offices or benefices after the resignation has been accepted. In all other matters of jurisdiction the power of the bishop and the vicar-general remains unaffected until certain notification is received.

The question now arises as to the degree of certainty the law demands, since the loss of jurisdiction on the part of the bishop and the vicar-general is dependent upon this certain knowledge. The canon simply states "certa notitia." The majority of canonists [12] interpret this to mean authentic certainty. This would signify that the bishop and the vicar-general could exercise jurisdiction until they received notification from official scources, or by receiving a document signed by a notary or chancellor.[13] The better opinion appears to be that "certa notitia" does not demand direct and authentic information, but rather that it would be sufficient to have reliable information.[14]

Resignation has been considered thus far from the aspect of express resignation. It must be remembered that tacit resignation, which affects all ecclesiastical offices not excluding the episcopacy, may be a cause also of an episcopal see becoming vacant.[15] Tacit resignation, or as it is sometimes called, equivalent resignation, is the result of certain explicitly determined facts, which, by a special disposition of law and of themselves, without the formalities of presentation, acceptance or declaration, produce the same effect as express resignation.[16] Canon

12 Cappello, *Summa Juris Canonici,* I, n. 399 (p. 411); Chelodi, *Jus De Personis,* n. 216 (p. 358); Augustine, *Commentary,* II, 478; Vermeersch-Creusen, *op. cit.,* I, n. 478 (p. 305).

13 Cf. Canon 374.

14 "Renuntians in officio tenetur permanere donec de Superioris acceptatione certum nuntium acceperit. Non tamen requiritus ex lege generali quod sit directum et authenticum, sufficit quod sit revera certum et quod referatur ad iam peractam acceptationem." — Maroto, *Institutiones Juris Canonici,* I, n. 683 (p. 809); Coronata, *op. cit.,* 531, footnote 4; Ayrinhac, *Constitutions,* p. 270.

15 De Meester, *Compendium,* II, n. 788, footnote 3 (p. 228); Cocchi, *Commentarium,* II, 524; Prümmer, *Manuale Juris Canonici,* p. 173; Klekotka, *Diocesan Consultors,* p. 161.

16 Cf. Maroto, *op. cit.,* I, n. 684 (pp. 809-10).

188 enumerates taxatively the facts which produce tacit resignation. The only probable fact which might affect the episcopal office is that of public defection from the faith.[17] This crime presupposes not an internal, or even external but occult act, but a public defection from the faith through formal heresy, or apostasy, with or without affiliation with another religious society. Simple schism without heresy would not suffice to constitute tacit resignation.[18] The public character of this crime must be understood in the light of canon 2197 n. 1. Hence, if a bishop were guilty of this violation and the fact were divulged to the greater part of the town or community, the crime would be public [19] and the see *ipso facto* becomes vacant. The jurisdiction of the vicar-general, furthermore, is immediately lost in this instance.[20]

Art. 3. *Vacancy by Privation of Office*

Privation of office implies that a bishop is deprived of his title to his see independently of his consent, because of some crime committed. A bishop may incur this ecclesiastical penalty by being guilty of a violation to which the law itself attaches the penalty, or by being the subject of a sentence imposed upon him by the Holy See.[21] There is only one case of privation *ipso facto* incurred which in all probability might effect a bishop. This instance, stated in canon 2398, has reference to a bishop who culpably neglects to be consecrated within six months from the time he receives his papal appointment to a diocese. Thus it might happen that a bishop-elect would take canonical possession of his diocese before his consecration, and then culpably neglect to receive the episcopal consecration within the prescribed time. The law states that such neglect

[17] Canon 188 n. 4.

[18] Blat, *Commentarium,* II, 125; Augustine, *Commentary,* II, 161; Vermeersch-Creusen, *Epitome,* I, n. 268 (p. 199); Ayrinhac, *General Legislation,* pp. 349-50.

[19] Cf. Vermeersch-Creusen, *op. cit.,* III, n. 384 (p. 185); "Quia res facti est, in aestimatione boni viri esse debet."—D'Annibale, *Summula Theologiae Moralis,* I, n. 242, footnote 49.

[20] Canon 371.

[21] Cf. Canons 2227, 1557.

would *ipso facto* deprive the bishop of his see.[22] Even in this case, nevertheless, a declaratory sentence would ordinarily have to be inflicted before the penalty would become efficacious. This appears quite evident from canon 2232, where it is stated that a delinquent who incurs a penalty *ipso facto* specified in the law, is excused from its observance before a declaratory sentence is pronounced, if the observance of the penalty would defame him. A bishop-elect, therefore, could scarcely avoid defamation by complying with the penalty, and consequently would not be efficaciously deprived of his see until the Roman Pontiff issued a declaratory sentence.[23] It may be concluded, therefore, that a bishop is never deprived from his office until the Roman Pontiff has pronounced either a declaratory or condemnatory sentence to that effect.[24]

Canon 430 § 1, consequently states that an episcopal see becomes vacant by privation of office only when the fact of privation is duly intimated to the bishop. Since this is generally a judicial procedure, the intimation would have to be of the nature of an authentic document, or at least official notification.[25]

ART. 4. *Vacancy by the Transfer of a Bishop*

The final cause of vacancy is the transfer of a bishop from his own see to another that is vacant. The Roman Pontiff alone is competent to effect the transfer of bishops and he does so to serve the necessity or greater utility of the Church. Transfers are freely enacted by the sovereign Pontiff and it matters not at all whether the bishop is willing or unwilling to be transferred, or whether the reason for such action be due to his culpability or to other causes.[26] Although a bishop

22 Canon 2398.

23 Augustine, *Commentary,* VIII, 103; cf. Vermeersch-Creusen, *Epitome,* III, n. 426 (pp. 210-211); Cocchi, *Commentarium,* V, 76-77; Sipos, *Juris Canonici,* p. 236.

24 Cf. De Meester, *Compendium,* II, n. 790 (pp. 230-31); Vermeersch-Creusen, *op. cit.,* I, n. 478 (p. 305).

25 Coronata, *Institutiones,* I, 531, footnote 4; Augustine, *op. cit.,* II, 478; cf. canon 192 § 3.

26 Cf. Prümmer, *Manuale Juris Canonici,* p. 172.

may be transferred to a see of equal, or even of less equal status than the one already possessed, it appears to be the present policy of the Holy See ordinarily to transfer suffragan bishops to metropolitan sees.

The exact time when a diocese becomes vacant by the transfer of its bishop according to canon 430 § 1 is diversely interpreted by present-day canonists. Owing to the fact that the terms *translatione* and *privatione* are joined by the article *ac*, the question arises as to whether *Episcopo intimata* modifies *privatione* only, or whether it extends also to *translatione*. Some canonists [27] maintain that *Episcopo intimata* applies also to *translatione*, with the result that the diocese does not become vacant by transfer until the bishop receives notification of the fact that the Holy See has taken such action. A concomitant result of this opinion is that the bishop and the vicar-general, according to canon 430 § 2, may validly confer ecclesiastical offices and benefices after the transfer has been announced in consistory and before the notification has been received. Other canonists [28] are of the opinion that the diocese becomes vacant the moment the transfer of the bishop is announced in public consistory. The effects which follow from this opinon are that, according to canon 430 § 2, the jurisdiction of the bishop and the vicar-general is prorogued from the time of this public announcement until certain notification of the pontifical acts is received, and that during this interval neither the bishop nor the vicar-general can validly confer benefices and ecclesiastical offices.

Although both opinions have foundation in the wording of the canon, it appears that the latter opinion is the correct interpretation of the law. Before the present Code of Canon law, a diocese became vacant when the transfer was announced in public consistory, and until the bishop received certain notifi-

[27] Coronata, *op. cit.*, I, 532; Chelodi, *Jus de Personis*, n. 216 (p. 358); Cappello, *Summa Juris Canonici*, I, n. 399 (p. 411); Augustine *Commentary*, II, 478; Cocchi, *Commentarium*, II, n. 315 (p. 336); Klekotka, *Diocesan Consultors*, pp. 86, 160.

[28] Wernz-Vidal, *Jus Canonicum*, II, nn. 359, 707 (pp. 353, 757-58); Sipos, *Juris Canonici*, p. 152, footnote 22; cf. Blat, *Commentarium*, II, 401.

cation of the pontifical acts, he retained his jurisdiction in all matters except with respect to the conferring of benefices and ecclesiastical offices.[29] This identity between former and present legislation demands, according to canon six, number two, that the present law be interpreted according to the approved authors of former legislation. And even if one should advance the argument that the wording of canon 430 § 1 leaves it doubtful as to whether the present Code has changed former law, canon six, number four would have to be complied with, and the former law retained.

The effect following from vacancy in this instance differs greatly from the other cases of vacancy, and marks an innovation in the present law from that of the past. In former times, the moment a bishop received authentic notice of his transfer, the governance of the diocese devolved upon the cathedral chapter.[30] According to the present law[31] the diocese of the transferred bishop does not become fully vacant (*plene vacat*) until the day on which the bishop takes canonical possession of his new see as prescribed by canons 333 and 334. The present Code, therefore, makes a distinction between vacancy and full vacancy in regard to the transfer of a bishop. The first type of vacancy arises when the bishop receives certain notification, while the latter does not take place until later. The law makes provision for the diocese during this interval in the following manner.

When the transferred bishop receives certain notification of the fact of his transfer, he immediately becomes obliged to retire within four months to his new diocese.[32] Since the reception of the notification does not co-incide with the beginning of the day, four months are calculated according to canon

[29] Urban VIII, breve, *Nobis super,* 20 Martii 1625—*Bullarium Romanum,* XIII, pp. 304-305; S.C. EE. et RR., 14 Dec. 1624—*Fontes,* n. 1720; Benedict XIV, *De Synodo Dioecesana,* lib. XIII, c. 16, n. 10; Wernz, *Jus Decretalium,* II, nn. 527-530 (pp. 267-69); Bouix, *De Capitulis,* p. 484.

[30] Cf. Urban VIII, breve *Nobis super,* 20 Martii 1625—*Bullarium Romanum,* XIII, pp. 304-305; S.C. EE. et RR., 14 Dec. 1624—*Fontes,* n. 1720; Benedict XIV, *De Synodo Dioecesana,* lib. XIII, c. 16, n. 10.

[31] Canon 430 § 3; cf. Canon 194 § 1.

[32] Canon 430 § 3.

34 §3 n.3.[33] Hence, if the bishop receives certain notice of his transfer on the tenth of May, the first day is not counted, and he is obliged, unless prevented by a legitimate impediment, to take canonical possession of the diocese *ad quam* before midnight on September the tenth.[34]

The second and very significant effect which results from the reception of certain notification of the transfer is that the bishop *ipso facto* becomes the Administrator (Vicar Capitular) of the diocese from which he is transferred, and the jurisdiction of the vicar-general ceases immediately.[35] During the entire period beginning with the time when notification was received and ending on the day on which he takes canonical possession of the new see, the transferred bishop possesses the jurisdiction, and has the same obligations as the Administrator elected by the Board of Diocesan Consultors.[36] He retains, moreover, the honorary privileges of a residential bishop,[37] and receives all the income of the *mensa episcopalis* according to canon 194 § 2.[38]

The entire disposition of the law governing the fact of vacancy arising from transfer and the effects outlined in canon 430 § 3 devolves upon the reception of certain notification. The all-important question, therefore, is the exact nature of the term *certa translationis notitia* employed by the legislator. Augustine [39] interprets this to mean authentic notice in the form of an official document, or at least official notice. He states that if the notice of "transfer is transmitted by telegraph or telephone, it must be done by persons acting in an official capacity, in other words, by the secretariate of State." Blat [40]

[33] Cf. Blat, *Commentarium,* II, 294, 401; Coronata, *op. cit.,* I, 532; Michiels, *Normae Generalis Juris Canonici,* II, 155; Cicognani, *Jus Canonicum,* II, 195.

[34] Canons 430 § 3, 333, 334.

[35] Canon 430 § 3, n. 1; cf. canon 315 § 2, n. 2.

[36] Canons 430 § 3, n. 1, 435-444.

[37] Canon 430 § 3, n. 2.

[38] Canon 430 § 3, n. 3.

[39] *Commentary,* II, 478; Cappello, *Summa Juris Canonici,* I, n. 399 (p. 411); Chelodi, *Jus De Personis,* n. 216 (p. 358).

[40] *Commentarium,* II, 401.

states that a trustworthy document is necessary, while Ayrinhac [41] considers reliable information as sufficient. Although official or documentary knowledge is less broad than reliable information, it will nevertheless clearly be seen that information, such as a letter or a telegram from a friend in Rome, or, a fortiori, a newspaper report, is certainly insufficient to contitute "certa notitia." The opinion of Augustine is substantiated by former law [42] and is therefore the correct interpretation of the present law. In the past it has been the practice of the Holy See to notify bishops of their transfers by a cablegram through the Apostolic Delegate to the United States. If this practice is still continued, notification from the Apostolic Delegate is authentic and official in the strict sense of the term.

[41] *Constitution,* p. 270; cf. Maroto, *Institutiones,* I, n. 693 (p. 821).

[42] ". . . ex testimonio, seu documento secretarii sacri collegii, vel alio modo huiusmodi absolutionis notitiam episcopus translatus habuerit."—Urban VIII, breve, *Nobis super,* 20 Martii 1625—*Bullarium Romanum,* XIII, 304; S.C. EE. et RR., 14 Dec. 1624—*Fontes,* n. 1720.

CHAPTER VI

THE BOARD OF DIOCESAN CONSULTORS

The Board of Diocesan Consultors takes the place of the cathedral Chapter as the council of the bishop. Whatever part the canons of the Code extend to the cathedral Chapter in the government of the diocese either during occupancy of see, or during vacancy or quasi-vacancy, is to be also the part of the Board of Diocesan Consultors. This is the statement of canon 427. It is the practical and very significant innovation which the present Code of Canon Law has introduced into the common discipline of the Church. Although the law prescribes norms to be followed during both the time of occupancy and vacancy, the present treatise will be devoted to a consideration of those canons only which affect the Board of Diocesan Consultors in the latter instance. Before proceeding, however, with a discussion on the particular rights and duties which are incumbent upon the Board during vacancy of see, it must first of all be established how these rights and duties are possessed by the Board, and how they must be exercised.

The law endows the *coetus consultorum dioecesanorum*[1] with certain rights and duties. These rights and duties are possessed, therefore, by the *coetus* itself, and not by the individual members who unite to form this gathering. From this it will be seen that the *coetus consultorum dioecesanorum* is an association of several physical persons, united by firm, precise bonds into one body politic, recognized by law as one moral person and endowed by law with rights and duties similar to that of an individual. In other words, the Board of Diocesan Consultors is a moral collegiate person.[2]

[1] Canon 427.

[2] Canon 100; Wernz-Vidal, *Jus Canonicum,* II, n. 698, (p. 752); Blat, *Commentarium,* II, 395; Cappello, *Summa Juris Canonici,* I, n. 475, (p. 500); Coronata, *Institutiones,* I, 525; Vermeersch-Creusen, *Epitome,* I, n.

The moral collegiate personality of the Board of Diocesan Consultors gives rise to very significant consequences. The most important of these is the perpetuity of life with which all moral persons, by their very nature, are endowed. When a moral person once comes into being it continues to exist until suppressed by legitimate authority, or when it ceases to have physical members for a period of one hundred years.[3] Hence, when a Board of Diocesan Consultors is legitimately instituted according to the norms of canons 423-425, by a fiction of law a moral collegiate person is created, and this legal person is endowed with perpetuity of life notwithstanding the continuous change of its physical members. Another very important quality of a moral person is that if but one individual of a collegiate moral person remains, the rights of all rest with this individual.[4] This would be found to be very significant, if, when the diocese becomes vacant, for some cause or other only one Consultor would have remained in office. In view of this legal disposition *all the rights* which common law extends to the Board of Diocesan Consultors during vacancy would devolve upon this individual Consultor.

Thus, having considered how the rights and obligations are possessed by the Board of Consultors, the next question concerns the manner by which these rights must be exercised. It must be remembered that the moral collegiate person—the Board of Diocesan Consultors—possesses the rights accorded it by law independently from the physical members, or, in other words, the individual Consultors. But since a moral collegiate person exercises its rights only through the physical persons who represent it, all acts of the Board of Consultors, in order to have juridical value, must be performed collectively. This signifies that the rights of the Board are exercised and determined, not by the will of an individual Consultor, but

475, (p. 304); Klekotka, *Diocesan Consultors,* pp. 31-38; Augustine *(Commentary,* II, 35, 468) denies that the Board is a moral collegiate person. This opinion was given shortly after the promulgation of the Code when this question was regarded as doubtful. Cf. Klekotka, *loc. cit.*

[3] Canon 102 § 1; Cf. Maroto, *Institutiones,* I, n. 463 (pp. 544-545).

[4] Canon 102 § 2; Cf. Maroto, *op. cit.,* I, n. 463 (p. 544); Wernz-Vidal, *op. cit.,* II, n. 656 (p. 704).

by the decisive vote of all the members as is required by canon 101. This generally requires that there be a convocation of the members of the Board, and a ballot cast on the negotiations to be undertaken.

The necessity of a convocation of the members of the Board of Diocesan Consultors gives rise to the question as to who shall do the summoning and preside over the assembly. In this respect the Board of Diocesan Consultors differs from the cathedral Chapter, insofar as the latter institution has its own independent existence distinct from its quality as the senate of the bishop and, therefore, may be convoked not only by the bishop, but also by its own head. Since, therefore, the Board of Diocesan Consultors has no head of its own during the time intervening the beginning of vacancy and the election of the Administrator, the duty of convoking the Board falls upon the senior member of the Board. This seniority is regulated by canon 106. "If there is an auxiliary bishop in the diocese," writes Woywod,[5] "and he does not belong to the consultors, he has no right to convoke them. Now, among the consultors themselves, one of a higher rank precedes the others of an inferior rank; if there are no prelates or dignitaries among them but all are merely priests, the seniority of ordination to the priesthood decides precedence, and, if several were ordained the same day, the senior in age precedes. The seniority in the office of consultor cannot be considered because all are supposed to be appointed at the same time and for three years only." It might be well to remark, incidentally, that too much emphasis cannot be placed upon the necessity that the Diocesan Consultors understand fully and at all times just who enjoys this precedence of seniority. It would probably be advisable to settle the question as soon as the members enter upon their duties of office, or at some session convoked shortly after their appointment. If this be neglected until vacancy arises, it would be but natural that unnecessary delay, and even confusion, might follow.

Although the assembled Consultors conduct themselves dur-

[5] *A Practical Commentary on the Code of Canon Law,* I, 155-56; cf. Klekotka, *Diocesan Consultors,* p. 108.

ing vacancy in the same manner as they do when, during occupancy of see, the bishop convokes them in those instances where the law demands their consent or advice, it would nevertheless be of practical value if the general principles governing collegiate acts were recalled in a general way. When the Board of Consultors are duly invested with certain rights by law, and they desire to exercise these rights, they must comply with the requirements made by law for all collegiate acts according to canon 101 § 1 n. 1; otherwise the acts are invalid. Over and above the prescriptions of the canon, there are several rules concerning elections which canonists regard as necessary for all collegiate proceedings.[6] The senior Consultor, therefore, must summon all the members of the Board, expressly stating the time and place where the meeting shall be held. Since the law does not demand a particular mode for a summoning,[7] the senior Consultors do so even by telephone, although this manner of issuing summons is not advisable, for it would be difficult to prove in such instances that summons were actually made, in case this question should arise after the meeting. If a Consultor has not been summoned, and for that reason missed being present at the meeting, the proceedings of the meeting are valid, but the Consultor thus neglected may demand that the competent superior[8] rescind the negotiations undertaken at the meeting, provided, however, that the lack of notification and absence from the meeting is proved, and also that he can furnish legal proof that he forwarded his objection to the competent superior within at least three days after obtaining knowledge of the meeting.[9] If, on the other hand, more than one-third of the members are not summoned, the acts of the assembly are null and void.[10] The lack of notice,

6 Canon 162; Maroto, *Institutiones*, I, nn. 467, 468 (pp. 546-7, 550-1); Vermeersch-Creusen, *Epitome*, I, n. 194 (p. 147-8); Coronata, *Institutiones*, I, 157; Chelodi, *Jus De Personis*, n. 99 (p. 176); Sipos, *Juris Canonici*, p. 281; Ayrinhac, *General Legislation*, p. 217.

7 Canon 162 § 1.

8 Cf. p. 154.

9 Canon 162 § 2.

10 Canon 162 § 3.

however, does not invalidate the proceedings, if those Consultors who were not called are nevertheless present.[11]

When the Consultors are legitimately convened, the business of the meeting must be clearly proposed to the assembly by the presiding Consultor and after a common deliberation the affairs must be voted on in canonical form. The absolute majority vote of those present and voting must be regarded as the decisive norm of action. Should it happen that an absolute majority is not attained in either the first or second ballot, the relative majority of the third ballot will decide.[12] Since the Code demands secret ballot only for canonical elections [13] it is not necessary that the Board employ secret ballot at any time, except, of course, when electing the Administrator. Hence the voting may be open and public.[14] The law does not specify the number necessary to constitute a quorum, and hence if the members are legitimately summoned, those who are present for the meeting on the appointed time and place may validly exercise the rights of the Board even though only one Consultor appears.[15]

During the limited period of time allotted by law to the Board of Diocesan Consultors for the exercise of its rights, the Board may, in virtue of its moral collegiate personality, function either collectively, or through its delegates. Hence, from the time the see becomes fully vacant up to the time when the Administrator is duly elected, the Board may, by a common agreement of all the Consultors, depute one or more priests (either Consultors or externs) who shall act in its name.[16] Thus, just as the cathedral Chapter was permitted

[11] Canon 162 § 4.

[12] Canon 101 § 1 n. 1; This does not apply to the election of the Administrator, as canon 433 § 2 demands an absolute majority, even after the second ballot. This will receive consideration in the following chapter.

[13] Canon 169 § 1 n. 2.

[14] Klekotka, *Diocesan Consultors*, p. 110.

[15] Cf. Wernz-Vidal, *Jus Canonicum*, II, n. 675 (p. 726); Augustine (*Commentary* II, 448) arbitrarily applies to Canon Law what is usual American Parliamentary law, and demands that three members are necessary to constitute a quorum.

[16] Coronata, *Institutiones*, I, 534; Cappello, *Summa Juris Canonici*, I, n. 400 (p. 411); Cf. Blat, *Commentarium*, II, 402-3.

to do during the whole period of vacancy before the Council of Trent, the Board of Diocesan Consultors may, by common agreement of the members and during the time it possesses power, authorize one or more to act in its name with respect to a particular act, or *ad universitatem negotiorum.*[17]

ART. I. *The Nature and Inception of the Administrative Rights of the Board During Vacancy*

Having thus considered how the Board of Diocesan Consultors possesses the rights extended to it by law during vacancy, and the manner by which these rights must be exercised, the discussion will next center about the rights themselves. Canon 431 § 1 states that when a see is vacant the governance of the diocese passes to the Board of Diocesan Consultors, unless there is an Apostolic Administrator in charge of the see, or the Holy See has otherwise provided. The Board of Diocesan Consultors, therefore, ordinarily comes into possession of the administration of the diocese when vacancy arises, and it is only by way of exception that the Holy See makes other provisions. But it must be remembered, however, that when other arrangements have been enforced by the Apostolic See, the Board of Consultors enjoys no more power after vacancy has become effective than it did before vacancy occurred, and any pretense on the part of the Board to exercise jurisdiction in such instances would result in invalidity of all action taken. It therefore becomes important to determine specifically when the governance of the vacant see does not devolve upon the Board.

Canon 431 § 1 expressly refers to the Administrator Apostolic. The reason why the governance of the diocese does not devolve upon the Board of Consultors when the see has an

[17] "Sane juxta antiquam Ecclesiae disciplinam, Sede Episcopali vacante, Diocesis administratio ad Capitulum cathedralis Ecclesiae devolvitur; quod olim per seipsum Diocesim toto tempore, quo sedes vacabat, administrare poterat, vel uni, aut pluribus Dioecesim administrandam committere, libera eidem relicta potestate deputatos eligendi, eisque delegatam jurisdictionem, sive quoad usum, sive quoad tempus arctandi, et constringendi."—Pius IX, Const., *"Romanus Pontifex,"* 28 Aug. 1873—Fontes, n. 565, p. 74; Cf. Historical Synopsis, pp. 34-35.

Administrator Apostolic is that the jurisdiction of this delegate of the Holy See does not cease with the death either of the Roman Pontiff who commissioned him, or of the bishop whose diocese he is administering.[18] Whether he be appointed permanently or only for a time, the jurisdiction of the Administrator Apostolic continues during the time of vacancy and ceases only when the new bishop appointed to the see has taken canonical possession of it.[19] Canon 312 states that the Administrator Apostolic may be appointed for sees which already have their ordinaries, as well as sees which are vacant, but in all instances the appointment is made only for special and grave reasons. Hence, if a bishop, through old-age, infirmity, physical or mental debility is unable to discharge properly the functions of his office, or if serious financial, religious, or political difficulties arise in a diocese and cannot be controlled by the bishop, it might be expected that the Holy See shall appoint an Administrator Apostolic to administer the see. If in the meantime the bishop should die, the Administrator Apostolic retains the governance of the see, and the Board of Diocesan Consultors must refrain from any attempt to infringe upon his rights.[20]

Another occasion on which the governance of a vacant see does not pass to the Board of Diocesan Consultors, is when the Holy See has given a bishop-coadjutor either to the bishop with the right of succession, or to the diocese. The bishop-coadjutor who enjoys the right of succession becomes the ordinary of the diocese the moment the see becomes vacant, provided, however, that he had taken legitimate possession of his office of coadjutor according to canon 353.[21] If the bishop-coadjutor was given to the see, his office continues when the see becomes vacant.[22] The bishops-coadjutor, how-

[18] Canon 318 § 1.

[19] Canon 318 § 2.

[20] S.C. EE. et RR., *Aquilana,* 4 Aug. 1578—*Fontes,* n. 1336; *Lycien.,* 17 Nov. 1590—*op. cit.,* n. 1436; *Lycien.,* 22 Dec. 1628—*op. cit.,* n. 1735; *Aprutina,* 24 Jan. 1749—*op. cit.,* n. 1864.

[21] Canon 355 § 1.

[22] Canon 355 § 2.

ever, must not be confused with auxiliary-bishops. The latter prelates are given to the person of the bishop and do not possess the right of succession. Their office ceases with that of the bishop, unless it is stated otherwise in the Apostolic letters of appointment.[23]

There is also a third instance when the governance of a vacant see does not devolve upon the Board of Diocesan Consultors. It has been observed previously that when a bishop receives official notification of his transfer, he immediately becomes the Administrator of the diocese and the jurisdiction of his vicar-general immediately ceases.[24] Should it happen that the Holy See would give the transferred bishop a vicar-general Apostolic to assist in the administration of the see until canonical possession of the new see is taken, the jurisdiction of the vicar-general Apostolic does not cease when the bishop assumes his new office.[25]

In all of these instances (which may be regarded as taxative as far as the United States is concerned) the Board of Diocesan Consultors does not receive the right to administer a see during vacancy. On all other occasions, however, the ordinary norm of canon 431 § 1 must be followed.

When the Apostolic See has not provided otherwise the governance of the diocese devolves upon the Board of Diocesan Consultors when the see becomes vacant. The Board of Consultors, consequently, is the successor to the bishop, has the right and duty to provide for the administration of the diocese, and is termed the *ordinarius loci.*[26] By a distinct grant, common law endows the Board with the ordinary jurisdiction of the bishop, thereby empowering the Board to do all that the bishop himself, in view of his ordinary jurisdiction, can do in both spiritual and temporal affairs, with the exception, however, of those rights expressly forbidden the Board by law.[27] The Board of Diocesan Consultors possesses,

[23] Canons 350 § 3; 355 § 2.

[24] Canon 430 § 3.

[25] Cf. Cocchi, *Commentarium,* II, 338.

[26] Canons 431 § 1, 198.

[27] Canon 435.

therefore, true ordinary episcopal jurisdiction in the strict sense of the term, since by the disposition of common law itself, such power is attached to the administrative office of the Board. It is, consequently, a distinct concession and in no manner a simple extension or increase of rights already possessed, or power delegated by way of privilege.[28] According to canon 435 § 1, the Administrator, who succeeds the Board of Diocesan Consultors in the office of governing the see, enjoys the same power and is bound by the same restrictions as the Board itself during its brief term of office. The administrative office of the Board of Consultors during vacancy, and that of the Administrator, is, therefore, one and the same office possessed successively by different persons. For this reason, all that will be stated in a subsequent Chapter with reference to the powers of jurisdiction and the prohibitions incumbent upon the Administrator, applies equally as well to the Board of Diocesan Consultors during the time they control the governance of the see.

The governance of the diocese, or in other words, the ordinary episcopal jurisdiction, devolves upon the Board of Diocesan Consultors the moment the see becomes fully vacant.[29] The diocese, therefore, is not left without someone possessing ordinary jurisdiction even for a brief interval. As soon as the bishop loses title, possession and jurisdiction of his office, according to the prescriptions of canon 430, whether this loss be caused by death, resignation, transfer, or deprivation, the governance of the see passes immediately into the possession of the Board who may then validly exercise its power. In all cases of vacancy, however, the Board of Consultors cannot licitly exercise jurisdiction until certain notifica-

[28] Cf. Bouix, *De Capitulis,* pp. 481-83; Leurenius, *Forum Beneficiale,* t. IV, tract. III, qq. 447, 455; Wernz-Vidal, *Jus Canonicum,* II, n. 709 (p. 759); Coronata, *Institutiones,* I, 533; et al.

[29] Canon 431 § 1; "Totam ordinariam episcopi jurisdictionem, *quae vacua sede episcopali in capitulum venerat,* ad Vicarium ab eo rite constitutum transire . . ."—Pius IX, Const., *Romanus Pontifex,* 28 Aug. 1873—*Fontes,* n. 565; Wernz-Vidal, *Jus Canonicum,* II, n. 709 (p. 759); Coronata, *Institutiones,* I, 534; Bouix, *De Capitulis,* pp. 483-85.

tion of the fact of vacancy is received.[30] Thus if there were uncertainty about the death of the bishop, as would possibly be the case when a bishop dies while away from the diocese, the vicar-general, by force of canon 430 § 2, has the right to continue in office and exercise jurisdiction. So also in the case of resignation or deprivation. The Board must possess certainty as to the fact that the bishop had actually been officially, or certainly notified with respect to the acceptation of his resignation, or to the infliction of a sentence of deprivation of office. It is only after this time, consequently, that the Board may begin to exercise the right of administering the see.[31]

Vacancy arising from the transfer of a bishop, it has already been observed, has its own particular norm, peculiar to the present discipline of the Church. According to canon 430 § 3, the diocese of a transferred bishop becomes fully vacant *a die captae possessionis dioecesis . . .* Hence, it is only on the day on which the transferred bishop takes canonical possession of his new see that the former see becomes fully vacant. Since vacancy begins in this instance with the beginning of the day, and since, furthermore, the time when vacancy arises is known to the Board, the latter may validly and licitly exercise jurisdiction from the very beginning of this day. Hence, if the bishop takes possession of his new see on June the first, the see *a qua* becomes vacant at mid-night between the thirty-first of May and June the first, and from that moment on, and no sooner, the Board may begin to administer the see.

30 S.C. EE. et RR., *Neritonen,* 24 Maii 1651—Ferraris, *Prompta Bibliotheca,* v. *Capitulum,* art. III, n. 37.

31 ". . . Et postquam huiusmodi absolutionis notitiam Episcopus habuerit, etiam ex testimonio, seu documento Secretarii Sacri Collegii, illico teneri eum abstinere ab exercitio ordinariae jurisdictionis, eamque transire in Capitulum sede vacante, et ita posse, et debere Capitulum statim ea jurisdictione uti . . ."—S.C. EE. et RR., 14 Dec. 1624—*Fontes,* n. 1720; cf. Urban VIII; breve, *Nobis super,* 20 Martii 1625—*Bullarium Romanum,* XIII, 304-5; Benedict XIV, *De Synodo Dioecesana,* lib. XIII, c. 16, n. 10; Leurenius, *Forum Beneficiale,* t. IV, tract. III, q. 543; Barbosa, *De Canonicis,* c. 25, n. 32; Bouix, *De Capitulis,* pp. 484-85.

A word may be said about the tacit resignation of a bishop. In the previous discussion on vacancy it has been noted that when a bishop tacitly resigns, as in the case of apostacy, heresy, etc., the see becomes fully vacant the moment the crime becomes public. According to a strict interpretation of the law, the jurisdiction of the bishop passes at that moment to the Board, who may validly and licitly begin to exercise its power, as long as there is certainty that the crime has become public. In practice, however, it would probably be more prudent on the part of the Board, instead of assuming the governance of the see immediately, to notify the Holy See without delay, and await for such provisions which the Supreme Authority might choose to make.

Before proceeding further with the discussion on the office of the Board of Consultors during vacancy, it may be well to state here the provisions to be made for the abbey *nullius* at Belmont, North Carolina, during its vacancy. Canon 327 § 1 states that during the vacancy of an abbey or a prelature *nullius* belonging to religious, the chapter of religious succeeds in the government, *unless the Constitutions provide otherwise;* to a vacant secular abbey or prelature, the chapter of canons succeeds; however, both chapters are obliged within eight days from date of notice of vacancy, according to canon 432 ss., to elect a Vicar Capitular, who shall rule the abbey or prelacy until a new abbot or prelate is elected. In conjunction with this latter prescription of the canon, the disposition of canon 432 § 2, which refers to the election of the Vicar Capitular, must be added. According to this latter legal norm, the religious chapter of an abbey *nullius* elects the Vicar Capitular, *unless the constitutions of the abbey nullius has other provision for the appointment of the Vicar,* and in such instances these constitutions are to be followed. In the case of the abbey *nullius* in this country, therefore, the Constitutions of the American-Cassinese Benedictine Congregation must be abided by.[32] The official translation of the above constitution is the following: "After the Abbot has heard the advice

[32] Cf. Wernz-Vidal, *Jus Canonicum,* II, n. 570 (p. 603); Vermeersch-Creusen, *Epitome,* I, n. 395 (p. 265).

of his capitulars in private, let him choose and appoint a Prior, an exemplary man, who should supply the place of the Abbot in the community and always be with the brethren. Let him watch especially over the regular discipline; and in those matters which pertain to divine worship, piety, and spiritual progress, let him both take the lead by example, and teach and direct others by word, warning, or punishment. *In the event of the Abbot's death, and until a new Abbot comes in possession, the jurisdiction passes over to him in the ordinary way; but if he should be wanting for any cause whatever, an Administrator must be elected by the Chapter.* When the Abbot is absent or dead, let the Prior govern the monastery with prudence and moderation, and not dare to change what the Abbot has appointed. When the Prior is hindered or absent the Subprior takes his place."[33]

This summarizes the norms to be followed when the abbey *nullius* in the United States becomes vacant. The statement of the constitution is sufficiently clear in itself and needs no further comment. It will readily be seen, consequently, that the subsequent articles which treat of the duties of the Board of Diocesan Consultors, especially that of electing the Administrator, do not apply to the religious chapter of the abbey.

Since the scope of this treatise is limited to the continental United States, and since furthermore Alaska comes within this territorial division, a word may be inserted here with respect to the administration of the vicariate-apostolic in that region during its vacancy or quasi-vacancy. The present law in this regard is found in canon 309, and is, for the most part, a restatement of the constitutions of Pope Benedict XIV. In the constitution *Ex sublimi,* promulgated by this Pontiff on January 26, 1753,[34] it was provided that where no coadjutor with the right to succession had been appointed, the vicar Apostolic was obliged to nominate a pro-vicar or vicar-general, who should immediately succeed him at the time of death. A

[33] *Declarationes in Regulam S.P.N. Benedicti et Statuta Congregationis Americano-Cassinensis,* Caput LXV, pp. 37-38.

[34] *Fontes,* n. 423.

second constitution *Quam ex sublimi* issued by the same Pontiff on August 8, 1755,[35] prescribed that vicars-general were to be appointed to those territories only which had no cathedral Chapters, for in these latter instances the Chapter appointed the Vicar Capitular to administer the vacant vicariate. The present law speaks not only of vicariates, but also of prefectures-apostolic, and enjoins these Ordinaries to appoint pro-vicars and pro-prefects in all instances, even though the particular territories have cathedral Chapters or Boards of Consultors. Canon 309 states, that Vicars and prefects shall as soon as they come into their territory, appoint a qualified pro-vicar or pro-prefect from among either the secular or regular clergy, unless a coadjutor with the right of future succession has been appointed by the Holy See. The pro-vicar or pro-prefect, the canon continues to prescribe, has no power during the lifetime of the vicar or prefect, except such as is committed to him by his superior. When the vicar or prefect goes out of office, or when his jurisdiction is impeded in the manner described in canon 429 § 1, the pro-vicar or pro-prefect must assume the entire government and retain it until the Holy See has made other provision. The pro-vicar or pro-prefect who succeeds in office in such cases, furthermore, must immediately appoint an ecclesiastic who shall succeed him in case of death, etc. If perchance it should occur that nobody was appointed as Administrator either by the vicar or prefect, or by the pro-vicar or pro-prefect, then the senior missionary present in the vicariate or prefecture is to be considered delegated by the Holy See to assume the government of the vacant vicariate or prefecture. Seniority, according to this canon, is determined by the letters of appointment of a missionary to the district; if several were appointed on the same date, the senior in the priesthood is preferred. The following canon states further that those who govern a vicariate or prefecture in virtue of the laws of the preceding canon must inform the Apostolic See as soon as possible. In the meanwhile, they have the faculties, both the ordinary ones accord-

[35] *Fontes,* n. 436.

ing to canon 294, and the delegated ones which the vicar or prefect had, unless they were given to them for reason of personal qualification.

This is the summary of the legislation with respect to the administration of vacant or quasi-vacant vicariates and prefectures Apostolic. Hence, in the Vicariate Apostolic in Alaska, the Board of Consultors does not participate in the governance of the vicariate during these periods, nor does it elect the Administrator.

Art. II. *The Duties of the Board During Vacancy*

It has thus been established that common law entrusts to the Board of Diocesan Consultors the office of administering vacant sees. This provision of law constitutes not only a right which the Board may exercise, and a right which no one save the Holy See can deprive it of, but also a grave duty. The welfare, both spiritual and temporal, of the vacant see is placed into the custody of the Board, and it rests upon the conscience of the Diocesan Consultors to discharge all duties with prudence, zeal and solicitude, so that nothing may be wanting in all that pertains to the right governance of the diocese, and the welfare of souls. The office of the Board, however, is of brief duration. It is intended by law to be provisional merely until a qualified priest shall be elected or appointed to succeed the Board in the administrative office. The Board of Diocesan Consultors ordinarily has the right and strict obligation to perform this election, and when such right and obligation exists, it constitutes one of the principal functions of the Board during vacancy. The following paragraph, therefore, will be given to a consideration of the duty incumbent upon the Board to elect an Administrator, determining specifically when the Board is to do so, and when it is forbidden, and the prescribed time when the election must be performed. The subsequent paragraphs of this article will comprise a discussion of other duties attached to the administrative office of the Board.

§ 1. The Duty of Electing an Administrator

According to canon 432, the cathedral Chapter, within eight days from the moment they receive certain notification of vacancy of see, must depute a Vicar Capitular to rule the diocese in its place. Should the Chapter for whatever reason fail to comply with this law within the prescribed time, the right to make the appointment devolves for this time on the metropolitan, or if the metropolitan see is vacant, on the senior suffragan bishop. This legislation, insofar as it effects the cathedral Chapter is a restatement of the law of the Council of Trent,[36] and insofar as it has brought the Board of Diocesan Consultors into its scope[37], has been a happy innovation and a sweeping abrogation of the particular legislation of the Second Plenary Council at Baltimore.

Prior to the promulgation of the present Code of Canon Law, Administrators in the United States were appointed by the bishop himself before death, and if the bishop, having failed to make the appointment, died, or if the see became vacant in any other fashion, the metropolitan, or if the metropolitan see were itself vacant, the senior suffragan bishop enjoyed the right to make the appointment.[38] The acts of the Council were ratified by the Holy See. When the present Code was promulgated, a doubt arose in the minds of many as to whether the existing discipline in the United States, with reference to the appointment of the Administrator, was abrogated. Canon 427, insofar as it extended to the Board of Diocesan Consultors the same legislation prescribed for the cathedral Chapters during vacancy, made it clear that the Board of Consultors received the administration of a diocese when the see became vacant. But since canon 431 § 2 states that if by special arrangement of the Holy See the archbishop, or another bishop, has the right to appoint an Administrator for a vacant diocese, such an Administrator has

[36] Sess. XXIV, *de ref.* c. 16—*Canones et Decreta,* p. 196.

[37] Canon 427.

[38] The Second Plenary Council at Baltimore, tit. III, c. II, nn. 97-98—*Acta et Decreta,* p. 68.

all those, and only those, faculties and powers which the Vicar Capitular has and he is held to the same obligations and penalties. It was at first thought that this canon had reference to the legislation of the Second Plenary Council at Baltimore, and that the metropolitans, or senior suffragan bishops, and not the Board of Diocesan Consultors, enjoyed the right to appoint the Administrator.[39] The Apostolic Delegate to the United States submitted the question to the Holy See. The Pontifical Commission for the Authentic Interpretation of the Code responded and expressly declared that the particular legislation of the Council at Baltimore was abrogated by the present law, and that the bishops in the United States could no longer in any case appoint an Administrator to administer the diocese after their death and that, in accordance with the prescriptions of canon 427 this power belonged to the Board of Diocesan Consultors. But, if special circumstances did not permit the carrying out of the law in all places, the Sacred Consistorial Congregation would give special instructions as to the manner of meeting these temporary conditions.[40]

The particular circumstances obtaining in the United States at that time were due, chiefly, to the fact that many dioceses had only two Diocesan Consultors in accordance with the minimum requirement of the Third Plenary Council at Baltimore.[41] This number was consequently at variance with the demands of canon 425 § 1 where it is prescribed that each diocese shall have at least six Diocesan Consultors, and in those dioceses where they are few priests at least four must be appointed. Since, therefore, this particular situation existed in many places it was felt incongruous that so few should be given the right to elect an Administrator. In order that the Church in America might have time to adjust itself to the prescriptions of canon 425 § 1, the Sacred Consistorial Congregation issued an indult for three years to the bishops of the United States, and later to those of Canada and New Found-

[39] Augustine, *Commentary*, II, 479-80.

[40] *Pontifical Commission*, Nov. 24, 1918—AAS, XI (1919), 75.

[41] Tit. II, c. II, n. 18—*Acta et Decreta*, p. 15.

land. According to the indult, the metropolitan, or during the vacancy of the archbishopric, the senior suffragan bishop was obliged to nominate the Administrator for those dioceses which did not have at least five or six Diocesan Consultors, and the Administrator thus appointed was to be ratified by the Apostolic Delegate.[42]

The Apostolic indult was in force only for the three years; it has long expired and has not since been renewed. The common law of the Church, consequently, now prevails to its fullest extent in the United States, and hence the Board of Diocesan Consultors possesses the right of electing the Administrator even though there be less than five Consultors in the diocese. This cannot be questioned, for canon 427 refers to the Board of Consultors simply as the *coetus consultorum diocesanorum* without specifying that at least five Consultors are necessary. Since, therefore, canon 425 § 1 permits that only four Consultors be appointed in dioceses where priests are few, it cannot be denied that such a Board has full authority to elect the Administrator.[43] The statement, therefore, that the Board of Diocesan Consultors is entitled to elect the Administrator only when there are at least five or six Consultors in the Diocese, is based entirely upon the disposition of the indult, and since the indult was given only for three years and is no longer in effect, the writings of American canonists on this point must be corrected.[44]

The question may be asked as to what must be done when the election is to take place and there are less than four Consultors in office. This may occur if a bishop fails to comply with canon 426 § 3, where it is prescribed that if any of the Consultors go out of office before their triennial term is expired, the bishop shall appoint others in their place. It may also happen that one or more Consultors would die, resign,

[42] S.C.C., 22 Feb., 1918—AAS, XI (1919), 75; 8 Maii, 1919—*op. cit.*, 233; cf. *American Ecclesiastical Review,* LX, 532 ss; LXI, 165.

[43] Cf. *Irish Ecclesiastical Record,* 5[s], XIII, 338.

[44] Cf. Augustine, *Commentary,* II, 469, 479-80; Woywod, *A Practical Commentary on the Code of Canon Law,* I. 155; Ayrinhac, *General Legislation,* p. 329; Augustine, *Rights and Duties of Ordinaries,* pp. 156-57.

or become physically or canonically hindered from fulfilling the duties of their office after vacancy occurred and before the Administrator is elected. In all cases of this nature it must be remembered that the Board of Diocesan Consultors is a moral collegiate person and as such possesses the right of electing the Administrator. Hence, in complete accordance with canon 102 § 2, even if there were only one Consultor left on the Board when vacancy of see arose, or when the election was to take place, this Consultor could licitly and validly exercise the corporate rights of the Board. He is fully entitled, therefore, to proceed with the appointment of the Administrator, provided, however, that he does not make a self-appointment.[45]

It has been stated previously that *ordinarily* the Board of Diocesan Consultors is obliged to elect the Administrator. There are instances, therefore, when the Board is strictly forbidden to perform the election. The most evident case of this kind is when the Board is obliged to elect the Administrator but fails to do so within eight days from the time they receive knowledge that the see is vacant. When the period of eight days has elapsed, the right of electing the Administrator no longer resides with the Board, but passes to the metropolitan or senior suffragan bishop.[46] So, too, does the Board forfeit its right to elect if the election indeed be held within the prescribed period of eight days, but not in compliance with canon 434 § 1.[47] In all these instances the Board is not permitted to proceed with the election, and if this be attempted it is without judicial effect, as will be seen more fully in the discussion on the devolution of the right of electing the Administrator.

Other occasions when the Board of Diocesan Consultors

[45] Cf. Canon 170; S.C.C., *Laquedoniensi*, 16 Martii 1912—AAS, IV (1912) 404; *Il Monitore Ecclesiastico,* XXIV (1912-13), 145 ss; Oesterle, *Praelectionis Juris Canonici,* p. 206; Coronata, *Institutiones,* I, 158, footnote 1; Wernz-Vidal, *Jus Canonicum,* II, n. 656 (p. 704); Ojetti, *Commentarium,* II, 144; Bouix, *De Capitulis,* pp. 544-45.

[46] Canon 432 § 2.

[47] Canon 434 § 3.

may not elect the Administrator may be briefly summarized in the following: when the Holy See has expressly forbidden the Board to proceed with the election; when, according to canon 431 § 2, the Holy See, by a special provision, has authorized an archbishop, or another bishop, to make the appointment; when the diocese already has an Ordinary, as in the case of bishops-coadjutor, Apostolic vicar-general, or Administrators Apostolic,[48] and finally when the Holy See appoints Administrators Apostolic to vacant sees. This latter case is quite frequently present when a bishop resigns from office, for very often when accepting a bishop's resignation, the Holy See commissions the bishop to administer the see until a newly appointed prelate takes possession of the diocese. It might also be expected that the Roman Pontiff would entrust the administration of the diocese to an Administrator Apostolic when a bishop is deprived of office.

When the duty of electing the Administrator is incumbent upon the Board of Diocesan Consultors, the election must be held, according to the prescriptions of canon 432 § 1, within eight days from the time the fact of vacancy becomes known to the Board. It is important to observe here that the period of eight days does not begin from the moment the see actually becomes vacant, but only from the time the Board learns that the see is vacant. Hence, it may happen that several days elapse before the Consultors receive word that the bishop has died, or that he has received official notification to the effect that his resignation has been accepted, or that a penalty of privation of office has been inflicted upon him. In all these instances, therefore, the Board has eight days' time to elect the Administrator beginning from the time when the Consultors become aware of their right to hold the election, *i. e.*, from the time when they learn that the diocese is vacant, for according to canonists, the time prior to this knowledge is *tempus utile*.[49]

[48] Cf. S.C. EE. et RR., *Aquilana*, 4 Aug. 1578—*Fontes*, n. 1336; *Lycien.*, 22 Dec. 1628—*op. cit.*, n. 1735; *Aprutina*, 24 Jan. 1749—*op. cit.*, n. 1864.

[49] Canon 35; Cicognani, *Jus Canonicum*, II, 200; Objetți, *Commentarium*, I, 204-5; Chelodi, *Jus De Personis*, n. 89 (p. 160); Cappello, *Summa Juris Canonici*, I, nn. 182, 400 (pp. 163, 411).

But when the Board has received the necessary knowledge, the period of eight days begins immediately, and the time, known as *tempus continuum*, does not admit of any suspension or interruption, no matter what cause might arise to hinder the Board from exercising its right.[50]

When the Board of Consultors learns that the see is vacant by the death, or resignation (express or tacit), or by the deprivation of the bishop of his office, the period of eight days is calculated according to the dispositions of canon 34 § 3 n. 3.[51] This signifies that since the time when the notification was received does not correspond with the beginning of the day, the first day is not counted. Hence, if the Board, on August the first, became aware of the fact that the diocese was vacant it would retain the right to elect the Administrator until mid-night August the ninth.[52] The same rule, however, does not apply when the see becomes vacant by the transfer of the bishop. In this case vacancy arises *on the day* the transferred bishop takes canonical possession of his see *ad quam*.[53] In this instance, therefore, not only vacancy itself, but also the knowledge of vacancy is co-incident with the beginning of the day. Hence, the period of eight days includes the first day according to the disposition of canon 34 § 3 n. 2.[54] Thus, if the transferred bishop takes canonical possession of his new diocese on the first of June, the obligation of electing an Administrator becomes incumbent upon the Board of Consultors at midnight between May 31 and June 1, and this right is retained by the Board until midnight on June the eighth.

[50] Canon 35; cf. Sipos, *Juris Canonici*, p. 286; Cicognani, *loc. cit.;* Augustine (*Commentary*, II, 124) seems to imply that the period of eight days is *tempus utile*.

[51] De Meester, *Compendium*, II, n. 793 (p. 233); Blat, *Commentarium*, II, 403; Ferreres, *Institutiones Canonicae*, I, nn. 175, 720; Coronata, *Institutiones*, I, 534; Michiels, *Normae Generalis*, II, 161.

[52] Cf. Ferreres, *op. cit.*, n. 720.

[53] "A certa translationis notitia Episcopus intra quatuor menses debet dioecesim *ad quam* petere eiusdemque canonicam possessionem assumere ad normam can. 333, 334, et a die captae possessionis dioecesis *a qua* plene vacat":—Canon 430 § 3.

[54] Cf. Footnote 47 supra.

The period of time within which the Board of Consultors must elect the Administrator is, therefore, accurately defined by law. If the Board fails to comply with these prescriptions, it loses the right to hold the election. It must be remembered, however, that the law speaks only of the loss of the right to elect. This does not include the loss of jurisdiction, for even in those cases where the Board has forfeited the electoral right, it retains the right to govern the vacant see until an Administrator is provided. This is clear from the dispositions of canons 435 and 438. The former canon states that the Board of Diocesan Consultors, after his election the Administrator, has ordinary episcopal jurisdiction in all things spiritual and temporal, with the exception of those acts which are explicitly forbidden in law. The latter canon prescribes that the Administrator, having made the profession of faith demanded in Canons 1406-1408, obtains jurisdiction immediately and does not need any confirmation of his election. These legal provisions leave no doubt with respect to the fact that the Board loses jurisdiction only when the Administrator receives it.

§ 2. The Necessity of Electing Economes

An Econome (*oeconomus*) is a steward, or procurator of ecclesiastical temporalities, i.e., the property and the revenues of the Church. Already in the fifth century[55] the office of the Econome was intimately associated with the administration of vacant dioceses. The Council of Trent made specific provisions with reference to this office when decreeing that in those dioceses where the cathedral Chapter has charge of the revenues of the see, it is incumbent upon the Chapter when appointing a Vicar Capitular, to appoint also one or more faithful and diligent Economes whose duty it shall be to take care of the property and revenues of the Church during the period of vacancy.[56] This decree has been restated verbatim in canon 432 § 1 of the present Code of Canon Law. In those

[55] Cf. Council of Chalcedon, can. 25, 26—Mansi, VI, 1230.

[56] Council of Trent, sess. XXIV, *de ref.*, c. 16—*Canones et Decreta*, p. 196.

dioceses, accordingly, where the Board of Diocesan Consultors has charge of the ecclesiastical revenues, the appointment of faithful and diligent Economes becomes imperative.

The only qualifications demanded by law for this office is that the candidate or candidates be faithful and diligent. They are elected by the Board at the same time and in the same manner as the Administrator. Theirs is the right to a decent support, their office expires, and they are obliged to render an account of their administration according to the same norms which govern the office of the Administrator.[57] The Economes, however, do not possess the independence which the Administrator enjoys, for they administer the temporalities under the authority and control of the latter.[58] Canon 433 § 3 makes the significant provision that the Economes and the Administrator may be one and the same individual.

The question now arises as to the necessity of the Board of Diocesan Consultors to elect Economes in this country. "In the United States," writes Ayrinhac,[59] "and in other countries also, the Diocesan Consultors have little to do with the temporal administration and the collecting of diocesan revenues, consequently the obligation of appointing the Oeconomus does not exist." This is the common opinion of other American canonists,[60] for generally speaking, the revenues of the Church in this country are administered by the bishop and his Diocesan Board of Administration according to the provisions of canons 1520-1528. The office of the Econome is generally regarded as quite useless in those countries also where the *mensa episcopalis* consists of a governmental pension, for in those instances the revenues are suspended during vacancy.[61] If it should happen, however, that the Board of Diocesan Consultors in any diocese has

57 Canons 432 §§ 1, 2; 433 § 2; 441; 443; 444.

58 Canon 442.

59 *Constitutiones of the Church,* p. 280.

60 Augustine, *Rights and Duties of Ordinaries,* p. 158; Smith, *Elements of Ecclesiastical Law,* p. 360.

61 Cf. Bouix, *De Capitulis,* p. 488; Badii, *Institutiones Juris Canonici,* I, 242, footnote 1; Cocchi, *Commentarium,* II, 340.

charge of the revenues, it would not follow that an Econome would have to be elected, for according to the provisions of canon 433 § 3 one and the same individual may be elected Administrator and Econome.

§ 3. Particular Duties of the Board After the Death of the Bishop

When a see becomes vacant by the death of the bishop the Board of Diocesan Consultors is obliged to inform the Apostolic See of the death of the bishop as soon as possible.[62] The term "*quantocius*" employed by the legislator has the signification that no delay be made in the matter, and hence this duty must be the first consideration of the Board. The canon states the report must be made to the Apostolic See. This means the Sacred Consistorial Congregation[63] for the United States is no longer under the jurisdiction of the Sacred Congregation of the Propagation of the Faith. It would not be sufficient if the Board omitted sending word to the Sacred Consistorial Congregation and informed only the Apostolic Delegate to the United States. Such action would not per se be in compliance with canon 432 § 4, for according to canon 7, the term "Apostolic See" includes the Roman Pontiff, the Sacred Congregations, the Roman Tribunals and Offices, through which the same Roman Pontiff does usually transact the affairs concerning the universal Church. The phrase "affairs concerning the Universal Church" excludes the Apostolic Delegate, for his activity is confined only to a particular portion of the Church universal. But, owing to the fact that the Apostolic Delegate, as the representative of the Holy See, is so intimately associated with the interests of the Church in the United States, it is only fitting and proper that he also be immediately informed of the bishop's death. Then, too, it might be said that the Board of Consultors may ask the Apostolic Delegate to relay the notice to the Holy See. If he consents to do so, the duty of reporting directly to the Holy See would not be incumbent upon the Board. It would un-

[62] Canon 432 § 4.

[63] Cf. Canon 248.

doubtedly be well to put this duty of the Consultors in the diocesan statutes.

The worthy and canonical burial of the prelate must next be given consideration. According to canon 397 n. 3, the first dignitary of the Canons of the cathedral Chapter has the right to conduct the funeral. This disposition of the law *per se* belongs to that category of legislation which has reference to the cathedral Chapter as an organization distinct from that of the senate of the bishop, and hence, according to a strict interpretation of canon 427, does not apply to the Board of Diocesan Consultors.[64] But in those dioceses where the Board of Consultors supplies the cathedral Chapter, this prescription would by analogy apply to the senior Consultor if neither custom nor diocesan statute provides for the worthy and canonical burial of the bishop. In the United States the chancellor, or secretary to the deceased bishop, generally assumes the duty of attending to the arrangements of the bishop's funeral, or the Administrator is elected soon enough either to make the arrangements himself, or to approve of those already made.

The phrase *defuncto justa funebria persolvere* found in canon 397 n. 3 directly comprises the duty of arranging for the recitation of the Office of the Dead, the Funeral Mass, and the canonical burial of the deceased according to canons 1205 § 2 and 1219 § 2.[65] It may be said, however, that the canon indirectly includes all the duties and arrangements which fall within the scope of general supervision of the obsequy.

[64] Blat, *Commentarium,* II, 395; Vermeersch-Creusen, *Epitome,* I, n. 475, (p. 303).

[65] Cf. Blat, *op. cit.,* II, 367; Coronata, *Institutiones,* I, 508.

CHAPTER VII

THE ELECTION OF THE ADMINISTRATOR

The previous chapter has been given to a consideration of the rights and duties of the Board of Diocesan Consultors during vacancy. It has been observed that the principal function of the Board is to elect one who shall succeed it in the administrative office of governing the vacant see. It has also been stated that this election must be performed by the Board within eight days from the time the Diocesan Consultors receive word that the see is vacant. The present chapter will be a discussion on the election itself.

The present law demands that the election of the Administrator be performed by the Board of Consultors acting collectively, and in compliance with the norms demanded for all canonical elections and postulations, safeguarding at the same time those particular requirements which the law prescribes for this particular election.[1] The election of the Administrator, therefore, is a true canonical election. Its liceity or validity depends upon a strict observance of all canons relative to canonical elections in general. According to canons 160-182, the Board may elect the Administrator either by secret ballot (scrutiny), or by compromise, or it may postulate a candidate for the office. Postulation[2] is a substitute for a canonical election proper and is the canonical manner of designating a candidate for an ecclesiastical office when the candidate whom the electors consider as best qualified for the office is afflicted with some impediment, such as age, from which the Church can and usually does dispense. From this it is apparent that it would be only by way of rare exception that a Board of Consultors would ever employ this method of pro-

[1] Canons 433 § 2, 160-182.

[2] Cf. Canons 179-182.

viding for the office of the Administrator. A general outline of election by scrutiny and compromise, therefore, will be regarded as sufficient when treating this duty of the Board. It may also be noted here that the accidental solemnities which generally accompany canonical elections need not be observed by the Board of Consultors.[3] The election of the Administrator, therefore, need not be preceded by the celebration of the Mass of the Holy Ghost, the absolution from censures, the examination of the electors, the oath to elect the most worthy candidate, and all other acts generally performed previous to a canonical election.[4]

ART. I. *The Convocation of the Electors*

A canonical election by scrutiny demands that there be a convocation of the college of electors. Since the Code does not specify which one of the Consultors shall summon the others to the election, it can safely be held that the Consultor who is first in precedence according to canon 106 shall be obliged to perform this duty.[5] If this Consultor be absent, e. g., in Europe, or on a vacation, or if he be hindered in any way from performing his duty, or even if he refuses to summon the Consultors, the right of convoking the Board passes to the Consultor next in order of precedence.[6]

The Consultor who is first in precedence, therefore, has the duty to convoke the others within the prescribed period of eight days from the time knowledge of vacancy has been received. He must determine the exact day, hour and place for the election.[7] The day and hour chosen should be such that it will be

[3] Cf. Cocchi, *Commentarium,* II, 341; Ayrinhac, *Constitution of the Church,* p. 274.

[4] Cf. Coronata, *Institutiones,* I, 262-64; Chelodi, *Jus De Personis,* n. 139 (p. 238); Maroto, *Institutiones,* I, nn. 627, 631 (pp. 753-55).

[5] Woywod, *A Practical Commentary,* I, 155; Klekotka, *Diocesan Consultors,* p. 108; cf. p. 90.

[6] Cf. Maroto, *op. cit.,* I, n. 617 (p. 734).

[7] Canon 162 § 1; The election may be held on any day, be it Sunday, or a Holy Day of Obligation, and at any time during the day or night. Cf. Maroto, *op. cit.,* I, n. 614 (p. 730); Wernz-Vidal, *Jus Canonicum,* II, n. 251 (p. 267); Coronata, *op. cit.,* I, 250.

morally possible for all the Consultors to be present. It is not necessary, however, to protract the time for the election to the last hour of the eighth day in order to make it convenient for the electors, nor is it permitted to anticipate a time which may reasonably be demanded for the others to attend.[8] The law does not prescribe any particular place where the Board must hold the election. Hence, the Consultor who summons the others is free to select the place. The determined place should be fitting and proper, so that the election may be performed without the danger of interference by externs. It should also be so situated so that it will be convenient for all electors to attend. In practically every instance the election of the Administrator will be held in the episcopal city, since canon 425 § 1 requires that the Consultors live either in the city itself or at least near by.

§ 1. Manner of Convocation

The Code does not demand that the electors be summoned in a special manner, and hence it is left to the judgment of the Consultor summoning to chose a reliable method. He may do so by word of mouth, or by mail, and although it is not strictly forbidden to do so by telephone or telegraph, the Holy See nevertheless discountenances this means; ordinarily this should not be done. If the summons be done by letter it is sufficient that this be sent to the domicile, quasi-domicile, or actual stopping-place of the Consultor.[9] It is advisable, however, that the Consultor who summons choose such means which will enable him to prove that the summons were actually made. Such proof would be demanded if a Consultor, who was not present at the election, would later maintain that he was not summoned and attempt, on these grounds, to rescind the election.[10] It would be well, therefore, if the one summoning would have witnesses with him when he issues the call to the Consultors, whether this be by word of mouth, or by letter. In the latter

[8] Maroto, *op. cit.*, I, nn. 615, 620 (pp. 731-2, 738).

[9] Canon 162 § 1.

[10] Cf. Canon 162 §§ 1, 2.

case the letter should be sent by registered mail and the receipt kept.

§ 2. Those to be Summoned

All the Diocesan Consultors must be summoned, since they comprise the collegiate body authorized to elect the Administrator.[11] Canonists,[12] however, commonly interpret the legal phrase *omnes de collegio* according to the norm prescribed by Pope Innocent III.[13] It follows from this that there is no necessity to summon those who are deprived of, or suspended from the use of the right to vote; or those who have expressly or tacitly renounced their right; or those who are visiting in very remote places, or otherwise hindered from being present for the election. Nor would there be a necessity of summoning an elector if circumstances rendered it impossible, or if serious harm or inconvenience would result from delaying the election.[14] Thus, if a Consultor were in Europe when the see became vacant, there would be no obligation of summoning him to the election. If, however, it would be possible for an absent Consultor to return in time for the election, he would be entitled to receive summons, and a reasonable opportunity of assisting at the election. It would then be left to the free choice of the Consultor to accept the invitation or to decline.

The necessity of convocation arises, not from the fact that the form of an election demands it, but because the individual Consultors, in view of their collegiate right to vote, are entitled in justice to be called for the election. This is readily seen from the tenure of canon 162 § 2 which states that if only one member of the electoral college were absent from the election by reason of not having been called, he has the right to petition a competent superior to rescind the election. Although the election would otherwise be valid, the judge of the court

[11] Cf. Canon 162 § 1.

[12] Wernz-Vidal, *op. cit.*, II, n. 252, footnote 23 (p. 267); Maroto, *op. cit.*, I, n. 618 (p. 734).

[13] C. 42, X, *de electione et electi potestate,* I, 6.

[14] Maroto, *loc. cit.;* Coronata, *op. cit.*, I, 252.

superior to that of the Board performing the election [15] could rescind the election if the neglected Consultor proved that his absence from the election was due to the omission of the summons, and also provided that he had sent in his written petition within three days from the moment he had heard of the election.[16] If, however, the action to have the election rescinded is not taken within three days, the right to rescind is lost, and the neglected Consultor tacitly ratifies the election.[17]

If it should happen that more than one-third of the number of Diocesan Consultors have not been summoned, e. g. if out of six Consultors, three were neglected, the election is *ipso jure* null and void,[18] nor can such an election be sanated even though the neglected Consultors give subsequent approval.[19] If, on the other hand, one-third or less would be neglected, the election would be valid, but anyone of the neglected Consultors could petition within three days from the time he learned of the election to have it rescinded. According to the prescription of canon 162 § 4, however, the mere neglect to issue summons is of no effect, if the uninvited Consultors come and exercise their right to elect. Hence, if all the Consultors are already present without being summoned, or even if the summons had been issued and the Consultors have assembled before the date set for the election, the Board could proceed then and there with the election of the Administrator.

Art. 2. *The Electorate*

After the summons of all Diocesan Consultors is legitamately made, which signifies that the place, day and hour for the election is made known to the Board, those Consultors who are present in the electoral chamber on the appointed time may proceed with the election of the Administrator.[20] It does not matter how many are present, as long as all or at least more

[15] Cf. p. 154.

[16] Canon 162 § 2.

[17] Cf. Wernz-Vidal, *Jus Canonicum*, II, n. 252 (p. 267).

[18] Canon 162 § 3.

[19] Maroto, *op. cit.*, I, n. 618 (p. 736).

[20] Canon 163.

than two-thirds of the Consultors have been legitimately summoned.[21] Hence, there is no necessity for those present to wait for the Consultors who have not come to the appointed place and at the appointed time, although the members present are free to decide to defer the election to a later time when all, or more of the Consultors can be present. This, however, is not obligatory.[22] It must be remembered that neither common law, nor any particular legislation, defines what constitutes a quorum for the election of the Administrator.[23] Thus, if only one Consultor were present he could proceed with the election.[24] As long as a Consultor has been invited to the election, the fact or cause of his absence has no legal effect. If, on the other hand, a Consultor is present and refuses to vote, he is to be regarded indeed as present, but his abstinence from voting would not affect the validity of the election. Then, too, if a Consultor is unjustly expelled from the electoral chamber, the election would indeed be valid, but the expelled Consultor would have grounds for rescinding the election.[25]

The right of electing the Administrator, therefore, is vested exclusively in those Consultors who are present in the room where the election takes place. There is one exception, however, to this general norm. According to canon 168, if a Consultor be present in the building where the election takes place, and because of infirmity, or sickness,[26] is unable to be present in the electoral chamber, the tellers (*scrutatores*) [27] shall go and take from him his voting in writing, without destroying the

[21] Canons 163, 162 § 3; Augustine's opinion (*Commentary*, II, 448) that at least three members are necessary to constitute a quorum is a matter of American Parliamentary and not Canon law.

[22] Cf. Maroto, *Institutiones*, I, n. 623 (pp. 747-48).

[23] Cf. p. 92.

[24] Canon 102 § 2; Coronata, *Institutiones*, I, 255; cf. p. 105, footnote 45.

[25] Coronata, *loc. cit.*

[26] Infirmity or sickness precludes mental disorders which would deprive the Consultor of the use of reason, for according to canon 167 § 1 n. 1, he would then be disqualified to vote.

[27] Cf. Canon 171 § 1.

secrecy of the ballot. According to Coronata,[28] it is not necessary for the validity of this vote that it be consigned to writing, since the canon in question contains no invalidating clause.[29] Those Consultors who are not present for the election are strictly forbidden to submit their votes by letter or proxy, nor is any Consultor entitled to more than one vote, even though he holds several offices, which, taken individually, and in other affairs, entitles him to a vote.[30]

Canons 165 and 166 have reference to externs, i. e., those individuals who are not members of the Board of Diocesan Consultors. According to the former canon, the election is *ipso facto* invalid if an extern is permitted by the Board to take part in the election. Only material presence, however, of such an individual would not vitiate the election, since the Code makes reference only to externs taking part in the election.[31] The latter canon states that if laymen interfere in any way with the election, or encroach upon its canonical freedom, the election is *ipso facto* invalid. Thus if a layman were freely and spontaneously admitted to cast his vote with the Consultors, or if he would, by force, propose candidates of his own choice, or if a civil official were petitioned for permission to hold the election, or if he demanded that a vote be cast for a particular individual, or if any secular power were present in the electoral chamber under the pretext of safeguarding the election, the election would have no juridical effect.[32] Invalidity of election, however, would follow in this instance only when the lay interference is permitted by the greater part of the Consultors voting.[33] The electors, nevertheless, who solicit or spontaneously admit such interference, are *ipso facto* deprived *pro ea vice* of the right of voting and if the one

[28] *Op. cit.*, I, 255.

[29] Cf. Canons 11, 15.

[30] Canons 163, 164.

[31] "Nullus collegio extraneus *admitti potest ad suffragium*, salvis privilegiis legitime quaesitis; secus, electio est ipso facto nulla."—Cannon 165.

[32] Maroto, *op. cit.*, I, n. 655 (p. 781); Coronata, *Institutiones*, I, 258; Ayrinhac, *General Legislation*, p. 335.

[33] Maroto, *loc. cit.;* Coronata, *loc. cit.*

elected has tacitly and knowingly [34] consented to such interference, he is *ipso facto* disqualified for the office of Administrator.[35]

Canon 167 gives a summary of those who are disqualified to vote in any canonical election. With the exception of one disqualifying cause, all refer to crime, and since only those priests who are distinguished by piety, exemplary life, learning and prudence, are appointed to the office of Diocesan Consultor,[36] this canon, generally speaking, has little effect upon the Diocesan Consultors. A general outline, however, of this legislation may prove to be of assistance should the very improbable occur that a Diocesan Consultor become disqualified to vote. The following, therefore, are disqualified to vote. 1. Those who are unable to perform an human act.[37] 2. Those who are under a censure which deprives them of the right to vote, provided, however, that a declaratory or a condemnatory sentence has been pronounced.[38] Hence, those who are excommunicated,[39] suspended from both office and orders,[40] under personal interdict,[41] *excommunicati vitandi*,[42] or affected with infamy of law,[43] are disqualified to vote in canonical elections after a condemnatory or declaratory sentence has been inflicted.[44] 3. Those who have affiliated themselves with an heretical or schismatical sect, either by placing their names on the official registers of these sects, or by

[34] Cf. Canon 2229 § 2.

[35] Canon 2390 § 2.

[36] Cf. Canon 423.

[37] Canon 167 § 1, n. 1.

[38] Canons 167 § 1, n. 3, 2265, 2232 § 1.

[39] Canon 2265, § 1, n. 1.

[40] Canon 2283; The suspension must include *ab officio,* for suspension *ab ordine* alone does not deprive one of the right to vote: cf. Wernz-Vidal, *Jus Canonicum,* II, n. 249, footnote 17 (p. 265) Coronata, *Institutiones,* I, 259.

[41] Canon 2275 n. 3.

[42] Canon 2265 § 2.

[43] Canon 2293.

[44] Canon 167 § 1, n. 3.

professing publicity, by an overt act, their allegiance to it.[45] 4. Those who have been deprived of the right of voting either by a sentence of a judge, or by a general or particular law which attaches this penalty of privation to specific delicts.[46]

In all instances, if one who is thus disqualified, is admitted to cast ballot, the election itself retains validity provided that the invalid vote of the disqualified is not decisive to the election.[47] If, however, a condemned or declared excommunicated Consultor be *knowingly* admitted to cast his vote, the election is null and void.[48]

Art. 3. *The Form of Scrutiny*

Scrutiny is a form of canonical election according to which the electors employ written and secret ballots. If the Board of Diocesan Consultors chooses this form of electing the Administrator, rather than that of compromise, it must abide by the norms prescribed by the Code under pain of an invalid or illicit election.

The Consultor who is first in precedence and who has convoked the others to the election must also preside over the function of actual voting. It is his duty to insist that the requirements of the law are complied with, although he may not disturb the freedom of the electors. He may, if he so chooses or sees fit, recall to the minds of the other Consultors before the actual balloting takes place, the qualifications which an Administrator must possess according to the requirements of the law. So also may he refer to the solemnities of the election, especially those which affect the substantial form. There is no law forbidding a free discussion among the electors present in

[45] Canon 167 § 1, n. 4; cf. Augustine, *Commentary,* II, 131; Coronata, *op. cit.,* I, 260.

[46] Canon 167 § 1, n. 5; cf. canons, 2291 nn. 8, 11; 729 et 2392 n. 2; 2256 n. 2; 2263; 2294, § 1; 2360 § 2; 2331 § 2; 2336 § 1; 2368 § 1.

[47] Canon 167 § 2; this would, indeed, be a difficult thing to prove when the election is done by scrutiny, since the secrecy of the ballot urn precludes, apparently, any investigation.

[48] Canon 167 § 2. The canon uses the word *scienter* which signifies that all ignorance, except *ignorantia affectata,* excuses from this penalty. Cf. Canon 2229; Maroto, *op. cit.,* I, n. 656 (p. 780); Coronata, *op. cit.,* I, 260.

regard to possible candidates, but the individual Consultor must always be given full liberty to cast his vote for the candidate whom he regards as best fitted for the office.

Before the election by scrutiny, the Consultors present must appoint by secret ballot at least two tellers (*scrutatores*) from the number of Consultors present. The tellers and the presiding Consultor must promise under oath to discharge their duties faithfully, and to keep secret the proceedings of the assembly even after the election is completed.[49] It is the duty of the tellers to see to it that secrecy be observed by the electors when casting their votes. If any voter choses to manifest his will by word of mouth, he must do so to the tellers, safeguarding, at the same time, the secrecy of his ballot. The tellers must immediately take down the vote in writing.[50] The tellers must also observe that only one vote is cast into the urn, or ballot box, at a time, and that the voters proceed according to the order of precedence.[51]

When all the votes are cast the tellers, in the presence of the presiding Consultor, must count the votes and compare this number with the number of electors.[52] If the number of votes cast is greater than the number of electors, the whole process is null and void and must be repeated.[53] If, on the other hand, the number of votes cast in less than the number of electors, this fact will not affect the validity of the election, for it only means that one or the other elector did not take advantage of his right to vote. When the number of votes cast is equal to, or less than the number of electors, the tellers, in the presence of the presiding Consultor, open the ballots, examine them in order to determine whether they are valid, and announce the results to the assembly of electors, precisely stating how many votes each candidate has received.[54]

[49] Canon 171 § 1; cf. Wernz-Vidal, *Jus Canonicum*, II, n. 257 (pp. 271-72) Vermeersch-Creusen, *Epitome*, I, n. 248 (p. 191); Maroto, *Institutiones*, I, n. 633 (pp. 756-57); Coronata, *Institutiones*, I, 264-65.

[50] Cf. Maroto, *op. cit.*, I, n. 634 (p. 658); Wernz-Vidal, *op. cit.*, II, n. 257 (p. 272); Coronata, *op. cit.*, I, 266.

[51] Canon 171 § 2; cf. Canon 106.

[52] Canon 171 § 2.

[53] Canon 171 § 3.

[54] Canon 171 § 2.

§ 1. Conditions Affecting the Validity of Votes

There are certain conditions specified in canon 169 which are necessary for the validity of a vote. In the first place, the law demands that the vote be freely given. Hence, any cause, such as absolute violence, and substantial error, which according to natural law itself destroys the freedom of an human act, would render a vote null and void. According to positive law, as stated in canon 169 § 1 n. 1, a vote is likewise invalid if the elector is compelled by grave fear or deceit,[55] directly or indirectly, to cast his vote for a particular candidate, or anyone of a specified number proposed. That the fear must be grave and the deceit real and that these causes have a determining effect on the vote, goes without saying. Nor does it matter whether this effect be intended.[56]

The canon continues to specify that any vote which is not secret, certain, absolute and determined is invalid.[57] Secrecy here refers to the act of voting[58] and is designed to secure the independence of the voter, and to remove probable evil results, such as partisanship, enmities, etc., which quite naturally would follow if it became known for whom an individual Consultor cast his vote.[59]

Owing to the fact that the secrecy demanded refers only to the act of voting, the law would not be violated, or the validity of the vote affected, if an elector manifested publicly, either before or after the election, the name of the candidate for whom he voted.[60] But if a vote is revealed to the electing assembly during the time of voting, either by the elector himself, or by the tellers, the secrecy is violated and the vote is invalid. But if one or the other elector, in the act of voting, manifested his ballot to another elector, the vote would still

[55] Cf. Canon 103 § 2.

[56] Ayrinhac, *General Legislation*, p. 335.

[57] Canon 169 § 1, n. 2.

[58] Cf. Wernz-Vidal, *op. cit.*, II, n. 254 (p. 270); Maroto, *Institutiones* I, n. 634 (pp. 758-59).

[59] Cf. Augustine, *Commentary*, II, 133; Ayrinhac, *General Legislation*, p. 335.

[60] Wernz-Vidal, *op. cit.*, n. 254 (p. 270); Coronata, *op. cit.*, 267.

be considered as secret, for, according to canonists, a vote is secret or public in the same juridical sense as a crime would be.[61] It must be remembered, finally, that this law of secrecy in balloting is a nullifying prescription, and hence, according to canon 16 § 1, the effect of the law follows even though one be ignorant of the legal disposition.

The vote must also be certain. This precludes any doubt as to the one voted for. Hence, if a Consultor voted for Rev. John Smith, and there were several priests in the diocese having this name, the vote lacks certainty, and is invalid. Thus, if a Consultor cast his vote for Father John Smith, of St. Peter Church, or parish in this city, the vote is certain. So also must the vote be absolute. This signifies that a vote which carries with it a condition, or imposes an obligation upon the candidate, is invalid. Thus, a vote would be invalid if the elector appended to the name "if he is thirty years old," or, "if he will not refuse the appointment." Lastly, a vote is invalid if it is not determined. Hence, if the vote reads "Rev. John Smith, or Rev. Patrick Jones," it is invalid, and must be discarded by the tellers when opening and examining the ballots after all votes are cast.

Canon 169 § 2 states that any condition attached to a vote before the election must be regarded as non-extant, while the following canon specified that any vote cast for oneself is null and void. The secrecy of the ballot urn, however, would render it extremely difficult to discover whether a Consultor voted for himself.

§ 2. The Destruction of the Ballots

After each scrutiny, or if there are several scrutinies in the same session, after each session, all ballots must be burned.[62] Hence, if on the first ballot a candidate received a sufficient number of votes to be elected, the ballots are then immediately burned. If, on the other hand, the required number of votes demanded several scrutinies, and this be done in one and the

[61] Cf. Canon 2197; Maroto, *op. cit.*, I, n. 659 (p. 785); Coronata, *loc. cit.*

[62] Canon 171 § 4.

same session, then the ballots are burned when the session comes to a close.

For convenience, rather than for unity of subject-matter, a word may be inserted in this paragraph with respect to the requirements of canon 171 § 5. According to this canon all proceedings of the election are to be recorded accurately by the one acting as secretary, and this record must be signed by the secretary, the presiding Consultor and the tellers, and carefully kept in the archives of the electoral body. The law states simply that the one acting as secretary must keep the record. Hence, one of the tellers may perform this duty, or if one of the Consultors has already been appointed to serve as secretary for the Board, as is done in some dioceses, he may continue in this capacity. The record, furthermore, must be kept in the archives of the electoral body. Since the law nowhere prescribes that the Board of Diocesan Consultors have its special archives, it would seem that the archives of the diocesan curia is the proper place for this record, as it is very important that this record be safeguarded. The particular reason for keeping this record is to enable the electoral college to prove that the proceedings of the election were canonical in case the validity of the election be challenged later, or a petition be placed to have it rescinded.

ART. 4. *The Form of Compromise*

Compromise, like scrutiny, is a canonical form of election. The Board of Consultors is free to choose either form in the election of the Administrator, according to the express grant in canon 433 § 2. Compromise as a method of designating a candidate differs from scrutiny insofar as the Consultors do not individually and immediately cast their vote for a candidate, but rather, by an express and unanimous consent of all the members, the Board transfers, for this occasion, its right of electing to one or several priests who shall, by the power thus received, hold the election in the name of the Board.[63] Compromise is ordinarily employed by a college of electors

[63] Canon 172 § 1; cf. Maroto, *op. cit.*, I, n. 638 (p. 762).

when dissention arises among the voters, or when repeated ballots have failed to give a particular candidate sufficient votes, or when there is difficulty in assembling all the electors at one and the same time.[64] With respect to the election of the Administrator, however, the Board of Consultors will find compromise a more convenient and efficient mode of electing in very many instances. The chief reason for this is that the number of Consultors on the Board is very frequently limited to four or six, and since the form of scrutiny ordinarily requires that there be two tellers and a secretary besides the presiding Consultor, scrutiny would be reduced to a situation where all the electors are officers in the election. It would seem, therefore, that especially in those instances where the Consultors are few in number, election by compromise would serve to an advantage.

The Board of Consultors is to decide whether the election shall be performed by scrutiny or by compromise. In order to arrive at a valid decision on this question the law demands that there be a free, express, written, and unanimous consent of all the Consultors.[65] This consent refers only to the choice between the forms of scrutiny and compromise, and does not have reference to the consent of the individual Consultor. That the consent must be unanimous is but natural, for the right to elect the Administrator resides in the Board itself, and therefore touches all the Consultors. Hence, the unanimous consent is in full accordance with the principle of canon 101 § 1, n. 2, which specifies that what touches all the members of a corporate body individually must be approved by all. Thus, even if one or two Consultors would refuse to consent to election by compromise, this form of election could not be employed by the Board.[66] It is not necessary, however, that the Board be assembled when giving individual consent, nor does the law demand that secrecy be maintained in doing so.

[64] Cf. Wernz-Vidal, *Jus Canonicum*, II, n. 258 (p. 274); Maroto, *op. cit.*, n. 638 (p. 763).

[65] Canon 172 § 1.

[66] Cf. Maroto, *Institutiones*, I, n. 639 (p. 764).

Hence, the consultors may express their will as to the choice between scrutiny or compromise, in any manner whatsoever.[67] When all Consultors agree that the election be performed by compromise, this consent of the Board must be put into writing in order to avoid misunderstandings and uncertainties, and remove possible occasions for future disputes.

The *Compromissarii,* or those chosen by the Board to perform the election in its name, may be one or several in number, and either Consultors themselves, or individuals who are not members of the Board.[68] They must be priests, however, and of good repute.[69] It is not necessary that there be a unanimous consent of the Board as to who in particular, or how many shall be the *Compromissarii,* since the unanimous consent has reference only to the form of election to be adopted. Hence, the appointment of the *Compromissarii* and all later considerations of the Board with respect to compromise, are governed by the absolute or relative majority vote of the Consultors, according to the prescriptions of canon 101 § 1, n. 1.[70]

Canon 172 §§ 3 and 4 describes the nature of the office of the *Compromissarii.* According to this prescription the *Compromissarii* are obliged, under pain of nullity of the election, to observe the conditions attached to the compromise, if these are not contrary to common law. If no conditions were attached, they must observe the canons regulating elections. Conditions contrary to the common law are considered as though not made. If the electors (Consultors) by compromise appoint only one person, this one cannot elect himself; if several are designated, no one of these can add his vote to that of the others who vote for him in order to effect his election.

It will be seen from this disposition of the Code that the Board, when appointing the *Compromissarii,* may attach con-

[67] Coronata, *Institutiones,* I, 276; Maroto, *Loc. cit.*

[68] Canon 172 § 1.

[69] Canons 171 §§ 1, 2; 167 § 1.

[70] Coronata, *op. cit.,* I, 276-77; Ayrinhac, *General Legislation,* pp. 338-39; Maroto, *op. cit.,* n. 639 (p. 764).

ditions to a compromise. Hence, the Board may demand that the *Compromissarii* elect an Administrator within a specified time, e. g., two days. Or the Board may also prescribe that one of the Consultors be elected, or that the metropolitan, or senior suffragan bishop be first consulted, etc. If no restrictions have been placed upon the power of the *Compromissarii* they must follow the common law governing elections.[71] Hence, they are obliged to perform the election before the period of eight days has elapsed; or they may elect only one Administrator; finally the one whom they elect must possess all the qualifications demanded for the validity of the election.[72] If, therefore, the *Compromissarii* fail to comply with the conditions placed by the Board (as long as these conditions do not conflict with common law), or the conditions otherwise demanded by common law, the election by compromise is null and void.[69] But if the election performed by the *Compromissarii* is valid in all respects, it has the same juridicial value as it would have in case the Consultors have voted themselves, and the Board is obliged to accept the results of the election.[73]

A compromise ceases and the right of electing an Administrator reverts back to the Board of Consultors in any one of three ways. In the first place the Diocesan Consultors may recall their consent to compromise. This revocation, however, must be made before the *Compromissarii* have begun to treat formally with respect to the election, or, in other words, before the election has taken a legal turn (*re integra*).[74] Hence, if the *Compromissarii* had already retired to a place to perform

[71] The prescriptions of the Code governing elections specify that the votes be secret, certain, absolute, collegiately given, etc., but the *Compromissarii* are not bound to follow the regulations of scrutiny, e.g., appointing tellers, etc., for election by compromise is a form distinct from scrutiny. Cf. Maroto, *op. cit.*, I, n. 641 (pp. 765-66); Coronata, *op. cit.*, I, 278.

[72] Cf. Canons 432 § 2, 433 §§ 1, 2.

[69] Canon 172 § 3.

[73] Maroto, *op. cit.*, I, n. 643 (p. 766).

[74] Canon 173 n. 1; cf. Maroto, *op. cit.*, I, n. 644 (p. 767); Coronata, *op. cit.*, I, 279.

the election, the Board is no longer able to revoke its consent. The revocation does not demand a unanimous consent of the Board, but an absolute, or relative majority vote, according to canon 101 § 1, n. 1 is sufficient.[75] The compromise ceases also when the *Compromissarii* have failed to comply with any one of the conditions placed by the Board, or those demanded by common law, or when the election itself is completed, whether this be valid or not.[76] In all instances the right of electing passes back to the Board of Consultors, except, however, when the law of devolution of the right of electing takes effect according to canons 432 § 2 and 434 § 3. The right of electing would not then pass back to the Board, but would devolve upon the metropolitan, or suffragan bishop. The prescriptions of the law in this regard will be considered in a subsequent chapter.

Art. 5. *The Conclusion of the Election*

The election of an Administrator comes to a close when, either by scrutiny or by compromise, a qualified candidate has received an absolute majority of the votes cast not counting the invalid ones.[77] In this respect the election of the Administrator differs from the ordinary election, for whereas elections in general permit a relative majority in the third ballot,[78] a candidate for the office of Administrator must receive an absolute majority of votes, even after the third ballot, in order to be elected validly.[79] Hence, if eight votes were cast in the election, the candidate receiving five votes is elected to the office. If the tellers discover that certain votes are invalid because they were not secret, certain, absolute and determined, or if the votes were invalid for any other reason,

[75] Cf. Footnote supra.

[76] Canon 173 nn. 2, 3.

[77] Canons 433 § 2; 167; 169; 170.

[78] Canon 101 § 1, n. 1.

[79] Canon 433 § 2; Cocchi, *Commentarium,* II, 341; Sipos, *Juris Canonici,* p. 286; Coronata, *Institutiones,* I, 535; *Ferreres, Institutiones,* I, 721; Blat, *Commentarium,* II, 405; Chelodi, Jus De Personis, n. 217 (p. 360) ; Ayrinhac, *Constitutiones,* p. 274; Augustine, *Commentary,* II, 484.

these must be deducted from the total number, and the absolute majority of those remaining will decide the election. Hence, if out of eight votes two are invalid, the absolute majority will be four. When it is determined which candidate has received sufficient votes, the presiding Consultor proclaims the results of the election.[80]

The next prescription of the law is that the results of the election be intimated without delay (*illico*) to the candidate duly elected.[81] When the one elected has received notification of his election directly and from the proper channels,[82] he must, within eight days from the time he received the notice, declare whether he accepts the election or not, otherwise he loses his right to the election.[83] The law expressly states *octiduum utile a recepta intimatione,* indicating that the candidate elected does not lose his right to the election, if for any reason the notice did not come to him or was delayed, or if he was not able to answer within that time.[84]

The Administrator-elect, therefore, remains free to accept or to refuse the office. If he has once refused, he has forfeited his right to the office even though he later regrets that he has done so, but this refusal does not disbar him from being elected again.[85] If, on the other hand, the Administrator-elect accepts his election, he obtains immediately the full right of the office *(jus in re),* since this election does not require confirmation by a superior.[86] In case the Administrator-elect refuses the election, the Board of Consultors, and not the metropolitan or senior suffragan bishop, must proceed, within a new period of eight days, with a second election. This is evident from the fact that the law governing the devolution of the right of electing is penal, and presupposes either negligence

80 Canon 174.

81 Canon 175.

82 Ayrinhac, *General Legislation,* p. 340.

83 Canon 175.

84 Canons 175; 35; cf. Michiels, *Normae Generales Juris Canonici,* II, 158.

85 Canon 176 § 1.

86 Canon 176 § 2, 438.

or fault on the part of the Board of Consultors.[87] Since in this instance the Board is neither negligent in its duty, nor at fault in any way, it would not incur the penalty depriving it of the right to repeat the election.

[87] Cf. Canons 432 § 2, 434 § 3; Coronata, *Institutiones,* I, 534; Augustine, *Commentary,* II, 486.

CHAPTER VIII

Administrators, The Number and Qualifications

Art. 1. *The Number*

It was the intention of the Fathers of the Council of Trent when instituting the office of the Vicar Capitular [1] that only one Vicar be appointed by the Chapter, for just as there is but one bishop in each diocese, so also ought there be but one Vicar Capitular, that the unity of governance might be preserved, and confusion which might arise from a lack of uniformity of official acts may be avoided.[2] But owing to the fact that in pre-Tridentine times the Chapters frequently appointed several vicars to act in their place,[3] the custom of appointing several Vicars Capitular to administer *in solidum* a vacant see was continued in some dioceses after the Council of Trent. The Sacred Congregation of the Council recognized the immemorial custom,[4] or at least tolerated prescribed custom to this effect, as in the case of France.[5]

The present Code of Canon Law has introduced a reform in this regard by reprobating all contrary customs, and prescrib-

[1] Sess. XXIV, *de ref.*, c. 16—*Canones et Decreta*, p. 196.

[2] "Cum autem tridentini Patres singulari numero usi fuerint, uno videlicet non pluribus eodem loco vicariis nominatis, satis superque ostenderunt, unum non plures, sede vacante, vicarios esse deputandos. Etenim ut unus in unaquaque dioecesi est Episcopus, ita etiam omnino congruit, ut unicus debeat esse Vicarius; hac enim tantummodo ratione servari potest unitas regiminis, et actuum uniformitas quae ad omnem confusionem praecavendam necessariae sunt."—S.C.C., *ad Canonicos Dioecesis Ruthensis*, 4 Sept. 1871—*Archiv Für Katholisches Kirchenrechts*, XXVII (1872), p. XIV; cf. S.C., EE. et RR., *Cassanen.*, 6 Aug. 1596—*Fontes*, n. 1557; *Bobiensi*, 12 Martii 1607—*op. cit.*, n. 1642; Ferraris, Prompta *Bibliotheca* v. *Capitulum*, art. III, n. 40.

[3] Cf. Historical Conspectus, pp. 34-36.

[4] "Congregatio Concilii censuit ex decreto Con., c. 16, Sess. 24 a Capitulo sede vacante unum tantum Vicarium esse eligendum. Ceterum non esse eo decreto sublatam consuetudinem duos, aut plures eligendi praesertim immemorabilem."—S.C.C., *Panormitana*, 21 Apr. 1592—*Fontes*, n. 2242; cf. Historical Conspectus, pp. 46-47.

[5] Cf. Bouix, *De Capitulis*, pp. 497-504; Wernz, *Jus Decretalium*, II, n. 795 (p. 607).

ing that the Chapter, under pain of a null and void election, may appoint only one Vicar Capitular.[6] Under no circumstances, therefore, may the Board of Diocesan Consultors elect more than one Administrator. Should it happen, however, that while a duly elected Administrator retains his office, the Board would attempt to elect other Administrators, the subsequent elections would, of course, be invalid, but this would not affect the status of the Administrator in office.[7] But if several Administrators were elected in one and the same session, the entire proceeding of the Board would be invalid, and no one of the several would be entitled to assume the office. In this case the Board would have to proceed with a new election, provided, however, that the period of eight days had not as yet elapsed. The devolution of the right of election in this instance, therefore, takes effect only after the eighth day, for canon 433 § 1 does not attach to such an invalid election, the penalty of immediate loss of the right of electing.

The prescription of the Code demanding that the Board of Consultors elect but one Administrator, does not prohibit the Administrator himself from appointing " pro-vicars," who shall function in the pastoral ministry under his power and guidance. This may be found necessary in very large dioceses, or in those places where the affairs of the see demands the services of many.[8] The " pro-Vicars," however, are merely delegates of the Administrator, and in no manner possess ordinary jurisdiction, for it is entirely beyond the capacity of the Administrator to confer ordinary episcopal jurisdiction upon others.[9]

[6] Canon 433 § 1.

[7] Cf. Blat, *Commentarium,* II, 404; Bouix, *De Capitulis,* p. 496; Bonal, *Institutiones Canonicae,* I, 654.

[8] "Quod si dioecesis latitudo, ac negotiorum multiplicitas plurim hominum operam exigat, nihil impedit quominus idem Vicarius unum vel plures tanquam provicarios sibi adsciscat, qui sua sub potestate ac nutu negotia ministerii pastoralis expediant."—S.C.C., *ad Canonicos Dioecesis Ruthensis,* 4 Sept. 1871—*loc. cit.;* Bargilliat, *Juris Canonici,* II, 41.

[9] Cf. Schmalzgrueber, *Jus Eccl. Univ.,* lib. I, tit. XXVIII, n. 32; Ferreres, *Institutiones Canonicae,* I, n. 725; Leurenius, *Forum Beneficiale,* t. IV, tract. III, q. 621.

ART. 2. *The Qualifications of the Administrator*

The Administrator of a diocese possesses an ecclesiastical office in the strict sense of the term,[10] and hence the fundamental prescriptions of the Code governing ecclesiastical offices in general will have their proportionate application. The Administrator, in common with all other candidates for ecclesiastical offices, must be worthy and fit, and must have the qualifications which are demanded by the common law, either for the validity, or for the liceity of the appointment.[11] When there is a choice between several candidates, all of whom possess the qualifications demanded by law, he is to be chosen who, after all things are considered, is regarded as being better fitted *(magis idoneus)* for the office, leaving aside all human considerations.[12] The law inculcates the necessity of choosing the better fitted candidate by way of admonition, rather than by prohibition, and adds that the choice should be made only after due consideration is given to all things concerned. Hence, the judgment remains with the Board of Consultors, or the metropolitan or senior suffragan bishop in case of devolution of the right to elect the Administrator. The condition of the diocese, therefore, will have to be balanced with the qualities of the candidates, and the one who is thought best fitted to serve the particular needs of the see should be elected to the office.

The appointment to any ecclesiastical office, moreover, presupposes that the candidate is canonically capable (*habilis*) of holding the office. Hence, anyone who is afflicted with an ecclesiastical penalty because of some crime committed, cannot be elected or appointed Administrator. Thus, the candidate must be free from excommunication,[13] interdict,[14] or suspension[15] and from infamy, whether of law or of fact.[16]

10 Canon 145.

11 Canon 153 §§ 1, 3.

12 "Assumatur, omnibus perpensis, magis idoneus sine ulla personarum acceptione."—Canon 153 § 2.

13 Canon 2265 § 1 n. 2.

14 Canon 2275 n. 3.

15 Canon 2283.

16 Canons 2293-2294; cf. Canons 2314 § 1, nn. 2-3; 2320; 2328; 2343 § 1, n. 2, § 2, n. 2; 2351 § 2, 2359 § 2.

Before a declaratory or a condemnatory sentence is imposed, an excommunicated, interdicted, or suspended cleric cannot licitly be given an ecclesiastical office, and after a sentence has been inflicted, such a promotion to office would be invalid.[17] Furthermore, if the Board of Consultors knowingly *(scienter)* [18] elect such an unworthy candidate, it is *ipso facto* deprived, for that time *(pro ea vice)* of the right of proceeding to a new election,[19] and the appointment of the Administrator would then rest with the metropolitan or the senior suffragan bishop, as the case might be.

Canon 434 explicitly specifies the positive qualifications necessary for the validity and the liceity of the election or appointment of the Administrator. The first paragraph of this canon enumerates certain qualifications which must be possessed by the Administrator, and if the Board elects one who is not thus qualified, the third paragraph continues to state that the metropolitan, or if the metropolitan see be vacant or it be question of electing an Administrator for the metropolitan see, the senior bishop of the province shall designate the Administrator, after having been duly informed of the election; all the official acts of the invalidly elected Administrator, furthermore, are *ipso jure* null and void. The second paragraph of the same canon is, for the most part, an enumeration of qualifications specified by the Council of Trent for the office of the Vicar Capitular.[20] Although the Code does not demand these latter qualifications for the validity of the appointment, the Board of Consultors, nevertheless, is strictly obliged to comply with these requirements under pain of an illicit election. The two categories of qualifications, therefore, will be given distinct consideration in the following paragraphs.

§ 1. Qualifications Necessary for the Validity of the Election

[17] Canon 2265 § 2; Canons 2275 n. 3, 2283.

[18] Cf. Canon 2229 § 2.

[19] Canon 2391 § 1.

[20] Council of Trent, sess. XXIV, *de ref.* c. 16—*Canones et Decreta*, p. 196.

Since it is the duty of the Administrator to exercise care for souls in both the internal and external forum,[12] the Administrator, in common with all other candidates for ecclesiastical offices to which the care of souls, either in the internal or external forum, is attached,[22] cannot validly be appointed to office unless he be a priest.[23] Furthermore, since the office of the Administrator is that of a superior and implies rank, precedence,[24] and jurisdiction,[25] the incumbent, in common with bishops,[26] abbots and prelates *nullius*,[27] vicars-general,[28] and officials of the diocesan court,[29] must have completed his thirtieth year of age.[30] The phrase *tricesimum aetatis annum non expleverit* found in canon 434 § 1, demands that the thirtieth anniversary be completed.[31] Hence, if a candidate celebrates his thirtieth birthday on the first of May, he cannot be validly elected to the office of Administrator until that day is completed. The prescripition of the present Code with respect to the priesthood and the necessary age, is a departure from former discipline, for, according to former practice, the Vicar Capitular needed only to have received tonsure and be twenty-five years old.[32]

The Administrator, like the vicar-general[33] and the synodal or pro-synodal judges,[34] may be an extra-diocesan priest,[35]

21 Cf. Canon 435 § 1.

22 Cf. Canons 232, 331, 320, 367, 445, 423, 453, 479, 1574.

23 Canons 434 § 1, 154.

24 Cf. Canons 439, 370.

25 Canon 435 § 1.

26 Canon 331 § 1, n. 2.

27 Canon 320 § 2.

28 Canon 367 § 1.

29 Canon 1573 § 4.

30 Canon 434 § 1.

31 Cf. canon 34 § 3, n. 3; Michiels, *Normae Generalis*, II, 157-58.

32 Cf. Leurenuis, *Forum Beneficiale*, t. IV, tract. III, qq. 559-560; Bouix, *De Capitulis*, 528; Wernz, *Jus Decretalium*, II, n. 795 (p. 607).

33 Canon 367 § 3.

34 Canon 1574 § 1.

35 Bouix, *op. cit.*, p. 521.

and hence the Board of Consultors remains free to elect any priest, either of the diocese or extern, as long as the candidate has the specified qualifications. A fellow-diocesan priest, however, should be given preference to one not of the diocese, if the former possesses the qualifications demanded by the Code.[36] According to former discipline, any cleric who has received a dispensation from the irregularity of illegitimacy of birth in order to be admitted into the clerical state, or to received an ecclesiastical office, was not eligible for the office of Vicar Capitular unless he first received a new and special dispensation.[37] The present law no longer places this as a requirement for the office of Vicar Capitular, or Administrator.[38] Hence, just as in the case of a vicar-general,[39] if a priest has once been dispensed from the irregularity of illegitimacy of birth, he need receive no further dispensation in order to be elected to the office of Administrator. The present Code, furthermore, does not prohibit the Board of Consultors from electing the official of the diocese, for canon 1573 § 7 explicitly states that if the official be elected Administrator, he is obliged to appoint a new official.[40]

The question may be asked as to whether religious priests may be elected to the office of Administrator. According to the prescriptions of canon 626 § 1, religious are not permitted to be promoted, without the authority of the Apostolic See, to ecclesiastical dignities, offices, and benefices which are incompatable with the religious state. The religious state is a permanent mode of living in common, by which the faithful, besides obeying the commandments, also observe the evangelical counsels embodied in the vows of obedience, chastity, and poverty.[41] A religious is anyone who has taken vows in any

[36] Cf. S.C.C., *Neritonen.*, 24 Jul. 1643—*Fontes*, n. 2646.

[37] Cf. Leurenius, *Forum Beneficiale*, t. IV, tract. III, q. 559; Bouix, *op. cit.*, pp. 528-29.

[38] Sipos, *Juris Canonici*, p. 287.

[39] Cf. Coronata, *Institutiones*, I, 483; Vermeersch-Creusen, *Epitome*, I, n. 435 (p. 283).

[40] Cf. Vermeersch-Creusen, *op. cit.*, III, n. 34 (p. 16).

[41] Canon 487.

religious institute.[42] And a religious institute is a society, approved by legitimate ecclesiastical authority, whose members strive after evangelical perfection by observing the special laws of that society and by making public vows, either perpetual or temporary, the latter to be renewed when the time expires.[43] All such individuals, therefore, come within the scope of the term "religious" found in canon 626 § 1, and no dignity, office or benefice which would conflict with their state of life can be bestowed upon them without the authority of the Apostolic See.

The general norm of the Code is that all dignities, offices and benefices which are not under the direction of religious are destined for the secular clergy, and if there be a doubt as to whether these are secular or religious, the law presumes that they are secular.[44] Hence, in secular dioceses a religious may not be given a secular benefice,[45] appointed vicar-general,[46] official, vice-official, synodal judge, and only under certain circumstances may they be advocates, procurators, and notaries.[48] A recent response of the Pontifical Commission for the Authentic Interpretation of the Code[48] has made it clear that religious may not be appointed to the office of Diocesan Consultor.[49]

It may be concluded from this general prohibition of religious being appointed to secular ecclesiastical offices, that religious are ineligible also for the office of Administrator, even

[42] Canon 488 n. 7.

[43] Canon 488 n. 1.

[44] Canon 1411 n. 2; cf. Schäfer, *De Religiosis*, p. 527; Vermeersch-Creusen, *Epitome*, I, n. 728 (475-76); Fanfani, *De Jure Religiosorum*, pp. 471-72.

[45] Canon 1442.

[46] Canon 367 §§ 1-2.

[47] Canon 1573, 1574, 1657 § 3, 2014; cf. Roberti, *De Processibus*, I, n. 98; Noval, *De Processibus*, I, n. 116; Wernz-Vidal, *Jus Canonicum*, VI, n. 87 (p. 80), footnote 9.

[48] 29 Jan. 1931—AAS, XXIII (1931), 110; cf. *Il Monitore Ecclesiastico*, March, 1931, p. 72; *Jus Pontificium*, XI (1931), 107.

[49] This question remained doubtful previous to this response: cf. Augustine, *Commentary*, III, 355; Klekotka, *Diocesan Consultors*, pp. 60-62.

though the law does not expressly take this office into account. The very fact, however, that the vicar-general in a secular diocese must be a secular priest, is indeed a strong argument for the opinion that religious may not be appointed Administrator in secular diocese, since the two offices bear a striking resemblence, and as far as qualifications are concerned, have very often been subject to one and the same norm.[50]

The next question centers about the appointment of secularized religious priests. A secularized religious,[51] according to the disposition of canon 642 may not, without a new and special indult from the Holy See, accept or hold certain ecclesiastical benefices or offices. The third paragraph of this canon explicitly states that a secularized religious may not hold any office or charge in the episcopal curia. Hence, such a cleric may not be vicar-general, official, chancellor, promotor of justice, defendor of the bond, etc.[52] The recent response of the Pontifical Commission has interpreted canon 423 to the effect that secularized religious are not to be appointed to the office of Diocesan Consultor.[53]

Since, therefore, a secularized religious is excluded from all offices of the diocesan curia, which is comprised of those clerics who assist the bishop, or the one who in place of the bishop rules the diocese, in the government of the see, it can scarcely be doubted that the prohibition extends to the office of the Administrator. Although no explicit pronouncement has as yet been made in this regard, it appears that the legislator implicitly includes the office of the Administrator among the offices prohibited to secularized religious, for it may be argued that if the restriction is placed upon all offices inferior to that of the Administrator, it *a fortiori* includes the superior office.

[50] Cf. Canons 434 §§ 1-2 et 367 § 1; 435 et 368; 439 et 370; S.C.C., *Nullius,* 12 Maii 1629—*Fontes,* n. 2509; cf. Pignatellus, *Consultationes Canonicae,* t. VII, consult. IV, n. 6; Quaranța, *Summa Bullarii* v. *Capitulum sede vacante,* p. 576.

[51] Cf. Canons 638-640.

[52] Cf. Canon 363 § 2.

[53] Cf. Footnote 48 supra.

The term "secularized religious" includes not only those religious who have become secularized since the promulgation of the Code, but those as well who have become thus before the new legislation had taken effect.[54] This legislation applies also to those who have pronounced only temporary vows, or who had taken the oath of perseverance, or made other promises according to their constitutions, provided, however, that they have been duly dispensed therefrom, and have been under the obligations for a period of at least six years.[55]

A third question in connection with the appointment of a priest for the office of Administrator, is whether a pastor, or a priest who actually exercises care for souls may serve as Administrator. Since the office of the Administrator is an ecclesiastical office in the strict sense, the answer to this question must be sought in an analysis of the general legislation of the Code with respect to incompatible offices, and by applying these norms to the offices of the Administrator and pastor, as the legislator does not expressly state that the two offices are incompatible.

According to the prescriptions of canon 156 § 1, it is strictly forbidden to anyone to confer two incompatible offices upon an individual. If a cleric accepts and obtains pacific possession of an office which is considered by law as being incompatible with the one he already possesses, he thereby tacitly tempts to retain the actual charge of both offices, he *ipso facto* loses title to both.[57] In one instance only may anyone accept and retain two incompatible offices. This is possible only by way of a special concession or dispensation from the Holy See according to the disposition of canon 156 § 3.

Ecclesiastical offices, according to canon 156 § 2, are said to be incompatible when the duties of each cannot be properly discharged by one and the same person. This remains true even in extraordinary cases when only a highly experienced and industrious person is able to do so.[58] Offices, consequently,

[54] *Pontifical Commission*, 24 Nov. 1920—AAS, XII (1920, 573.

[55] Canon 642 § 2.

[57] Canon 2396.

[58] Maroto, *Institutiones*, I, n. 595 (p. 706).

are incompatible if each requires residence, or the presence of the incumbent in distinct places, or demands his whole attention and time. Thus the Code specifically states that a pastor may have title to only one parish;[59] a vicar-general may not be a canon penitentiary, or a pastor or one having the care of souls, except in the case of necessity.[60] A judge may not be notary in one and the same case;[61] a religious superior general or provincial may not be the Econome of the institute;[62] or a promoter or justice may not act as defender of the bond when there is a multiplicity of duties and cases.[63] The law, however, does not regard two offices as incompatible when one is held in title and the other only temporarily.[64] resigns his former office.[56] Furthermore, if the individual at-
Hence, a pastor may assume the administration of a nearby vacant parish;[65] or a cleric who already has title to an office may be commissioned for a time to perform duties that are incompatible with those attached to his office.[66] The question therefore remains as to whether or not the office of pastor, or of one encompassing the care of souls, is incompatible with that of the Administrator. Since the present law prescinds from any express statement on the question, former practice must be given consideration.

The Sacred Congregation of the Council had decided upon several occasions that a pastor having actual care of souls either within the episcopal city, or outside of it, is ineligible for the office of vicar-general or Vicar Capitular.[67]

59 Canon 460 § 1.

60 Canon 367 § 3.

61 Canon 1585 § 2.

62 Canon 516 § 3.

63 Canon 1588 § 1.

56 Canon 188 n. 3.

64 Canon 1439 § 1.

65 Canon 472 n. 2.

66 Maroto, *op. cit.*, I, n. 595 (p. 707).

67 " Sacra, etc. respondit Parochum habentem curam animarum extra vel intra civitatem consuevisse Sacram Congregationem improbare, ut in Vicarium Episcopi, vel Capituli eligatur."—S.C.C., *Nullius,* 12 Maii 1629—*Fontes,* n. 2509; cf. Leurenius *Forum Beneficiale,* t. IV, tract. III, q. 558; Pignatellus, *Consultationes Canonicae,* t. VII consult. 4, n. 6.

These decisions, however, were given for particular cases and consequently lacked the force of general law. No general law, therefore, directly prohibited all pastors from being elected to the office of Vicar Capitular.[68] But owing to the fact that the Vicar Capitular was obliged to reside in the episcopal city, and even in the episcopal palace,[69] pastors not residing in the episcopal city were indirectly prohibited from being appointed to the office of Vicar Capitular because such appointment would entail a violation of the law of residence incumbent upon pastors.[70] Pastors who had actual charge of souls within the episcopal city, however, were generally permitted, according to the decisions of the Sacred Congregation of Bishops and Regulars, to be appointed either vicar-general or Vicar Capitular.[71] According to law and practice before the present Code, therefore, pastors who resided outside the episcopal city could not be validly appointed to the office of Vicar Capitular because of the law of residence, and not because it was regarded impossible for one and the same individual to perform the duties attached to each office.[72] The interpretations given by the Sacred Congregation of Bishops and Regulars, and the common opinion of earlier canonists, will throw light upon the true significance of present legislation in this regard.

68 Cf. Wernz, *Jus Decretalium,* II, n. 795 (p. 607); Hermes, *De Capitulo Sede Vacante et Impedita,* p. 128.

69 "Iste tenetur *habitare in episcopio,* ut, ex mente Sacrae Congregationis super Episcopis, resolvit Ricclus (resol. 116, n. 1 et 2)";—Pignatellus, *op. cit.*, t. VII, consult, 4, n. 8; Bouix, *op. cit.*, p. 527.

70 Council of Trent, Sess. XXIII, *de ref,* c. 1—*Canones et Decreta,* p. 153; Pignatellus, *op. cit.,* n. 6; Leurenius, *loc. cit.;* Quaranta, *Summa Bullarii* v. *Capitulum sede vacante,* p. 576.

71 "Interrogata, an sede episcopali vacante canonici eligere valeant in vicarium capitularem canonicum ejusdem ecclesiae, qui in eadem civitate, et ecclesia curam quoque gerit animarum, ipsa affirmative respondit; et generatim, quo parochus urbanus tam episcopi, quam capituli vicarius deputari possit (si habeat alia requisita) declaravit in Auriensi 19 Martii 1610, et 19 Julii ejusdem anni."—Pignatellus, *loc. cit.*

72 Cf. Leurenius, *loc. cit.;* Pignatellus, *loc. cit.;* Bouix, *op. cit.,* pp. 525-528; Wernz, *loc. cit.;* Hermes, *loc cit.;* Bonal, *Institutiones Canonicae,* I, 662.

Among modern canonists there are but few who have given this question any consideration. De Meester[73] regards an office to which is attached the actual care of souls as incompatible with that of the Vicar Capitular, and maintains that anyone who possesses such an office is ineligible for the latter. Coronata[74] and Vermeersch-Creusen[75] are of the opinion that if a pastor be elected to the office of Vicar Capitular, he may compatible. The opinion of these canonists, however, appears to be too rigorous an interpretation of the present law, for it lacks the moderation of former discipline which, even in the presence of prevailing legislation, is still justifiable. Canon 156 § 2 explicitly states that two offices are incompatible when it is impossible for one person to do justice to both. Now, since the present Code nowhere expressly states that the office of the pastor and that of the Vicar Capitular are incompatible, there is no reason for believing that the office of pastor in the episcopal city is any more incompatible with the office of Vicar Capitular according to the present law than it was before the Code was promulgated. Furthermore, since the present law does not oblige the Vicar Capitular to reside in the episcopal city, but rather that he keep residence in the diocese the same as the bishop,[76] a pastor who has charge of souls outside of the episcopal city could retain his office and that of the Vicar Capitular without violating the law of residence attached to both offices. It may be said, *salvo meliori judicio,* that *per se* a parochial office *within the diocese* and the office of Vicar Capitular or Administrator are not incompatible according to the present discipline. It appears, however, that a pastor should not be appointed or elected Vicar Capitular or Administrator, unless there is a necessity for doing so. This seems to be more in accord with the spirit of the law, for insofar as former discipline in this respect applied the same norms to the office of vicar-general and Vicar

[73] *Compendium,* II, n. 796 (p. 234).

[74] *Institutiones,* I, 535, footnote 8.

[75] *Epitome,* I, n. 480 (p. 306).

[76] Canon 440, 338; cf. pp. 206-208.

Capitular alike,[77] it would appear entirely congruous to apply to the office of Vicar Capitular the same disposition which the present law provides for the vicar-general. Since the Code prescribes that a pastor or any other having charge of souls may be appointed vicar-general only in case of necessity,[78] so also ought the same norm be followed in the election or appointment of the Vicar Capitular or Administrator. Experience has shown that Boards of Diocesan Consultors in the United States have quite frequently found it necessary to elect pastors to serve in the office of Administrator, chiefly because certain pastors were regarded as being best fitted for the office, or because capable priests who were neither pastors, nor had actual charge of souls, had refused to accept the office. In any case the appointment of pastors to the office of Administrator in the United States is tacitly approved. If, consequently, it be found necessary in the future to elect a pastor, it would be advisable for the Administrator when assuming office to appoint a parochial assistant[79] to assist him in his parochial ministry.

The first and second conditions for the valid election of an Administrator, therefore, are that the candidate be a priest, and that he has completed his thirtieth year of age. The same paragraph of canon 434 continues to state that anyone who has been presented, nominated, or elected to the vacant see cannot be validly elected to be its Vicar Capitular or Administrator. This prescription of the Code is taken from the Constitution *"Romanus Pontifex"* of Pope Pius IX, who attached the penalty of excommunication reserved to the Holy See, for anyone who would violate the law.[80] The same penalty was incurred, according to the Constitution, by bishops-elect who interfered with the administration of the diocese before they had taken canonical possession of it.

[77] Cf. Footnotes, 67, 71. supra; Benedict XIV, *De Synodo Dioecesana,* lib. II, c. 9, n. 3.

[78] Canon 367 § 3.

[79] Cf. Canons 455 § 2, n. 1, 476.

[80] 28 Aug. 1873—ASS, VII, 403-404; the penalty was abrogated by the present code. Cf. De Meester, *Compendium,* II, n. 796 (p. 234); Prümmer, *Manuale Juris Canonici,* p. 202.

In the United States no individual or group of individuals enjoy the right of presenting, nominating, or electing candidates for the episcopacy, and hence the election of an Administrator will scarcely ever be vitiated by a failure on the part of the Board of Consultors to comply with this legal prescription. The only semblance of presenting candidates to bishoprics in the United States is the method established by the Sacred Consistorial Congregation,[81] whereby the bishops of this country choose possible candidates for the episcopacy and forward the names to the Holy See through the Apostolic Delegate to the United States. The manner of proposing names does not create the juridical effect of a *jus ad rem* but serves merely to acquaint the Holy See with suitable candidates to vacant dioceses. Under the present circumstances, therefore, the only way the Board of Consultors could perform an invalid election by failing to comply with this third condition, is by electing a bishop-elect to the office of Administrator before he has taken canonical possession of the see. It must be remembered, however, that if an Administrator is duly elected and later receives word of his promotion to the see which he is administering, he may continue in the capacity of Administrator until he has taken canonical possession of the diocese.[82]

The present law prescribes only three qualifications, therefore, which are necessary for the valid election of the Administrator. If these conditions be neglected by the Board of Consultors, the election is null and void, and the acts of the Administrator are invalid. The right of electing, furthermore, is *ipso facto* forfeited by the Board *pro ea vice,* and the appointment rests with the metropolitan or senior suffragan bishop, as the case may be.[83]

§ 2. Qualifications Necessary for the Liceity of the Election

Canon 434 § 2 prescribes certain qualifications for the law-

[81] 25 Julii 1916—AAS, VIII (1916), 400-404; cf. Augustine, *Commentary,* II, 120-123.

[82] Canons 334 § 2; 443 § 2.

[83] Canon 434 § 3.

ful election of a candidate to the office of Administrator. Much in common with other superior offices in the Church which encompass the duty of caring for souls,[84] the office of the Administrator can lawfully be held only by a doctor or licentiate of theology or of Canon Law, or one who is at least well versed in these sciences as required for the proper discharge of the attached duties. The incumbent must also possess integrity of life, piety, sound doctrine and prudence.[85] The legislator does not demand that these qualifications be possessed by a candidate as a condition for the validity of the election, nor does he determine the exact degree in which they must exist for liceity, but rather leaves this to the prudent judgment of the Board of Consultors. It is the duty of the Board, therefore, to take all things into account and to elect that cleric who, to the best of their knowledge, possesses these qualifications in the highest degree.[86]

The Council of Trent[87] had decreed that the Vicar Capitular must be a doctor or licentiate of Canon Law. This disposition of the Council had given rise to much controversy, but after many decrees and decisions of the Sacred Congregation of the Council and of the Bishops and Regulars, the following rule became the common teaching:[88] if there were doctors of Canon Law among the canons of the cathedral Chapter and these were otherwise fit, the validity of the election demanded that one of them be chosen; a cathedral Canon who was not a doctor but otherwise capable had to be preferred to a doctor who was not fit; if there were a cathedral Canon who was not a doctor, but otherwise capable, the Chapter was not obliged to choose a doctor who was not a Canon; finally, the doctorate of theology did not satisfy the requirements of the Council of Trent.

The present legislation, it has been observed, has discarded the dispositions of former law which have only too frequently

[84] Cf. Canons 331 § 1, nn. 4-5; 320 § 2; 367 § 1; 1573 § 4; 1589 § 1.

[85] Canon 434 § 2.

[86] Canon 153 § 2; cf. S.C.C., *Carniolen.*, 22 Sept. 1714— *Fontes,* n. 3138.

[87] Sess XXIV, *de ref.* c. 16—*Canones et Decreta,* p. 196.

[88] Cf. Historical Conspectus, pp. 51ss.

proven to be grounds for invalid and rescinded elections of Vicars Capitular. The present law requires, of course, that the doctorate or licentiate of theology or canon law be received from an institution which has faculties from the Holy See to confer degrees,[89] but neither degree is demanded for the valid election of the Administrator. Nor does the present law require that the Vicar Capitular be chosen from the membership of the cathedral Chapter. Hence, if the Board of Diocesan Consultors elects an Administrator who is neither a doctor, nor a Consultor, even though there are doctors and capable Consultors available, the validity of the election cannot be challenged on these grounds. But owing to the fact that it was the intention of the Council of Trent, that, when all things are equal, a member of the cathedral Chapter must be preferred,[90] canonists [91] teach that the same norm should be followed in present practice, although this is given only by way of admonition. There is, of course, much wisdom in this advice, for it is but natural that since a cathedral Canon or a Diocesan Consultor holds an office so closely associated with the governance of the diocese, such a one is more capable than others to function in the office of Vivar Capitular or Administrator. Vidal,[92] however, establishes a norm to be followed in the election of a Vicar Capitular, which may be of some assistance to a Board of Consultors when electing the Administrator. The canonist advises that the auxiliary-bishop of the preceding prelate, or the vicar-general of the deceased bishop be the first choice of the Board, even though they do not belong to the Board of Consultors. If for any reason it

[89] Canon 1377.

[90] "Cum alias haec S. Congregatio censuerit in Vicarium Capitularem eligi posses etiam aliquem extra Capitulum, si tamen quis de gremio Capituli reperiatus habilis, istum ceteris paribus esse praeferendum:"—S.C.C., *Neritonen.*, 24 Jul. 1643—*Fontes*, n. 2646; cf. *Camplen.*, ii maii 1624—*op. cit.*, n. 2450; *Triventina*, mense dec. 1586—*op. cit.*, n. 2167.

[91] Blat, *Commentarium*, II, 405; Sipos, *Juris Canonici*, p. 287; Cocchi, *Commentarium*, II, 342; Raus, *Institutiones Canonicae*, p. 224-25; De Meester, *Compendium*, 11, n. 796, (pp. 234-35); Ferreres, *Institutiones*, I, 302; Chelodi, *Jus De Personis*, n. 217, (p. 360).

[92] *Jus Canonicum*, II, n. 709, (p. 761).

is felt that the office should be held by another, a member of the Board of Consultors who is endowed with the required qualifications, merits to be elected in preference to those who are not Consultors. This advice is not wanting in value, for it is true that an auxiliary-bishop, or a vicar-general is in a position to be an expert in administering the affairs of a diocese, and further, in either instance there would not be a question of the necessary qualification, for these dignities require practically the same qualifications as those demanded for the office of Administrator.[93]

[93] Cf. Canons 331 § 1, nn. 4-5; 367 § 1; 434.

CHAPTER IX

The Devolution of the Right of Electing the Administrator

The legal enactment of the Council of Trent [1] forms the source from which is derived the present law governing the devolution of the right of electing the Vicar Capitular or Administrator. According to this prescription, the Board of Diocesan Consultors loses the right of electing the Administrator when either it fails, for any reason whatever, to make the appointment within eight days from the time notice of vacancy is received, or when it elects one who lacks the qualifications demanded by law for the validity of the election.[2] When either of these circumstances contemplated by law is verified, the right of electing devolves upon the metropolitan, or if the metropolitan see is vacant upon the senior suffragan bishop.[3] The same disposition of law applies also to those vacant dioceses which are immediately subject to the Holy See, or an abbacy or prelature *nullius,* when the chapter fails to appoint a Vicar Capitular within the prescribed time. In such instances the right to make the appointment devolves upon the metropolitan chosen once for all as superior in such matters, unless in the case of an abbacy or religious prelature *nullius*. the respective constitutions have a special provision for such emergencies.[4] As it has already been stated, there are no dioceses in the United States which are immediately subject to the Holy See, nor is there a prelature *nullius*. The particular constitutions of the American-Cassinese Benedictine Congregation, it has been observed, govern the administration of the abbey *nullius* at Belmont, North Carolina. Since, in this in-

[1] Sess. XXIV, *de ref.* c. 16—*Canones et Decreta,* p. 196.

[2] Canons 432 § 2 et 1, 434 § 3 et 1.

[3] Canons 432 § 2, 434 § 3.

[4] Canons 432 § 3, 285.

stance, the Prior supplies the Abbot Ordinary as soon as the abbey *nullius* becomes vacant, the question of the devolution of the right of electing an Administrator will scarcely occur. It may happen, however, that the Prior would die during the period of vacancy. The religious chapter would then, according to the constitutions, have to elect an Administrator. If the chapter would fail to perform the election within eight days, the right to make the appointment would then pass to the metropolitan, according to the common law of the Church.[5]

ART. I. *The Causes and Time of Devolution*

Before considering the causes which give rise to devolution of the right to elect the Administrator, attention must be called to a strange condition which might possibly present itself in those dioceses where the Board of Diocesan Consultors takes the place of the cathedral Chapter. It is not altogether impossible that a diocese be without a Board of Consultors when vacancy arises. According to canon 426 §§ 1 and 2, the office of Diocesan Consultors extends over a period of three years, and when the triennial term has expired, the bishop must either appoint others, or reappoint the same Consultors for another term of office. This rule must be followed every three years. Now, it always remains possible that a bishop might fail, either through inadvertance or neglect, to appoint new Consultors, or confirm the former ones when their term of office has elapsed. If the see becomes vacant in any manner before the bishop had made this provision, the vacant see will be without a Board of Consultors, and the former Consultors will no longer possess the right to administer the see or to elect the Administrator. In such instances the metropolitan or the senior suffragan bishop, as the case may be, would then be obliged to appoint the Administrator.[6] It appears that this appointment to be made by the metropolitan or senior suffragan

[5] Cf. *Declarationes in Regulam S.P.N. Benedicti et Statuta Congregationis Americano-Cassinensis*, caput LXV, pp. 37-38; canon 432 § 3.

[6] Cf. S.C.C., decis., 28 Aug. 1683, et 14 Apr. 1685—Richter, *Canones et Decreta*, p. 375, n. 24; Benedict XIV, *De Synodo Dioecesana*, lib. 11, c. 9, n. 2.

bishop should take place as soon as possible, since the diocese would be without a superior who possesses ordinary episcopal jurisdiction. It must be remembered, however, that if the triennial term of the office of the Diocesan Consultors expires after the see becomes vacant, the Consultors remain in office until the new bishop takes possession of the diocese, and he is then to provide within the first six months according to canon 426 § 4. Likewise, it might be recalled that if there is but one Consultor remaining in office at the time vacancy arises, or when the election of the Administrator is to take place, he can exercise the rights proper to the Board itself.

If the Board of Diocesan Consultors elects one who is not a priest, or a priest who has not completed his thirtieth year of age, or one who is presented, nominated or elected to the vacant see in question, the election is invalid, and the right of appointing the Administrator devolves for this one time (*pro ea vice*) upon the metropolitan, or the senior bishop of the province, as the case may be, and the latter may proceed to exercise his right as soon as he has ascertained the nullity of the election performed by the Board.[7] In this case the Board loses its right *pro ea vice,* which signifies that it is not permitted for the Board to repeat the election, even though the period of eight days has not as yet elapsed, and if the Board attempts to do so, the subsequent election is invalid.[8]

The other causes contributing to the devolution of the right of electing the Administrator take effect only after the expiration of the period of eight days from the time knowledge of vacancy has been received. Canon 432 § 2 states that if the Board of Consultors fails, for any reason whatever, to make the appointment within this prescribed period of time, the right of electing devolves upon the metropolitan or senior suffragan bishop. The phrase *quavis de causa* employed by the legislation is general in scope and includes any cause, whether culpable or inculpable, which might precipitate in the failure

[7] Canon 434 § 3.

[8] Cf. Capello, *Summa,* I, n. 401, (p. 413); Chelodi, *Jus De Personis,* n. 217, (p. 360); Coronata, *Institutiones,* I, 534.

of the Board to provide the diocese with an Administrator. Hence, if within the period of eight days, the Board refuses to exercise its prerogative, or neglects to do so, or if, after repeated ballots, it fails to come to an agreement as to the candidate to be elected, the right of electing is *ipso facto* forfeited, and any attempt to elect after this time would produce invalid results.

The failure of the Board to provide the see with an Administrator within the prescribed period of time may be due, also, to another cause. According to canon 433 § 2, the validity of the election performed by the Board demands compliance with the substantial form of a true ecclesiastical election. Hence, if the Diocesan Consultors violate the common law in this respect, the election is null and void. The same applies also to those instances where the Board elects more than one Administrator in one and the same election.[9] In either case, the invalid election would be a contributing cause to the devolution of the right of electing.[10] But since neither canon 433 § 1 and 2, nor *per se* the general law governing all canonical elections in this respect,[11] deprives the electoral body *pro ea vice* of the right of electing, the Board of Consultors is at liberty to repeat the election in this instance. But if the Board fails to correct the invalid election before the end of the eighth day, the right of electing, by force of canon 432 § 2, devolves upon the metropolitan or senior suffragan.[12]

The question now arises as to what constitutes the substantial form of a canonical election. Authors differ in this regard. Maroto [13] maintains that the validity of a canonical election whether by scrutiny or by compromise depends upon a compliance not only with those canons which contain an invalidating clause, but with norms of solemnity as well, which,

[9] Canon 433 § 1.

[10] Cocchi, *Commentarium*, II, 340; Coronata, *Institutiones*, I, 534; Blat, *Commentarium*, II, 403; Sipos, *Juris Canonici*, p. 286; Chelodi, *Jus De Personis*, n. 217, (p. 360); Cappello, *Summa*, I, n. 410, (p. 413).

[11] Cf. Canon 2391 § 2; Maroto, *Institutiones*, I, n. 660, (p. 789).

[12] Chelodi, *loc. cit.*; Cappello, *loc. cit.*

[13] *Op. cit.*, I, n. 660, (pp. 786-789).

by their very nature, are necessary for the validity of the election. Thus he holds the opinion that the appointment of tellers for an election by scrutiny is necessary for the maintenance of secrecy, and consequently, for the validity of the election.[14] Vidal,[15] on the other hand, subscribes to the opinion that a canonical election is invalid because of the lack of substantial form only when those prescriptions which contain a nullifying clause are violated. He argues on the strength of canon 11 which states that only those laws are to be regarded as nullifying which expressly or equivalently mention that an act is null and void. The opinion of Vidal, it is believed, may be applied to the election of the Administrator. The reason for this assertion is that the appointment of tellers for elections wherein a great number of electors participate, as in the case of the election of a religious superior, appears, indeed, to be necessary for the maintenance of the secrecy of the election, and therefore necessary for the validity of the same. But when there are only four, six, or eight Consultors voting, it seems that the secrecy of the scrutiny may very well be safeguarded without the presence of tellers, since the presiding Consultor can easily guard against any abuse in this respect. The following conditions, therefore, constitute the substantial form of the election of an Administrator:

1. That the election be performed within eight days from the time knoweldge of vacancy has been received by the Board.[16]

2. That only one Administrator be elected.[17]

3. If the election be performed by scrutiny, at least two-thirds of the Consultors must be summoned to the election.[18]

4. That no one who is not a Consultor be allowed to take part in the election.[19]

[14] This opinion is held also by Vermeersch-Creusen, (*Epitome*, I, n. 248, p. 191), and Coronata (*Institutiones*, I, 264).

[15] *Jus Canonicum*, II, n. 257, (pp. 273-74).

[16] Canon 432 §§ 1-2; cf. Canon 161.

[17] Canon 433 § 1.

[18] Canon 162 § 3.

[19] Canon 165.

5. That laymen interfere in no way with the canonical freedom of the election.[20]

6. That the candidate receive an absolute majority of votes even after the third ballot, and that this absolute majority be attained after the votes which are invalid according to canon 167 § 1, 169 § 1, 170, are subtracted from the total number of votes cast.[21]

7. That a Consultor who is excommunicated by a declaratory or condemnatory sentence be not admitted knowingly to the election.[22]

8. That the number of votes cast be not greater than the number of voters.[23]

9. That simony be entirely dissociated from the election.[24]

10. If the election be performed by compromise, that the *Compromissarii* be priests, and that they comply with the conditions attached to the compromise by the Board, and the requirements placed by common law.[25]

These are the conditions necessary for the valid election of the Administrator. If the Board fails to comply with any one of them, and neglects to correct the invalid act within the period of eight days, the right of electing devolves upon the metropolitan or senior suffragan.[26] But if the election suffers from a defect other than those mentioned above, the matter may be placed before a competent superior who shall examine the defect and either rescind the election, or sanate it.[27] Thus, if one Consultor had not been summoned to the election and thereby was deprived of his right to vote, he can apply to the competent superior within three days from the time he became acquainted of the fact that the election had been held,

20 Canon 166; cf. canon 2390 § 2.

21 Canon 433 § 2, 167 § 2; cf. p. 128-9, supra.

22 Canon 167 § 2.

23 Canon 171 § 3.

24 Canons 729, 2392, n. 2.

25 Canons 172 §§ 2-3; 323, 427 et 432 § 1.

26 Chelodi, *Jus De Personis*, n. 217, (p. 360); Cappello, *Summa*, I, n. 410, (p. 413).

27 Wernz-Vidal, *Jus Canonicum*, II, n. 257, (p. 274).

and if he proves that he was actually neglected in the summons, the election must be rescinded.[28] This gives rise to two questions. In the first place, who is the competent superior to judge the case? Secondly, does the Board of Consultors lose its right to repeat the election if the period of eight days has already elapsed? The competent superior is the judge of the court superior to the Board which performed the election.[29] The judge of the court superior to a Board of Consultors of a suffragan see is the metropolitan court,[30] and the court superior to a metropolitan Board of Consultors is, by analogy with canon 1614 § 2,[31] the court of second instance to the metropolitan court.[32] In this instance, if the election is rescinded, the right of electing the Administrator does not devolve upon the metropolitan or senior suffragan bishop, for the electing Board neither failed to provide the see with an Administrator within eight days (since a rescinded election presupposes that the election itself is invalid), nor did it fail to comply with the prescriptions of canon 434 § 1.[33] Hence, if the superior judge decides either administratively or judicially, that the election be rescinded, the Board which performed the election is obliged to repeat the election within eight days from the time the decision or sentence is received.[34]

ART. 2. *The Metropolitan, or the Senior Suffragan Bishop*

When the conditions thus specified are present, the right of electing the Administrator devolves upon the metropolitan when a suffragan Board of Consultors has failed to comply with the law. When a metropolitan Board has failed in its duty, the senior suffragan bishop receives the right to make the appointment. If a suffragan see becomes vacant during

[28] Canon 162 § 2.

[29] Cf. Bouix, *De Capitulis*, p. 530; Hermes, *De Capitulo Sede Vacante et Impedita*, p. 136.

[30] Canon 1594 § 1.

[31] Cf. Roberti, *De Processibus*, I, 250; Wernz-Vidal, *Jus Canonicum*, VI, n. 145, (pp. 125-26).

[32] Cf. Canon 1594 § 2.

[33] Chelodi, *loc. cit.*; Capello, *loc. cit.*

[34] Bouix, *loc. cit.*; Hermes, *loc. cit.*

the vacancy of the metropolitan see, the senior suffragan bishop and not the Administrator, or the Board of Consultors of the metropolitan see receives the devolutive right.[35] All canonists, with the exception of Augustine,[36] agree that the senior suffragan bishop spoken of in this connection is the bishop who is the senior in the province, not by age or ordination, but by promotion to the suffragan see, according to canons 284 and 292. Since these canons speak of the duties of the senior suffragan bishop (who is senior by reason of promotion to a suffragan see) during the vacancy or quasi-vacancy of the metropolitan see, it can scarcely be said that this interpretation of the term " senior suffragan bishop," found in canons 432 § 2 and 434 § 3, is offset by a response of the Pontifical Commission for the Authentic Interpretation of the Code given on November 10, 1925,[37] for this response refers only to honorary rights and is but a logical conclusion drawn from canon 106.

The metropolitan or senior suffragan bishop may not interfere with the election of the Administrator before the right of electing has devolved upon them. If the metropolitan or senior suffragan bishop would proceed to appoint the Administrator before this time, and without the free consent of the Board of Consultors who enjoys the right to perform the election, the appointment would be without legal effect. But as soon as the metropolitan, or senior suffragan bishop is duly informed that the eight days have elapsed and the Administrator has not been elected, or that the one elected does not possess the qualification required by canon 434 § 1, he may, without informing the Board of Consultors of the vacant see, appoint the Administrator.[38] The metropolitan or senior suffragan bishop is regarded as being duly informed *(agnita rei*

[35] Canons 432 § 2, 434 § 3; for the former discipline with respect to the last case mentioned see Benedict XIV, *De Synodo Dioecesana,* lib. II, c. 9, n. 2; Richter, *Canones et Decreta,* p. 375, n. 24.

[36] *Commentary,* II, 483.

[37] AAS, XVII (1925), 582.

[38] Augustine, *op cit.,* II, 482-83; Pellegrinus, *Praxis Vicariorum,* p. I, sect. 4, subsect. 1, n. 29.

veritate)[39] when he has information which would constitute proof for a prudent man that the condition actually exists, and if there be a necessity for doing so, the matter must be placed before the Sacred Consistorial Congregation.[40] Mere heresay or rumor, therefore, would not justify action in this instance.

The right of electing the Administrator which the metropolitan or senior suffragan bishop receives by way of devolution, comprises the right only of supplying that which was lacking on the part of the Board of Consultors. Hence, this devolutive right does not concede any powers of jurisdiction over the vacant see, nor does it excuse the metropolitan or senior suffragan bishop from the norms prescribed by law for the Board of Consultors. The devolutive right, therefore, must be exercised within eight days, and the candidate appointed to the office must possess all the required qualifications.[41] If the metropolitan or senior suffragan bishop should neglect the appointment of the Administrator, the right of doing so would then rest with the Sacred Consistorial Congregation.[42] It appears, contrary to the opinion of Augustine[43] and Coronata,[44] that the Sacred Consistory should appoint the Administrator also when the metropolitan or senior suffragan has invalidly appointed an Administrator because of a non-compliance with the conditions of canon 434 § 1.

39 Canon 434 § 3.

40 Blat, *Commentarium,* II, 406.

41 Bouix, *De Capitulis,* p. 533.

42 Pellegrinus, *Praxis Vicariorum,* p. I, sect. 4, *subsect.* 1, n. 29; Monacelli, *Formularium Legale Practicum,* p. II, tit. 16, form. 8.

43 *Commentary,* II, 486.

44 *Institutiones,* I, 534.

CHAPTER X

The First Duties and the Independence of the Administrator

Since the election or appointment of the Administrator need not be confirmed or ratified by anyone, the incumbent receives possession of his office when he accepts his duly performed election or appointment.[1] Before exercising the power of jurisdiction, however, the Administrator must take the profession of faith according to the dispositions of canons 1406-1408.[2] The Administrator, consequently, must make the profession personally, and not by proxy, before the Board of Diocesan Consultors, using the formula of profession approved by the Apostolic See.[3] When the profession is made, he confirms his act by a *juramento corporali,* by touching the book of the Holy Gospels with his hand;[5] he then signs the copy from which he read the profession.

Although practically all the individuals enumerated in Canon 1406 are obliged also to take the anti-modernist oath *(adjuratio modernismi),* it appears that the Administrator is not obliged to do so. Veermeersch-Creusen [5] explicitly states that he is not bound to do so, while Prümmer [6] includes him among the number of those upon whom this duty is incumbent. The statement of Vermeersch-Creusen seems safe to follow, for neither the motu proprio *Sacrorum Antistium* (September 1, 1910) of Pope Pius X,[7] nor the subsequent declarations of

1 Canons 176 § 2, 438.

2 Canon 438.

3 Canons 1406 § 1, n. 4; 1407; this formula is found in the fore-part of the *Codex Juris Canonici.*

4 Benedict XIV, *De Synodo Dioecesana,* lib. V, c. 11, n. 8; Wernz, *Jus Decretalium,* III, n. 19.

5 *Epitome,* I, n. 483, (p. 307).

6 *Manuale Juris Canonici,* p. 505.

7 AAS, II (1910), 669; cf. *Fontes,* n. 689.

the Sacred Consistorial Congregation [8] specifically mention the Vicar Capitular or Administrator among those obliged to take the oath.

The wording of canon 438, which places the obligation of making the profession of faith, gives rise to no little doubt as to the correct significance of the law. The canon reads: "Vicarius Capitularis, edita fidei professione de qua in can. 1406-1408, statim jurisdictionem obtinet, quin necessaria sit ullius confirmatio." The presence of the ablative absolute *edita fidei professione* before the words *statim jurisdictionem obtinet* makes it doubtful whether the jurisdiction of the Administrator is dependent upon the profession of faith. If the affirmative be held, then all official acts of the Administrator would be invalid in case he accidently omitted making the profession. Most canonists have not given consideration to the difficult and simply state the canon in their texts. Without making reference to this canon, Cocchi [9] and Vidal [10] state that as soon as the Board of Consultors legitimately designates the Administrator, by a disposition of the law itself, the entire ordinary episcopal jurisdiction devolves upon the Administrator. This implies that the jurisdiction of the Administrator is not dependent upon the profession of faith. Blat [11] and Chelodi [12] appear inclined to regard the profession as a necessary condition for the acquisition of jurisdiction. Coronata [13] and Augustine [14] have taken the problem into account and have come to a *salvo meliori judicio* conclusion that the profession is not necessary for jurisdiction.

[8] 25 Sept., et 25 Oct. 1910—AAS, II (1910), 741, 856-57; cf. *Fontes*, nn. 2075, 2077; 17 Dec. 1910—AAS, III (1911), 25.

[9] "Postquam Capitulum cathedrale deputaverit Vicarium Capitularem, ipso facto tota ordinaria jurisdictio Episcopi . . . ex juris dispositione in eum transit."—*Commentarium*, II, 342-43.

[10] "Si Capitulum cathedrale *personam* Vicarii capitularis legitime designavit, ipso facto ex juris dispositione in eundem transit *tota jurisdictio ordinaria* Episcopi . . ."—*Jus Canonicum*, II, n. 710, (p. 761).

[11] *Commentarium*, II, 409.

[12] *Jus De Personis* n. 217, (360).

[13] *Institutiones*, I, 538.

[14] *Rights and Duties of Ordinaries*, p. 164.

The prescriptions of canon 1406-1408, which govern the discipline with respect to profession of faith, do not state whether the law demands the fulfillment of this duty as a condition for the acquisition of jurisdiction in particular cases. Canon 2403, furthermore, seems to imply that the profession of faith is not necessary for jurisdiction, for it states that if those who are obliged by canon 1406 (the Vicar Capitular or Administrator is expressly mentioned in the canon) to make the profession of faith fail to do so, they shall be warned canonically and a suitable time be given them within which they must comply with the obligation; if they permit the fixed time to go by and contumaciously persist in their refusal, they shall be punished even by privation from office, benefice, dignity or charge, and in the meantime they shall not be entitled to the income from the benefice, office, dignity or charge. Certainly this disposition of the penal Code seems to imply that the profession of faith does not carry with it such momentous effects as to be a *sine qua non* condition for jurisdiction, for if such were the intention of the legislator it might rightly be expected that the penalty provided for those who refuse to comply with the law would not be relatively so lenient, but rather that the office would *ipso facto* be forfeited. From this it would seem that the ablative absolute *edita fidei professione* in canon 438 is a temporal, and not a conditional, clause.

If one were to apply to this ablative absolute the principles established by canonists [15] for the interpretation of ablative absolutes in rescripts, the ablative absolute in canon 438 would signify that the legislator wished to express more forcefully the grave obligation incumbent upon the Administrator to make the profession of faith, but that this obligation is not a *sine qua non* condition for the acquisition of jurisdiction.[16] This opinion appears to be more in keeping with the general

[15] Cf. Vermeersch-Creusen, *Epitome,* I, n. 131, (pp. 110-11); Magnin, *Dictionnaire de Droit Canonique,* v. *Ablatif absolu dans les rescrits,* col. 94; Ojetti, *Commentarium in Codicem,* I, 216; Cappello, *Summa,* I, n. 149, (p. 130); Michiels, *Normae Generalis,* II, 211; Chelodi, *Juse De Personis,* n. 77, footnote 4, (p. 136).

[16] Cf. Coronata, *loc. cit.*

spirit of the Code, and may be regarded as the correct interpretation of canon 438.

The second duty incumbent upon the Administrator is that he report his election to the Apostolic See (Sacred Consistorial Congregation). The law seems to demand this report, however, only when the Administrator is elected to govern a see made vacant by the death of the bishop.[17] This appears to be the meaning of the canon, for when a see becomes vacant by the transfer of the bishop, the transferred bishop becomes the Administrator, while in the cases of resignation and privation of office, the Holy See generally makes provision for the diocese when forwarding notice of the acceptance of the resignation, or of the penalty of privation. It must be remembered, however, that the duty of reporting to the Holy See in this instance binds both the Board of Consultors and the Administrator, and two distinct reports will consequently have to be made. In both instances, it might be added, propriety would demand that the Board and the Administrator inform also the Apostolic Delegate to the United States.

As soon as the Administrator is elected, he and the Board of Diocesan Consultors is entrusted with the custody of the secret archives of the diocese. According to canon 379 § 3, the secret archives must have a lock which requires two different keys to open it. One of the keys is kept by the bishop, or Administrator Apostolic, and the other by the vicar-general, or if there is no vicar-general, by the chancellor. As soon as the bishop takes possession of his diocese he must appoint a priest who shall take possession of his key in case the diocese becomes vacant or quasi-vacant. Immediately after the election the priest who has possession of the bishop's key gives it to the Administrator, while the former vicar-general or the chancellor turns his key over to the Diocesan Consultor who is senior in office.[18] But before the keys are given to the Administrator and senior diocesan Consultor, the priest in

[17] "Capitulum quanțocius de morte Episcopi et deinde electus in Vicarium Capitularem de sua electione Sedem Apostolicam certiorem faciant."—canon 432 § 4.

[18] Canon 381 § 1, n. 2.

question and the vicar-general (or chancellor) must seal the archives with the seal of the diocesan curia.[19]

The ordinary episcopal jurisdiction which the Board of Diocesan Consultors receives when the see becomes vacant passes in its entirety to the Administrator after he has duly been elected or appointed.[20] His election or appointment, therefore, establishes him as the successor of the bishop and the sole possessor of ordinary episcopal jurisdiction in the vacant see. This was the intention of the Fathers of the Council of Trent when instituting the office of the Vicar Capitular, but owing to the fact that the decree promulgated [21] did not explicitly vindicate the independence of the Vicar Capitular, certain abuses arose whereby the cathedral Chapter often encroached upon the prerogatives of the Vicar. Previous to the year 1736, the Sacred Congregation of the Council had occasionally decided that the Chapter was permitted to restrict the power of the Vicar and to appoint him for a limited period of time.[22] Although the Sacred Congregation of Bishops and Regulars, and most of the decisions of the Sacred Congregation of the Council, had always proclaimed the independence of the Vicar Capitular, there were many canonists who maintained that the Chapter, by force of the adverse decisions of the latter Congregation, was permitted to restrict the Vicar's power and term of office.[23] Pope Pius IX, in his celebrated Constitution "*Romanus Pontifex*" August 28, 1873,[24] recounted these aberrations from the correct mind of the Fathers of the Council of Trent, and brought all dispute in this matter to a close with an authentic statement now found in the present Code of Canon Law.

[19] Canon 381 § 1, n. 2.

[20] Canon 435 § 1.

[21] Sess. XXIV, *de ref.* c. 16—*Canones et Decreta*, p. 196.

[22] Cf. S.C.C., *Cameneten.*, 4 Dec. 1632—*Fontes*, n. 2548; *Salernitana*, mense Jul. 1589—*op. cit.*, n. 2212; Scarfantoni, *Animadversiones*, lib. IV, tit. 7, n. 61. Bouix, *De Capitulis*, pp. 508, 512.

[23] Cf. Garcia, *De Beneficiis*, p. V, c. 7, n. 25; Barbosa, *De Canonicis et Dignitatibus*, c. 42, n. 21; Pignatellus, *Consultationes Canonicae*, t. IX, consult. 159, n. 4; Scarfantoni, *loc. cit.*.

[24] *Fontes*, n. 565.

The Board of Consultors, therefore, when electing the Administrator cannot reserve to itself any part of the jurisdiction, or limit the term of his office, or make any other restrictions.[25] If, indeed, the Board would attempt to do so, the conditions and restrictions would be regarded as not made, but the validity of the election would in no way be affected by them.[26] Since the Board of Diocesan Consultors loses all powers of jurisdiction as soon as the Administrator is legitimately appointed, it immediately reverts back to its original status of the Council of the Bishop, or of his successor, the Administrator. The Administrator retains his jurisdiction in its complete form until his office ceases in any fashion according to the prescriptions of canon 433. Hence, since the Board of Consultors no longer possesses jurisdiction, it is powerless to remove the Administrator from office, to limit his term of office, to demand that he render account of his administration to them, to demand that he first obtain a special mandate from them before performing certain acts, or to proceed judicially against him, just as the Board, during the occupancy of see, is powerless to infringe in any way upon the independence of the bishop, for when the Administrator is once duly elected or appointed to office and accepts the same, the jurisdiction of the Board is lost, and all these acts demand jurisdiction.[27]

[25] Canon 437.

[26] "Quamobrem pro nullis habendae sunt limitationes, seu quoad jurisdictionem, seu quoad tempus adjectae a Capitulo electioni Vicarii capitularis, qui idcirco, iis non obstantibus, officium semel sibi rite collatum toto tempore, quo Sedes Episcopalis vacua fuerit, totamque ordinariam jurisdictionem Episcopalem libere et valide exercere perget, donec novus Episcopus Apostolicas canonicae suae institutiones Litteras . . . exhibeat."—Pius IX, const., *Romanus Pontifex,* 28 Aug. 1873—*op. cit.*, p. 75; cf. canon 169 § 2.

[27] Cf. Canons 437, 443, 444; Bouix, *op. cit.*, pp. 504-512, 549-553.

CHAPTER XI

The Powers of Jurisdiction

The nature and extent of the powers of jurisdiction which, according to the present discipline, constitute the administrative office of those who govern vacant episcopal sees, is substantially the same as that which the law of the decretals accorded to the cathedral Chapter during vacancy.[1] The present Code of Canon Law provides that this administrative office, with all its rights, duties and special prohibitions, may be held by different individuals when a diocese becomes vacant. When the Holy See has not made special arrangements, and ordinarily it does not do so, the Board of Diocesan Consultors comes into possession of the office as soon as vacancy arises.[2] When the duly elected or appointed Administrator accepts the office, it passes immediately and in its entirety into his possession, and is retained by him until the new bishop takes canonical possession of the diocese, or until he loses the office according to the disposition of canon 443.[3] According to the special prescription of the Code, the same office is held also by a transferred bishop from the time he receives authentic notification of his transfer until he takes canonical possession of his new see[4]; by a Vicar Capitular who, according to a special provision of the Apostolic See, is appointed by an archbishop or other bishop[5]; by an Administrator who is elected by the Board of Consultors to administer a quasi-vacant see[6]; and finally by an Administrator Apostolic who is commissioned for

1 Canons 431 § 1, 435-436; cf. Historical Conspectus, pp. 28ss.

2 Canons 427, 431 § 1, 435 § 1.

3 Canon 435, § 1, 437; Pius IX, const., *Romanus Pontifex*, 28 Aug. 1873, *loc. cit.*

4 Canon 430 § 3 n. 1.

5 Canon 431 § 2.

6 Canons 429 § 3.

a limited period of time.[7] In all instances, consequently, the administrative office is one and the same according to the present law, nor is any distinction to be made with respect to the nature and extent of jurisdiction no matter who of the specified individuals receives the office.

In order that an adequate appreciation of the powers of jurisdiction of the administrative office may be had, it is necessary that a few observations be made with respect to the episcopal office. According to the provisions of Canon Law, residential bishops are constituted teachers and rulers of certain portions of the Church. They are given ordinary jurisdiction which they can exercise over every one of their subjects both immediately and through local pastors. This power is called ordinary because it is permanently connected to the episcopal office itself, so that it regularly follows the office whoever may be the holder and does not exist without it.[8] For this reason residential bishops are known in law as Ordinaries, or Ordinaries of the place.[9] Their power is called jurisdiction since it is the power of ruling given by Christ to His Church.[10]

The scope of the ordinary jurisdiction of bishops encompasses all ecclesiastical matters, both spiritual and temporal, and includes the capacity to legislate, to judge, and to punish.[11] The Code clearly sets forth the object, limitations and mode of exercise of this power when dealing with each matter in particular. Hence in the third book of the Code, the jurisdiction of the bishop is considered in its relation to Sacred Things, while in the fourth book, to Judicial Trials, and in the fifth, to ecclesiastical Penalties. But besides legislative, judicial and coercive power, the law endows the office of bishops with executive power. This prerequisite of ordinary episcopal jurisdiction constitutes residential bishops as guardains of ecclesiastical discipline in their particular jurisdictions; gives them

[7] Canon 315 § 2.

[8] Canon 197 § 1.

[9] Canon 198.

[10] Canon 196.

[11] Canon 335 § 1.

the right and the duty to promote obedience to all Church enactments by exhortation, warning, rebuke, punishment, and any other way suggested by zeal and prudence.[12] Bishops cannot, however, dispense from the general laws of the Church unless the legislator himself has either implicitly or explicitly empowered them to do so.[13] In all these instances the bishop acts in the name of the Roman Pontiff, and the powers exercised are therefore vicarious. But since the Code itself upon many occasions [14] attaches this vicarious power to the office of the bishop, or Ordinary, it is called ordinary vicarious in contradistinction to delegated power.[15] Hence, Canon 197 § 2 states that ordinary power may be either proper or vicarious. But the power granted to Ordinaries by way of indults or privileges, enabling them to dispense from the general law of the Church, is not ordinary power, even though these concessions be given habitually, as in the case of quinquennial faculties. This power is delegated and not ordinary, since the bishop receives this power by force of a commission and not from the office he has received.[16]

Besides jurisdiction, bishops, by force of their episcopal consecration, enjoy the power of Orders. This consecration empowers them to administer the sacraments of Confirmation and of Holy Orders.[17] Ecclesiastical law, furthermore, reserves to them all consecrations which require the use of Holy Oils, and it is only by way of a special privilege or indult that those who are not bishops, may perform consecrations, such as altars, chalices, churches, etc.[18]

[12] Canon 336.

[13] Canon 336 § 1, 81.

[14] Cf. Canons 81; 1245 §§ 1-2; 1313 n. 1; 1320; 1028; 1030; 990 § 1; 1043; 1045; 2253 n. 2; 2245 § 2; 2253 n. 3; 2237 § 1; et al.

[15] A good discussion of this subject may be found in Kearney, *The Principles of Delegation*, pp. 60-71; cf. Maroto, *Institutiones*, I, n. 829; Wernz-Vidal, *Jus Canonicum*, II, n. 599, (p. 631); De Meester, *Compendium*, II, n. 681, (p. 147); Cocchi, *Commentarium*, II, n. 118; Chelodi, *Jus De Personis*, p. 202.

[16] Cf. Kearney, *op. cit.*, p. 69.

[17] Canons 712 § 1, 951, 240 § 1, n. 22.

[18] Canons 1147 § 1; 1155; 1169 §§ 2, 5; 1199 § 2.

The powers of bishops, therefore, is divided into two categories—the power of jurisdiction and the power of Orders. All power of jurisdiction has reference to governing or ruling the diocese, and is divided into ordinary, either ordinary proper, or ordinary vicarious, and delegated power. This general outline may serve to an advantage in understanding the powers of jurisdiction which comprise the office of those who administer a diocese when vacancy arises.

Canon 431 § 1 states that in case of vacancy of see, the governance of the diocese devolves upon the Board of Diocesan Consultors, unless there is an Administrator Apostolic, or the Apostolic See has otherwise provided. This indicates that the Board of Consultors comes into possession of the office of the bishop as the ruler of the diocese. And since the power of ruling in the Church is the power of jurisdiction,[19] at the vacancy of a diocese, according to canon 435 § 1, the ordinary jurisdiction of the bishop in temporal and spiritual affairs devolves on the Board of Diocesan Consultors; after the election of the Administrator, that power is vested in the one elected, except in matters wherein his jurisdiction is expressly denied by the law. By the very disposition of the law itself, therefore, the Board of Diocesan Consultors and later the Administrator possesses ordinary and not delegated episcopal jurisdiction. They become the successors to the bishop, and are the Ordinary of the diocese.[20] In consequence of this the Board and later the Administrator may exercise the legislative, judicial, coercive, and executive rights of the bishop by force of their ordinary episcopal jurisdiction proper; they can also dispense from the general laws of the church in all instances where the bishop himself, by force of his ordinary vicarious power, can dispense.

The second paragraph of canon 435 continues to state that the Board of Consultors and after the election, the Administrator, can perform all acts which canon 368 § 2 ascribes to the vicar-general. This has reference to the execution of re-

[19] Cf. Canon 196.

[20] Canon 198.

scripts of the Holy See which were sent to the bishop, and the power to exercise habitual faculties given to the local Ordinary by the Holy See. This empowers the Board of Consultors, and later the Administrator, to make use of the jurisdiction delegated to the bishop by the Apostolic See. The same paragraph of canon 435 grants those who function in this administrative office, certain rights with respect to the power of Orders.

But since the administrative office of the Board of Consultors and the Administrator is merely provisional, and meant to serve the diocese only until a new bishop takes possession of the see, it is but natural that the law should expressly state that the Board of Consultors and the Administrator may do nothing which would prejudice the rights of the diocese or of the succeeding bishop,[21] and that during the time of vacancy no innovation shall be undertaken which would change the status of the see.[22]

This is a general statement of nature and extent of the jurisdiction of the administrative office of the Board of Consultors and the Administrator. In the following paragraphs, in which a more detailed description of this jurisdiction will be given, all that has reference to this administrative office shall be attributed to the Administrator, although it must be remembered, that the same applies to the Board of Consultors during its limited term of office. The discussion will take the following order: the ordinary episcopal jurisdiction, the delegated jurisdiction, the power of Orders, the rights of the Administrator in particular, and the prohibitions in general and in particular.

ART. I. *Ordinary Episcopal Jurisdiction*

The Administrator is the successor to the bishop and not his inferior, for he possesses the ordinary episcopal jurisdiction in spiritual and temporal affairs with the exception, however, of certain prohibitions expressly stated in the law.[23] Being the

[21] Canon 435 § 3.

[22] Canon 436.

[23] Canon 435 § 1; Pius IX, const., *Romanus Pontifex*, 28 Aug. 1873—*Fontes*, n. 565; cf. Cocchi, *Commentarium*, II, 343; Ayrinhac, *Constitutions of the Church*, 275.

successor to the bishop, he is known as the "Ordinarius loci," [24] and as a consequence of this fact, the object, limitations and mode of exercise of his jurisdiction is governed by the same norms of law as those of the bishop, excepting, of course, the special prohibitions. In the same manner as the bishop himself, therefore, the Administrator enjoys legislative, judicial, coercive and executive power which he may exercise over everyone of his subjects.[25]

§ 1. Legislative Power

The Administrator is fully empowered by law to enact for the whole diocese, laws of a permanent character, even though these be contrary to the laws enforced by the bishop, or the prescriptions of the diocesan synod. His legal enactments oblige all within the jurisdiction, and retain effect even after the new bishop takes canonical possession of the diocese. The Administrator cannot make laws, however, which are contrary to those of a superior such as common law itself, the particular legislation enforced by the Holy See, or the laws established by a Plenary or Provincial Council; nor can the Administrator promulgate such laws as would change the status of the diocese, or prove prejudicial to the rights of the succeeding bishop.[26] Obviously, the power of legislating includes the capacity to issue precepts which effect individual persons. Fagnanus,[27] however, voiced a bit of prudent advice to the effect that it is better for those in power to abstain from the use of legislative power, since the time of vacancy of see is not opportune for the performance of any act which might affect the status of the diocese.

[24] Canon 198.

[25] Cf. Canon 335, 336; Capello, *Summa*, I, n. 402 (p. 414); Cocchi, *op. cit.*, 344; Ayrinhac, *op. cit.*, pp. 275-76; Sipos, *Juris Canonici*, 287; Raus, *Institutiones Canonicae*, 225.

[26] Canons 435 § 3, 436, 81; Reiffenstuel, *Jus Can. Univ.* lib. III, tit. IX, n. 66; Schmalzgrueber, *Jus Eccl. Univ.*, lib. III, tit. IX, n. 30; Leurenius, *Forum Beneficiale*, t. IV, tract. III, p. 470.

[27] *Commentaria*, lib. III, c. I, n. 14.

§ 2. Judicial Power

The Administrator is also the "Judge Ordinary" of the diocese. In the same manner as the bishop himself, he is fully competent to judge, either personally or by his delegate, all criminal and contentious cases which come within the competence of the court of first instance, or within the administrative power of the bishop.[28] The Administrator is also obliged to see to it that the diocese has an official. Ordinarily this provision is already made, for the official who was appointed by the bishop does not lose his office when the see becomes vacant.[29] If the official of the diocese and the vicar-general is one and the same individual, the former office is not lost when vacancy arises; and if the Administrator was himself the official, or if the official had gone out of office, the Administrator is then obliged to appoint a qualified priest to fill the office.[30]

A question may be raised here as to whether the Administrator, as the ordinary of the diocese, can appear in court to prosecute the rights of the cathedral Church,[31] or of the *mensa episcopalis*,[32] according to the disposition of canon 1653. In former discipline[33] the cathedral Chapter and the Vicar Capitular could not, without leave of the Holy See, prosecute in court for the rights of the cathedral Church, or the *mensa episcopalis*, nor could they even continue the procedure already

[28] Canon 1672 § 1; cf. Roberti, *De Processibus*, I, 145; Noval, *De Processibus*, I, n. 110; Vermeersch-Creusen, *Epitome*, III, n. 32, (p. 15); Raus, *op. cit.*, 225.

[29] Canon 1573 § 5.

[30] Canon 1573 §§ 6-7; Cappello, *op. cit.*, n. 402, (p. 414); Chelodi, *Jus de Personis*, n. 218, footnote 3, (p. 361).

[31] This includes both the spiritual and temporal rights of the Cathedral Church; cf. Canon 1182 § 1; Vromant, *De Bonis Ecclesiae Temporalibus*, p. 81; Wernz-Vidal, *Jus Canonicum*, VI, n. 209, (p. 178).

[32] The *mensa episcopalis* is the episcopal benefice with all the temporal rights annexed to the episcopal office. This concerns all revenues, chiefly, which contribute to the support of the bishop. Cf. Noval, *De Processibus*, I, n. 258; Wernz-Vidal, *Jus Canonicum*, VI, n. 209, (p. 177).

[33] Cf. Fagnanus, *Commentaria*, lib. III, c. I, n. 14; Reiffenstuel, *op. cit.*, lib. III, tit. IX, n. 74; Schmalzgrueber, *op. cit.*, lib. I, tit. XI, n. 53; Leurenius, *op. cit.*, t. IV, tract. III, q. 500.

begun by the bishop before the see became vacant. The present law has abrogated this limitation of the judiciary power of the Board of Diocesan Consultors, and the Administrator, for canon 1653 § 1 attributes this right to the *ordinarii locorum* without further modification. Since, therefore, the Administrator is known in law as the *ordinarius loci,*[34] he is fully entitled to defend in court the rights of the cathedral Church or the *mensa episcopalis* according to the prescriptions of the present Code.[35] It must be remembered, however, that if the Administrator is a bishop, he must, by force of canon 1655 § 4, be represented in court by a procurator or an attorney.

§ 3. Coercive Power

Since the Administrator possesses the power to make laws, impose precepts and judge, he may also attach penalties to his laws and precepts, and enforce his judicial sentences by applying the penalties prescribed by the Code.[36] The Administrator, consequently, may inflict various penalties, including censures, on all violators of the divine or ecclesiastical, of general or particular law. He may, therefore, inflict excommunication, interdict and suspension, deprive clerics of office and depose them because of crime, and do all things necessary for correction, right order and discipline, just as the bishop himself can do within the limits of his ordinary jurisdiction.[37]

The power of absolving from censures and ecclesiastical penalties is closely correlated with coercive power. Since the Administrator possesses ordinary jurisdiction, he can absolve from all sins and censures, either *a jure or ab homine* and in both the forum of conscience and in the external forum, in the same manner as the bishop himself can do. In normal

[34] Canon 198.

[35] Blat, *Commentarium,* IV, 150; Noval, *op. cit.,* n. 258; Coronata, *Institutiones,* I, 537, footnote 9.

[36] Canon 2220 § 1; cf. Cocchi, *Commentarium,* V, 86, 158; De Meester, *Compendium,* III, n. 1770, (p. 205); Vermeersch-Creusen, *Epitome,* III, n. 411, (p. 203); Raus, *Institutiones,* p. 437; Capello, *De Censuris,* n. 11, (p. 12).

[37] Leurenius, *Forum Beneficiale,* t. IV, tract. III, qq. 472, 475; Schmalzgrueber, *Jus Eccl. Univ.,* lib. III, tit. IX, n. 31; Bouix, *De Capitulis,* p. 566.

cases, which signifies that there is neither urgent need, nor danger of death, the Administrator may absolve from all censures *ab homine* which the bishop had reserved to himself, and he is able to impart the absolution even though the person afflicted has changed domicile or quasi-domicile.[38] So also may the Administrator, or his delegate, absolve his subjects everywhere and peregrins from all censures incurred *a jure* and reserved by law to the bishop or Ordinary.[39]

In occult cases, according to the prescriptions of canon 2237 § 2, the Administrator, or his delegate, may remit all penalties which are stated in common law as being incurred *latae sententiae* except those censures which are reserved in a most special or special manner to the Apostolic See. In all public cases, the Administrator may remit all penalties *latae sententiae* established by common law, except those contentious cases which are brought before the ecclesiastical court, or all cases reserved simply, especially, or most especially to the Holy See, or all penalties entailing disqualification for benefices, offices, and dignities in the church, penalties referring to active and passive vote, and privation thereof, perpetual suspension, infamy by law, and privation of the privileges or favors granted by the Holy See.[40]

§ 4. Executive Power

The general principle governing the executive power of residential bishops is contained in canon 336. This power also comes within the scope of ordinary jurisdiction, and consequently is a right and a duty of the Administrator. As a guardian of ecclesiastical discipline in the vacant diocese, the Administrator must watch over the application of laws both general and particular. His, therefore, is the right and duty to exercise vigilance lest abuses creep into ecclesiastical discipline especially in regard to the administration of the sacraments and sacramentals, divine worship and the veneration of saints, preaching of the word of God, indulgences, and

[38] Canons 2253, n. 2; 2245 § 2.

[39] Canons 2253 § 3.

[40] Canon 2237 § 1.

the fulfillment of bequests in favor of pious causes; he must guard the integrity of faith and morals in both the clergy and laity, and see to it that the faithful, especially the children and illiterate, are properly instructed in Christian doctrine, and that the schools for children and young men and women are conducted according to the principles of the Catholic religion.[41]

It would, indeed, be far beyond the scope of this treatise to consider in particular these rights and duties of the Administrator. Nor does it seem necessary for doing so, for the Administrator possesses the same prerogatives as the bishop himself in all matters, excepting a few specified acts which will be given consideration in subsequent paragraphs. Thus, for instance, the delegated jurisdiction to hear confessions both of seculars and of religious, is given to secular priests as well as to exempt and non-exempt religious by the Administrator.[42] It is his right and duty as Ordinary of the diocese to examine the priests before giving the faculties, unless their theological learning is plainly known from other sources.[43] And if the faculty had been granted, and a serious doubt arises later as to whether the priest who was approved continues to be capable, the Administrator may recall him for examination, even though there be a question of a pastor.[44] So also is it the right of the Administrator to give the faculty of preaching to the secular clergy as well as to the non-exempt religious;[45] to exempt religious according to the norms of canons 1338 and 514 § 1.

Executive power includes also the right to dispense from the law. Canon 80 states that a dispensation, which is a relaxation of the law in a particular case, may be granted by the lawgiver, his successor or superior, and by those to whom the faculty of dispensing has been delegated. Since, therefore, the Administrator is the successor to the bishop, he may dis-

[41] Canon 336 § 2.
[42] Canon 874 § 1.
[43] Canon 877 § 1.
[44] Canon 877 § 2.
[45] Canon 1337.

pense his subjects from laws enacted by his predecessor in office, or from those which he himself has promulgated. Furthermore, canon 82 provides that bishops and other diocesan Ordinaries can dispense from diocesan laws and from laws of provincial and plenary councils, according to the rule contained in canon 291 § 2. His right to dispense extends also to all diocesan statutes which were enacted in the diocesan synod, or outside of it.

The power of the Administrator to dispense from the general laws of the Church is the same as that of the bishop. The general provision of the law in this regard is found in canon 81. It is here stated that Ordinaries inferior to the Roman Pontiff cannot dispense from the general laws of the Church, not even in a particular case, unless this power has been conceded to them implicitly or explicitly, or when recourse to the Holy See is difficult and there is at the same time danger of causing great harm by the delay, and the case is one in which the Holy See usually dispenses. Canon 82 places in the same category with general laws of the Church, those laws which the Roman Pontiff has enacted for a particular country or diocese. When, under given circumstances, the bishops or Ordinaries legitimately dispense from the general laws of the Church, they do so, consequently, in the name of the Holy See. But since, as it was noted in a previous article, the Code itself explicitly attaches this power to the office of the bishop or Ordinary in certain matters, the power of dispensing is ordinary,[46] and at the same time vicarious. Hence, this ordinary vicarious jurisdiction of the bishops is ordinary power,[47] and consequently forms a part of the ordinary episcopal jurisdiction of the Administrator.

The Administrator, as Ordinary of the diocese, may dispense from the general laws of the Church, and those special laws enacted by the Roman Pontiff for a particular country or diocese, in the following instances:

[46] Cf. Canon 197 § 1.

[47] Cf. Canon 197 § 2.

1. When there is a doubt of fact (*dubium facti*) with respect to these laws, the Administrator may dispense, provided there is question of laws from which the Roman Pontiff usually dispenses.[48]

2. In those instances in which recourse to the Holy See is difficult and at the same time there is a grave danger in delay, provided the needed dispensation be one of those which the Holy See is wont to grant.[49]

3. In individual cases and for a legitimate reason, the Administrator can dispense any subject or individual family, also outside the diocese, and peregrins in the diocese, from the obligation of keeping the Holydays of Obligations, and from the law of fast or abstinence, or from both fast and abstinence combined.[50]

4. When there is a great concourse of people on a particular occasion, or for a cause of public health, the Administrator may dispense the whole diocese from the obligations of fast or of abstinence, or of both obligations.[51]

5. He may dispense from the banns of matrimony according to the dispositions of canons 1028 and 1030.

6. He may dispense from all irregularities arising from occult crime except voluntary homicide or effective abortion, or others which are brought before the civil or ecclesiastical court.[52]

7. He may dispense from certain matrimonial impediments and from the canonical form of marriage according to the prescriptions of canons 1043 and 1045.

These are the principal instances when the Administrator may dispense, by force of ordinary jurisdiction, from the general laws of the Church. Ordinaries are empowered, however, to dispense further from the general law by reason of habitual faculties, indults and rescripts granted by the Holy

[48] Canon 15.

[49] Canons 81, 82.

[50] Canon 1245 § 1.

[51] Canon 1245 § 2.

[52] Canon 990 § 1.

See. But since, on these occasions, the power is delegated, and does not form a part of the ordinary jurisdiction of the Administrator or other ordinaries, consideration will be given to this particular matter in the following article.

Since the powers of jurisdiction of the Administrator are ordinary, he may delegate it to another, either totally or in part, unless the law expressly restricts the power of delegation.[53] The Administrator, however, cannot appoint a vicar-general and transfer to him ordinary jurisdiction in the same manner as the bishop does when appointing a vicar-general. And even in those instances when the Administrator, for reasons of protracted sickness, infirmity, absence, or any other similar impediment, delegates all his powers to another, he alone retains the ordinary episcopal jurisdiction, while the other exercises only delegated power.[54]

Art. 2. *Delegated Jurisdiction*

The powers of jurisdiction thus far considered have reference to those rights and duties which the Administrator may exercise in the governance of the see by reason of the office which he has received. The present article will be given to a brief discussion on those powers which the Holy See has delegated to bishops or Ordinaries by reason either of the dignity or office of the bishops or ordinaries, or by reason of the person. An example of the first type of delegated power is had in the case of habitual faculties granted to Ordinaries by the Holy See, e.g., the quinquennial faculties. Special rescripts, indults and privileges which the Apostolic See concedes to bishops or Ordinaries belong to those powers delegated to the person of the recipient. In all cases, however, delegated power is not connected with the office, but is a right committed to a person.[55]

[53] "Qui jurisdictionis potestatem habet ordinariam potest eam alteri ex toto vel ex parte delegare, nisi aliud expresse jure caveatur."—Canon 199 § 1.

[54] Cf. Schmalzgrueber, *Jus. Eccl, Univ.*, lib. I, tit. 28, nn. 32-33; Leurenius, *Forum Beneficiale*, t. IV, tract. III, q. 621; Ferreres, *Institutiones Canonicae* I, n. 725; Bonal, *Institutiones*, I, 670-71; Augustine, *Rights and Duties of Ordinaries*, p. 164; Coronata, *Institutiones*, I, 539.

[55] Canon 197 § 1.

Canon 435 § 2 states that the Board of Diocesan Consultors, and after his acquisition of office, the Administrator possesses all the rights contained in canon 368 § 2. This concession of power refers to the jurisdiction delegated to the bishop, or to Ordinaries in general, by the Holy See. According to canon 368 § 2, consequently, the Administrator is empowered to execute the rescripts of the Holy See which are sent to the bishop or his predecessor in the diocese, unless the law has stated otherwise. Furthermore, the same canon extends to the Administrator the right to use the faculties which are habitually given to the Ordinary by the Holy See according to the dispositions of canon 66.

Habitual faculties granted to Ordinaries, or to the bishop himself, are explained fully in the latter canon. These faculties, accordingly, comprise not only those given perpetually, but also those granted for a definite period of time, or for a certain number of cases.[56] The quinquennial faculties granted to Ordinaries are faculties given for a limited period of time, while faculties which empower the Ordinary to dispense, for example, ten times from the impediment of consanguinity in the second degree of the collateral line, are powers delegated for a certain number of cases.

The second paragraph of canon 66 explains further the dispositions governing habitual faculties. The canon states that unless habitual faculties are conceded for personal reasons *(industria personae)*, or unless the indult or rescript provides otherwise, they do not expire with the authority of the bishop or other Ordinaries mentioned in canon 198 § 1, to whom they have been granted by the Apostolic See, even though those thus delegated have already begun to execute the faculties; but they pass over to those who succeed them in office. This provision, it is evident, refers not to habitual faculties granted by the Holy See to Ordinaries in general, as in the case of quinquennial faculties, but habitual faculties extended to a particular Ordinary. Thus Bishop———, of a certain diocese. may be given habitual faculties empowering him to dispense

[56] Canon 66 § 1.

from certain general laws of the Church because of the peculiar conditions or circumstances prevailing in his diocese. Hence, under the prescribed conditions, the Administrator can execute these faculties given to the bishop, vicar-general, or official, even though the bishop or the others have already begun to execute them. Likewise, when the diocese is provided with a new bishop, vicar-general, and official, they can execute the faculties which were given to the Administrator, even though he had already begun to apply them.[57]

Immediately upon assuming his office, the Administrator must, therefore, acquaint himself with the nature and extent of the quinquennial faculties given by the Holy See to Ordinaries, and likewise with the other habitual faculties extended to the bishop. It may easily be learned whether the particular habitual faculties have been given to the bishop *ex industria personae,* for such faculties are usually addressed to the bishop by name and not to the Ordinary of the diocese.[58] The phrase *etiam si ipse eas exsequi coeperit* signifies that even though the bishop had already begun to execute them, this fact does not diminish the power of the Administrator for as long as the execution has not been completed, he may change the will of his predecessor by either denying, or permitting the faculty to be executed.[59]

Paragraph the third of canon 66 provides that the faculties imply all the power necessary for their exercise. Hence, the faculty of dispensing includes also the faculty of absolving from ecclesiastical penalties, if by chance such action is necessary in order to qualify one to receive the dispensation. The dispensation, however, does not remove the penalty, but simply suspends it in order that the person receiving the dispensation may *hic et nunc* be capable of receiving the favor. But, since papal faculties are favors granted by the Holy See, it

[57] S.C.S. Offic., litt. encycl. 20 Febr. 1888, n. 3—*Collectanea S.C. Prop. Fide,* n. 1985, (*Fontes,* n. 1109); cf. decr. 20 Apr. 1898, n. 1—*Fontes,* n. 1198; 24 Nov. 1897—*op. cit.,* n. 1193; 3 Maii 1899, nn. 1, 3—*op. cit.,* n. 1223; 20 Dec. 1899—*op. cit.,* 1232; 5 Sept. 1900—*op. cit.,* n. 1247.

[58] Cf. Ojetti, *Commentarium,* I, 289; Maroto, *Institutiones,* I, n. 705, (p. 844).

[59] Cf. Vermeersch-Creusen, *Epitome,* I, n. 153, (p. 121).

must be borne in mind that certain penalties disqualifying individuals from validly receiving pontifical favors. Hence, a person who is excommunicated, personally interdicted or suspended by a declaratory or condemnatory sentence, cannot validly receive papal favors, nor can the Administrator dispense from the penalties, unless the faculties expressly make mention of the fact of excommunication, interdict, or suspension.[60]

Since the rescripts and habitual faculties spoken of above is jurisdiction delegated to the Administrator as the successor to the bishop, he can subdelegate it to others, either for one act or habitually, unless subdelegation is forbidden in particular instances.[61] But if the Administrator received faculties from the Holy See which were granted to him as a strictly personal delegation *(industria personae)* he cannot subdelegate the faculty to others.[62]

Art. 3. *The Power of Orders*

The Administrator does not receive, by virtue of his appointment to office, the power of orders.[63] Canon 435 § 2, however, expressly concedes to the Administrator the faculty to invite any bishop into the vacant diocese for the purpose of exercising pontificals,[64] and if he is a bishop, he may do so himself, provided, however, that the throne and baldachine are not used. Since only residential bishops can grant the use of the throne and baldachine to other bishops whom they invite to pontificate in the diocese,[65] the Administrator, even

60 Cf. Canons 36 § 2, 2265 § 2, 2275 n. 3, 2283; Ojetti, *op. cit.*, I, 290-91; Michiels, *Normae Generales,* II, 187-196.

61 Canon 199 § 2.

62 Canon 199 § 2.

63 Leurenius, *Forum Beneficiale,* t. IV, tract. III, q. 466; Pellegrinus, *Praxis Vicariorum,* p. I, sect. 4, subsect. 2, n. 6; De Meester, *Compendium,* II, n. 792, (p. 232); Bargilliat, *Juris Canonici,* II, n. 875, (p. 44); Cocchi, *Commentarium,* II, 343.

64 The exercise of pontificals includes all functions in which the laws of liturgy call for the use of the pontifical insignia of the crozier and the mitre.—Canon 337 § 2.

65 Canon 337 § 3; S.C.R., decret., 12 Junii 1899—*Decreta Authentica S.C.R.*, III, n. 4023; cf. 26 Martii 1919, V, n. 3—AAS, XII (1919), 177.

though he possess the episcopal character himself, cannot grant this permission to any other bishop.[66] In all pontifical functions during the vacancy, therefore, the episcopal throne and baldachine may not be used, but may be supplied by faldstool (*faldistorium*) placed at the epistle side of the altar.[67]

The Administrator may invite into the vacant diocese any bishop to administer the sacrament of Confirmation, or to perform any consecration, and, if he is a bishop he may do so himself, for the law places no limitations upon these powers of orders during vacancy.[68] But the Administrator may not confer sacred orders, nor may he permit any bishop to do so, except according to the prescriptions of canons 958 § 1, n. 3, § 2, and 959. This particular prohibition shall receive special consideration in subsequent pages.

Since canon 1147 § 1 states that consecrations can be validly performed only by consecrated bishops, and by those who are given this faculty either by law or by Apostolic indult, the Administrator who is not a bishop must have a special faculty to consecrate chalices, patens, portable altars (altar stones), bells, etc.[69] Such faculties have been included in the quinquennial faculties granted to Ordinaries by the Holy See in the past, and if the Apostolic See continues to make this concession, the Administrator who does not possess the episcopal character then enjoys the power to perform the consecrations specified in the faculties. It will be necessary, therefore, that the Administrator consult the quinquennial faculties in this matter.

ART. 4. *Rights of the Administrator in Particular*

It would, indeed, be too cumbersome a task to consider all the rights of the Administrator in particular, since he enjoys

66 S.R.C., decret. 4 Nov. 1905—*Il Monitore Ecclesiastico*, VII (1905-06), 492; De Meester, *op. cit.*, II, n. 792, (p. 232); Vermeersch-Creusen, *Epitome*, I, n. 481, (p. 306); Cappello, *Summa*, I, n. 403, (p. 416).

67 Cf. Augustine, *Commentary*, II, 490.

68 Cf. Canons 783, 1155, 1147 § 1; Coronata, *De Locis et Temporibus Sacris*, pp. 2-3; Augustine, *Commentary*, IV, 108, VI, 4.

69 Cf. Canons 1160 §§ 2, 5; 1199 § 2; 1155.

ordinary episcopal jurisdiction. Such a discussion would necessarily encompass the entire field of the jurisdiction of the bishop himself. The present article, therefore, will be confined to those salient and necessary acts of ordinary jurisdiction which the Code explicitly attributes to the Administrator. Among these particular rights, there are some which have no qualifications attached to them by law, and hence the Administrator can exercise them at any time during the period of vacancy. There are others, however, which the law permits the Administrator to exercise only under certain conditions. The former rights may be styled non-conditional rights, and the latter conditional. These will be considered in the following paragraphs.

§ 1. The Non-conditional Rights of the Administrator

I. It is of vast importance that the Administrator be given the right to fill vacancies arising on the Board of Diocesan Consultors, for if he were unable to do so and all the members of the Board would either die or resign during the period of vacancy, the Administrator would be left without his episcopal senate. This would place the Administrator in a precarious position, for, according to the Code,[70] the validity of certain acts demands the advice or consent of the Board. It must be remembered, however, that the Diocesan Consultors remain in office until the new bishop takes possession of the see when their triennial term of office expires during vacancy.[71]

Canon 426 § 5 provides, therefore, that the Administrator shall, with the consent (not merely advice) of the remaining members of the Board, appoint substitute Consultors when any of the members die or resign from office during vacancy of see. These substitute Consultors, according to the same canon, need the confirmation of the bishop, however, in order to continue in office after the new bishop has taken possession of the diocese.

A question may be advanced here as to whether the Admin-

[70] Cf. Canons 105 n. 1; 425 § 5; 373 § 5, 113; 958 § 1, n. 3; et al.

[71] Canon 426 § 4.

istrator, by force of canon 428, can remove a Consultor from office, even though there is a just cause and this be done with the advice of the other members of the Board. The Code does not explicitly forbid such procedure on the part of the Administrator, yet the context of canons 425 § 1 and 426 § 5 implicitly indicate that the Administrator does not enjoy the prerogative of the bishop in this respect. Since canon 425 § 1 demands that there be at least six Consultors in each diocese, and in those dioceses where priests are few at least four, and since furthermore, canon 426 § 5 empowers the Administrator to make substitutions on the Board only when vacancies arise from death or resignation, Blat [72] maintains that the Administrator may remove Consultors according to canon 428, provided there are at least four or six Consultors still remaining on the Board. Cappello [73] and Chelodi [74] concluded from the disposition of these canons that the Administrator is permitted to remove a Consultor from office only in case crime is committed for which any cleric may be removed from office. In this instance, they maintain, that the removal would have to follow the prescription of canon 428.

In practice, however, prudence would dictate that the Administrator should abstain from any attempt to remove a Consultor from office unless this be motivated by urgent need. But if the Administrator would feel confident that the condition of affairs would be ameliorated by the removal of an undesirable Consultor, it would possibly be more diplomatic to urge, either by himself or through the other Consultors, this undesirable member to resign, and then he could substitute another according to the norm of canon 426 § 5.

2. The Administrator may remove the chancellor or notary from office, or suspend them from their activities for a time, but this can be done only with the *consent* of the Board of Consultors.[75]

[72] *Commentarium*, II, 395.

[73] *Summa*, I, n. 479, (p. 502).

[74] *Jus De Personis*, n. 215, (p. 357).

[75] Canon 373 § 5.

3. Since the power of the Administrator to appoint pastors is circumscribed by certain legal restrictions,[76] the legislator has made provisions whereby the parochial ministry shall not be neglected, nor the spiritual interests of the faithful suffer during the vacancy of the episcopal see. The Administrator, accordingly, has not only the right but also the duty to appoint parochial vicars according to the prescriptions of canons 472-476.[77]

When a parish becomes vacant during the vacancy of the episcopal see, it is incumbent upon the Administrator to appoint, as soon as possible (*quamprimum*),[78] a parochial Administrator (*vicarius occonomus*) who shall govern the parish. And if the parochial Administrator be a religious, the Diocesan Administrator must obtain the consent of the proper religious superior before making the appointment.[79] If there is no diocesan statute which specifies what is necessary for the proper support of the parochial Administrator, the Diocesan Administrator must assign a part of the parochial revenues for this purpose.[80]

Just as the Administrator is obliged to provide a vacant parish with a parochial Administrator, so also must he see to it that vicar substitutes (*vicarius substitutus*) take charge of the parochial affairs when pastors are absent. Consequently, when a pastor is absent from his parish for more than a week, whether this be due to his vacation or whether it is brought about by some sudden and urgent call, the vicar substitute whom the pastor has left in charge of the parish must be approved by the Diocesan Administrator, and if the pastor in question be a religious, the substitute vicar must be approved by both the Diocesan Administrator and the proper religious superior.[81] Likewise when a pastor, who was judicially de-

[76] Canon 455 § 2, n. 3.

[77] Canon 455 § 2, n. 1.

[78] The delay should not extend beyond three days. Cf. Blat, *Commentarium,* II, 444; Coronata, *Institutiones,* I, 574, footnote 1.

[79] Canon 472 n. 1.

[80] Canon 472 n. 1.

[81] Canons 474, 465 §§ 4-5.

prived of his parish, appeals to the Holy See for redress, the Administrator must appoint a vicar substitute to administer the parish until the Apostolic See has settled the difficulty.[82]

Canon 475 treats of the appointments of vicars adjutant or coadjutant. According to this prescription of the Code the diocesan Administrator has the right and the duty to appoint a vicar adjutant to take the place of those pastors who are unable to discharge their parochial duties because of old age, mental disorders, inexperience, blindness or any other permanent cause which incapacitates the pastor.[83] If the vicar adjutant is to assume only a part of the pastor's duties, or if the pastor is of sound mind, the Administrator must specify the rights and the obligations of the vicar adjutant in the letter of appointment.[84] Such appointments may be freely made by the Administrator, and although he may first consult the pastor in this regard, he is, nevertheless, not obliged either to obtain the consent or the advice of the pastor, and can proceed with the appointment even though the pastor is unwilling.[85]

The present law speaks only of permanent inability of the pastor. Hence, temporary inability would not ordinarily justify the appointment of a vicar adjutant, since it might suffice to give the pastor an assistant (*vicar co-operator*). But if the appointment of a vicar adjutant proves insufficient to provide for the good of souls, the Administrator must remove the pastor according to the prescriptions of canons 2147-2161.[86] Finally, if there is no provision at hand for the support of the adjutant, the Administrator must make arrangements for this matter.[87]

82 Canons 474, 1923 § 2.

83 Canon 475 § 1; if the inability of the pastor can be satisfactorily supplied by the appointment of an assistant *(vicarius co-operator)*, the Administrator would have to resort to such procedure. Cf. Ayrinhac, *Constitution*, p. 358.

84 Canon 475 §§ 2-3.

85 Cf. Canon 105; Wernz-Vidal, *Jus Canonicum*, n. 473, (p. 801); Coronata, *op. cit.*, I, 575; Ayrinhac, *op. cit.*, p. 358

86 Canon 475 §§ 1, 4.

87 Canon 475 § 1.

The Administrator enjoys also the right to appoint assistants (*vicarii cooperatores*) to assist those pastors who, in the judgment of the Administrator, are unable to give fitting care for the parish because of the large number of parishioners, or other causes.[88] Since the Administrator possesses the same prerogatives as the bishop in this regard, the appointment is the right of the Administrator and not of the pastor, but the Administrator must give the pastor a hearing (*audito parocho*) before making the appointment.[89] When the assistant belongs to a religious order, as in the case of a parish belonging to a religious community, he is presented by the religious superior who is competent to do so according to the constitutions of the particular institute, and the assistant is approved by the Ordinary of the place (Administrator).[90]

According to the disposition of canon 477, the Administrator is empowered to remove *ad nutum* any secular parochial administrator, vicar substitute, adjutant or assistant, nor is he obliged to obtain the advice or consent of either the Board of Diocesan Consultors, or the pastor. In the case of religious parochial vicars, their removal may be enacted by the Ordinary of the place (Administrator) having notified the religious superior, or *vica versa*.[91]

4. According to the stipulations of canon 455 § 2, n. 2, the

[88] Canons 455 § 2, n. 1; 476 § 1.

[89] Canon 476 § 3; whether or not the appointment of the assistant would be invalid in case the Administrator failed to hear the pastor is a question, for canonists take both sides of the problem in applying canon 105 n. 1 to canon 476 § 3. Bastnagel, (*The Appointment of Parochial Adjutants and Assistants*, pp. 187-237) gives this matter a scholarly and exhaustive study, and establishing a *dubium juris* he concludes, ". . . it seems indicated to acknowledge the extrinsic probability of the less common opinion, and hence, not to be disturbed about the consequences of acts which superiors might execute in violation of the demand of canon 105 n. 1 (*audito parocho*). Yet, whilst the validity of the act might remain intact . . . it is hardly conceivable that such a legal fiction of doubt with regard to the requirement *ad validitatem* should lend encouragement to the non-observance of a law which still continues imperative in its full obediential sanction, despite the cherished possibility of its lack of nullifying force."—ibidem, p. 228.

[90] Canon 476 § 4.

[91] Canons 477 § 1, 454 § 5.

Administrator may, at any time during vacancy or quasi-vacancy of the see, confirm the election, or accept the presentation of a candidate to a vacant parish, or grant to the elected or presented priest the canonical institution as pastor. "In the United States," writes Augustine,[92] "there is neither election nor presentation to hamper the free choice of the bishop" when appointing a pastor to a vacant parish. This, of course, is true with respect to all secular parishes. But in the case of parishes which are entrusted to the charge of Religious, however, the superior presents the pastor and the Ordinary has the right to examine him as to his fitness for the position, and if he finds him qualified he must give him the canonical institution." [93] Since in this instance true canonical presentation is had, the Administrator, by force of canon 455 § 2, n. 2, can give institution to such candidates for the parochial office any time during the period of vacancy.

§ 2. The Conditional Rights of the Administrator

There are three rights which the Administrator may exercise only after the elapse of one complete year from the time of vacancy. And if the Administrator should find it necessary to perform any of these acts within the first year of vacancy he must with the possible exception of the right to grant dimissorial letters, petition the Holy See in order to obtain the proper faculties. The period of one year is calculated according to the prescriptions of canon 34 § 3, nn. 1, and 3.[94] Hence, if a diocese became vacant on the first of June, 1931, the year of vacancy would be completed at midnight the first of June, 1932.

1. According to the norm of canon 113, the Administrator is strictly forbidden to grant incardination or excardination to any cleric before the diocese is vacant for one year, and after this time may he do so only with the *consent* (not merely

[92] *Commentary* II, 524; cf. Woywod, *A Practical Commentary,* I, 163; Coady, *The Appointment of Pastors,* pp. 104-5; Ayrinhac, *Constitutions,* pp. 319-320.

[93] Canon 456; Woywod, *op. cit.,* I, 163.

[94] Cf. Blat, *Commentarium,* II, 423.

advice) of the Board of Diocesan Consultors. This legal restriction, like others specified in the Code, prevents any undesirable change in the status of the vacant diocese, and likewise avoids the possible chance of the Administrator prejudicing the rights of the succeeding bishop by incardinating undesirables into the diocese.

2. The power of the Administrator with respect to issuing dimissorial letters is stipulated in canon 958. Canon 955 § 1 states the general rule that everyone shall be ordained by his own bishop, or with dimissorial letters granted by his own bishop. Hence, dimissorials are nothing other than the written consent of a bishop permitting one of his subjects to be ordained by another bishop. Since the term "ordain" includes all orders, even tonsure,[95] it is necessary that dimissorials be granted even for those entering the clerical state.

According to the prescriptions of canon 958 § 1, n. 3, the Administrator may, with the *consent* of the Board of Consultors, grant dimissorial letters to his subjects after the first year of vacancy; within the first year he may, with the consent of the Board, grant dimissorial only to the *arctati*, i.e., those who must be ordained on account of a benefice they have received or are to receive, or on account of some certain office which must be filled on account of the needs of the diocese.

In those countries where the right of patronage exists, or where the civil government, by a special agreement with the Holy See, enjoys the right to appoint to ecclesiastical offices and benefices, the Vicars Capitular may frequently be able to grant dimissorial letters within the first year of vacancy. The Administrators, nevertheless, are permitted to do so when the needs of the diocese demand that a certain office be filled without delay. Such instances may be present in times of great distress, such as war, plague, etc., which would cause a shortage of priests and thereby leave parishes without pastors. Likewise in some dioceses of this country there is a great want of priests with the result that many parochial charges are without pastoral care. Under such circumstances the Admin-

[95] Canons 950 et 955.

istrator could, with the consent of the Board of Diocesan Consultors, grant dimissorial letters.

A few observations, however, must be made with respect to the right of the Administrator to grant dimissorials. In the first place he may *at no time* give those permission to be ordained who have been rejected by the bishop.[96] This provision of the Code protects the authority of the bishop and the unity of the government, and at the same time keeps undesirable candidates out of the sanctuary. The Administrator may, however, grant dimissorials within the first year of vacancy for those whom the bishop, when on the verge of death, had given orders to be ordained.[97] Furthermore, when the Administrator is entitled by law to grant dimissorial he may, if he is a bishop, do the ordaining himself,[98] and he likewise has the right to examine the candidates, whether these be secular or religious.[99] So also may the Administrator who enjoys the right to grant dimissorials, dispense from the law of the "interstices" in the same manner as the bishop himself.[100] Testimonials,[101] however, must not be confused with dimissorials, for these may be given by the Administrator at any time during the term of office.

The present discipline provides for an Administrator who would violate the prescriptions of canon 958 § 1, n. 3. Accordingly, if an Administrator would grant dimissorials without the consent of the Board of Diocesan Consultors, or if he should do so even with this consent but when he is not empowered to do so by law, he would incur *ipso facto* suspension *a divinis* reserved to no one.[102]

96 Canon 958 § 2.

97 S.C.C., *Mexicana*, 24 Apr. 1700—*Fontes*, n. 2978.

98 Canon 959.

99 Canon 997.

100 Canon 978; "Ad I. Congregatio respondit facultatem remittendi interstitia Episcopo competentem ex causis comprehensis in c. xi, xiii et xiv, Sess. 23, transire in Vicarium Capituli sede vacante."—S.C.C., *Asturicen.*, 21 Apr. 1591—*Fontes*, n. 2228; cf. Bargilliat, *Juris Canonici*, II, 43; Bonal, *Institutiones Canonicae*, I, 665.

101 Cf. Canon 993 n. 4.

102 Canon 2409.

3. The third conditional right of the Administrator has reference to the conferring of parishes and parochial benefices of free collation. According to canon 455 § 1, the right to nominate and institute pastors belongs to the bishop, except for parishes reserved to the Holy See. The same is true for benefices, both parochial and otherwise, for according to canon 1432 § 1 the appointment to benefices in a diocese is a right of the proper Ordinary. Hence, the bishop alone enjoys the right to confer parishes and benefices in his own diocese, unless the Holy See reserves this right to itself. Since the Holy See does not ordinarily reserve, by a special act, parishes or benefices to itself, nor does it frequently occur that these become thus reserved by the law itself,[103] it can be said that the bishop, in practically every instance, enjoys the right of free collation with respect to all secular parishes and benefices in his diocese.[104]

Canons 455 § 1 and 1432 § 2 specify that when a diocese has been vacant for one full year, the Administrator is fully empowered by law to confer parishes and parochial benefices of free collation; it matters not at all whether these parochial benefices be removable or irremovable. This disposition of the present law is a decided departure from former discipline, for according to previous legislation Vicar Capitular was not permitted to confer benefices of free collation at any time during the period of vacancy.[105]

[103] Cf. Canon 1435.

[104] With reference to papal reservations, Coady *(The Appointment of Pastors,* p. 103) states that the Roman Pontiff is wont to reserve to himself those parishes which were held by priests at the time of their promotion to the episcopacy. Whether or not common law reservations are going to be applied to the parochial benefices in the United States is a question entirely beyond the scope of this treatise. American canonists seem to be of the opinion that the United States will be exempt from such a complication of the universal law of the Church. Cf. Coady, *op. cit.,* p. 102; "In the United States all the secular pastors are freely appointed by the bishop," writes Woywod *(A Practical Commentary,* I, 163), "because we have no parishes that are reserved to the Holy See, nor have we any parishes where other persons have the right to elect or present the pastor."

[105] Cf. c. 1, *de institutionibus,* III, 6, in VI°; c. un., *ne sede vacante,* III, 8, in VI°; c. 2, X, *ne sede vacante,* III, 9; Wernz, *Jus Decretalium,* II, n. 795, (p. 609); Schmalzgrueber, *Jus Eccl. Univ.,* lib. III, tit. IX, n. 11.

The question of the canonical status of the parishes in the United States was one much discussed in this country shortly after the promulgation of the present Code of Canon Law. Students in ecclesiastical law, however, have given the question full consideration, and have come to the conclusion which leaves no room for doubt that all parishes in the United States, whether these be removable or irremovable, are true canonical parishes and parochial benefices.[106] The Administrator must consequently abide by the canons governing the appointments to ecclesiastical offices of free collation,[107] when making these parochial appointments. He must remember, furthermore, that according to the prescriptions of canon 1437, no one can confer a benefice upon himself. Hence, he cannot appoint himself to a parish even though he would probably be appointed to it during the occupancy of the see on account of his seniority. It must be borne in mind, furthermore, that if the Administrator attempts to appoint pastors before the specified time, unless the Holy See especially authorizes him to do so, such appointments are utterly invalid.[108]

Art. 5. *Prohibition in General and in Particular*

Obviously, the matters of primary interest and importance for one called upon to administer a vacant episcopal see center chiefly about the restrictions which the law attaches to the administrative office, since in all other affairs, both spiritual and temporal, the Administrator, in view of his ordinary episcopal jurisdiction, has the same juridical capacity in the governance of the diocese as the bishop himself.

Since the office of the Administrator is, by its very nature, only transitory and since, furthermore, a diocese is a moral person and is regarded by law as a minor whose rights are

106 Cf. Ryder, *Simony*, pp. 81-87; Coady, *The Appointment of Pastors*, pp. 65-71; Augustine, *Canonical and Civil Status of Parishes*, pp. 63 ss; Woywod, *op. cit.*, pp. 160-61; Ayrinhac, *Constitutions*, p. 300; Golden, *Parochial Benefices in the New Code*, pp. 97-107.

107 Canons 152-159; Blat, *Commentarium*, II, 423.

108 Vermeersch-Creusen, *Epitome*, I, n. 497, (p. 313); Cf. Canons 455 § 2, n. 3; 1432 § 2.

safeguarded, executed and defended primarily by its proper guardian, the bishop, it is but natural that the law should place certain restrictions upon those acts of the Administrator which would result in an infringement upon, or a prejudice to, the rights of the diocese or of the succeeding bishop.[109]

Canon 436 states the general prohibition: "Sede vacante nihil innovetur." This prescription is a restatement of the preceptive rubric of the ninth title in the third book of the decretals. In view of this identity of present and former legislation, the disposition of the Code must be understood in the light of approved and accepted interpretation which recognized canonists placed upon this particular portion of the decretal law.[110]

The general restriction *Ne sede vacante aliquid innovetur* of the law of the decretals was interpreted by canonists[111] as signifying that those who administer vacant sees are forbidden to perform all acts which contain or which are likely to effect a true innovation or change in the status of the diocese, or prejudice the rights of the succeeding bishop. And if such changes or prejudices are actually enacted, they are without juridical consequence, and are revocable without restoration of any loss suffered by the parties concerned.[112] But since the law is directed solely to avoid any injury or deterioration to the status of the see and the rights of the succeeding bishop, those in charge of the administration are fully entitled to better the condition of the diocese in any manner they see fit.[113]

When commenting on this law of the decretals, canonists

[109] Cf. Canons 435 § 3, 436, "Attendentes igitur, quo episcopali sede vacante, non debet aliquid innovari, cum non sit, qui episcopale jus tueatur."—c. 1, X, *ne sede vacante aliquid innovetur,* III, 9; c. ult., X, *ne sede vacante aliquid innovetur,* III, 9; Vermeersch-Creusen, *op. cit.,* I, n. 482, (p. 306); Bargilliat, *Juris Canonici,* II, 42.

[110] Canon 6 n. 2; cf. Blat, *Commentary,* II, 407-8; Vermeersch-Creusen, *loc. cit.;* Coronata, *Institutiones,* I, 537.

[111] Reiffenstuel, *Jus Can. Univ.,* lib. III, tit. IX, n. 16; Schmalzgrueber, *Jus Eccl. Univ.,* lib. III, tit. IX, nn. 1-4.

[112] Reiffenstuel, *op. cit.,* lib. III, tit. IX, n. 13.

[113] Reiffenstuel, *op. cit.,* lib. III, tit. IX, n. 16; cf. Vermeersch-Creusen, *loc. cit.;* Augustine, *Commentary,* II, 489-90; Coronata, *loc. cit.*

enumerated various acts which were gathered from scattered sources. These prohibitions, with the exception of certain aspects of the power to alienate ecclesiastical property, are expressly stated in the present Code of Canon Law. Besides the general prohibition, therefore, to refrain from performing any act which will change the status of the diocese or prove prejudicial to the succeeding bishop, the Administrator must abide strictly by the following prescriptions of the Code.

1. Canon 435 § 3 states the general principle that the Administrator and the Board of Diocesan Consultors are not allowed to do anything that might be prejudicial to the rights of the diocese or the future bishop. To this general prohibition, the same canon expressly adds that the Administrator, any member of the Board of Consultors, and outsiders, lay or cleric, are strictly forbidden to remove, destroy, conceal, or change, personally or through others, any document belonging to the episcopal curia. This canon expresses the desire of the Church that great care be taken of all important documents pertaining to diocesan government. The Code, furthermore, provides a particular sanction to this prescription, for, according to canon 2405, anyone who is guilty of a violation of this law *ipso facto* incurs excommunication simply reserved to the Holy See. The Administrator furthermore, may deprive the violators from office or benefice, while if he himself be guilty,[114] the Holy See would be justified in removing him from office.[115]

"By documents," writes Augustine,[116] "are understood the papers or entries mentioned in canon 1813 § 1; but not only

[114] Canon 2405 employs the term "Vicarius Capitularis." Since penalties must be strictly interpreted, canonists hold that this penalty would not be incurred by a transferred bishop who is acting as Administrator (canon 430 § 3, n. 1), nor by an Apostolic Administrator (canon 431 § 1), and it remains doubtful whether the excommunication would be incurred by a vicar general, or delegate of the bishop during quasi-vacancy of see. (Canon 429); cf. Cappello, *De Censuris*, n. 365, (p. 316); Cocchi, *Commentarium*, V, 400.

[115] Cf. Canons 2405, 443 § 1; Vermeersch-Creusen, *Epitome*, III, n. 611 (p. 320).

[116] *Op. cit.*, VIII, 507; cf. Cocchi, *loc. cit.*; Cappello, *op. cit.*, n. 366, (pp. 316-17).

such as are issued by the diocesan officials and abstracts of which are kept in the diocesan archives, but also such as are sent to, or received by, the episcopal court; in other words, all documents which concern persons, property, or rights of the diocese, as, e.g., petitions, accusations, criminal and civil acts, dispensations, appointments, concursus and examination papers, establishments, dedications, consecrations of churches and chapels, parishes and missions, inventories, deeds, abstracts, receipts, and also civil documents addressed to the diocesan court. Private letters, unless they bear on ecclesiastical as connected with civil or criminal procedure, do not belong to the diocesan court."

This prescription of the Code does not appear to prohibit, however, the Administrator from removing documents from the diocesan archives according to the disposition of canon 378.[117] Hence, the Administrator may permit documents to be removed from the archives, and if necessary may give the one having the documents three days' time for their return. The one who removes the documents from the archives, however, must leave a signed receipt for it with the chancellor. Coronata [118] observes that the Administrator does not seem to be forbidden to destroy documents according to the norms of canon 379 § 1. This beyond doubt is true according to a strict interpretation of the canon. It appears, however, that canon 382 discountenances such action on the part of the Administrator, although no strict prohibition is made here. In practice, certainly it would be more prudent if the Administrator would leave this matter to the new bishop.

A word may be inserted here with respect to the unsealing of the secret archives of the diocese during vacancy. According to canon 382, the secret archives are not to be opened or unsealed during the period of vacancy, except in urgent cases. If circumstances necessitate this, the law requires that the Administrator, in the presence of two Diocesan Consultors, shall unseal and open the archives. He may examine the papers

[117] Coronata, *Institutiones,* I, 537; Blat, *Commentarium,* II, 407

[118] *Loc. cit.*

alone in the presence of the Consultors, but he is not allowed to take any of them away. When the inspection has been made, he must again seal the archives. If the seal has been removed and the archives opened, the Administrator must report the affair to the new bishop and state the reason why such action was taken.[119]

2. The Administrator may not convoke a diocesan synod during the period of vacancy.[120] This prescription differs from earlier discipline, for in former times the Vicar Capitular was permitted to do so when a year had elapsed from the time the last synod was held.[121] But since the present law demands that a synod be held in each diocese only once in every ten years,[122] the restriction placed upon the power of the Administrator in this respect does not appear to be too exacting.

3. The Administrator is forbidden by law to reserve to himself sins and censures.[123] This prohibition is striking in so far as it is an exception to the general rule that those who possess the ordinary power to grant faculties for hearing confession and inflicting censures, enjoy the right also of reserving to themselves certain sins and censures.[124]

4. Since the Administrator is not expressly authorized by law to grant indulgences, he is not permitted to do so, for canon 912 explicitly states that besides the Roman Pontiff, only those can by their ordinary power grant indulgences who are expressly authorized to do so by law.[125] According to former discipline the Vicar Capitular was forbidden to grant indulgences even though he already possessed the

119 Canon 382 § 2.

120 Canon 357 § 1.

121 Benedict XIV, *De Synodo Dioecesana,* lib. II, c. 9, n. 6; Bouix, *De Capitulis,* pp. 578-79.

122 Canon 356 § 1.

123 Canon 893 § 1.

124 Canon 893 § 1.

125 Cf. De Meester, *Compendium,* II, n. 789, (p. 236); Vermeersch-Creusen, *Epitome,* I, n. 482, (p. 306); Oesterle, *Praelectiones,* p. 207; Raus, *Institutiones,* p. 226; Augustine, *Rights and Duties of Ordinaries,* p. 163; Coronata, *op. cit.,* I, 536.

faculty.[126] In view of canon 912, this restriction no longer applies, for the present law does not forbid those who already enjoy the right to grant indulgences, e. g., a titular bishop, who is an Administrator, to exercise this right during the vacancy of the diocese.

5. The Administrator is not allowed to fix the fee to be paid by priests, who, for convenience, say mass in a very poor church, in order that by this fee the expenses of the sacred utensils and other requirements of Holy Mass may be defrayed.[127]

6. According to canons 1573 § 5 and 1590 § 1, the Administrator cannot remove from office the official of the diocese, or the defender of the bond, or promotor of justice. But should it occur that any of these officials would commit a crime which, according to the penal Code, would either warrant or necessitate their removal from office, the Administrator could then take action against them but only by instituting a canonical trial in order to effect their removal.[128]

7. Canon 492 § 1 specifies that the Administrator cannot found religious congregations. This signifies that he cannot found a religious institute which has simple vows, either perpetual or temporary.[129] But since this canon has reference only to religious congregations, a question may be advanced as to whether the Administrator according to canon 497, can give the required consent for the erection of exempt religious houses, whether these belong to regulars, or nuns with solemn vows. This canon attributes this right to the Ordinaries of the particular territories and makes no mention of the inability of the Administrator to give the required consent. Since the Administrator is the successor to the bishop and is the Ordinary of the place,[130] it appears that the law *per se* does not deny him this

126 S.C.C., 13 Nov. 1688—Benedict XIV, *De Synodo Dioecesana*, lib. II, c. 9, n. 7.

127 Canon 1303 §§ 2-3.

128 Noval, *De Processibus*, I, n. 116; Roberti, *De Processibus*, I, 167.

129 Canon 488 n. 2.

130 Canon 198.

right. Melo [131] and Coronata,[132] however, maintain that since the erection of monasteries is a transaction of greater import and among those acts which naturally result in a change of the status of the diocese, the Administrator, by force of canons 436 and 435 § 3, is not permitted to give the required consent. Schäfer,[133] Larraona,[134] and Goyeneche,[135] on the other hand, modify the above opinion by stating that the Administrator can do so as long as the erection of the exempt religious house will not effect an innovation in the diocese. This appears to be the more acceptable opinion. An innovation would certainly take place, and the Administrator would be forbidden to give his consent, if, by the erection of the exempt religious house, a religious institute, which heretofore did not exist in the diocese, were introduced.[136]

8. The Administrator cannot erect, or give consent for the erection or aggregation of pious associations of the faithful.[137] The term pious association includes, according to canon 700, secular tertiaries, confraternities and pious unions.

9. All administrative acts which touch upon the question of parishes and benefices in any way, are matters intimately connected with the status of the diocese and the prerogatives of the bishop himself. It is but natural, therefore, that the powers of the Administrator in this respect be greatly circumscribed by law. It has been previously observed that the Administrator is permitted to confer parishes and parochial benefices, (which include all parishes in the United States), after the first year of vacancy has elapsed. This is the only concession given

131 *De Exemptione Regularium*, p. 122.

132 *Op. cit.*, 536.

133 *De Religiosis*, p. 127.

134 *Commentarium pro Religiosis*, V (1924), 424 ss.

135 *Op. cit.*, I (1920), 115.

136 Cf. Vermeersch-Creusen, *Epitome*, I, n. 482, (p. 306); Vermeersch, *De Religiosis*, I, n. 104; S.C. EE, et RR., 10 Feb. 1633—Ferraris, *Prompta Bibliotheca*, v. *Vicarius Capitularis*, art. II, n. 66.

137 Canon 686 § 4; cf. S.C. Indulg., respons. 15 Nov. 1878—*Decreta Authentica S.C. Indulg. Sac. Reliq.*, n. 438; ASS, XI, 353; Fanfani, *De Jure Religiosorum*, n. 550, (p. 544).

by the Code to the Administrator with respect to the question of parishes and benefices, exclusive, of course, of the right to appoint parochial vicars.

According to canon 1432 § 2, the Administrator is strictly forbidden to confer perpetual benefices other than parochial, which are of free collation. This prescription of the Code beyond doubt has little reference to the United States, for it appears that the only non-consistorial benefices in this country are the parochial benefices.[138] There always remains, however, the possibility of such benefices in this country, for the present law acknowledges the authority of the bishop as sufficient for the erection of any benefice inferior to the episcopacy, and not reserved to the Holy See.[139] It is clear from the definition of a benefice given in canon 1409, that offices such as chaplaincies in Catholic hospitals, etc., may be erected into true ecclesiastical benefices,[140] but it appears that such ecclesiastical offices have not, up to the present time, been erected into benefices in the United States.

The Administrator is also forbidden to give permanency to removable parishes by declaring them irremovable.[141] He is likewise not permitted to unite, or to suppress parish churches, either *aeque* or *minus principaliter* with one another or with non-curate benefices according to the prescription of canon 1423 §.[142] Lastly, the Administrator cannot permit an exchange of benefices.[143] An exchange of benefices signifies that two clerics, who have title to their respective benefices,

[138] Woywod, *The New Code of Canon Law*, p. 298.

[139] Canon 1414 § 2.

[140] Cf. Woywod, *The Homiletic and Pastoral Review*, XXVIII (1928), 1185; Ryder, *Simony*, p. 79; Golden, *Parochial Benefices in the New Code*, p. 4.

[141] Canon 454 § 3.

[142] An *aeque principalis* union of benefices is the union of two or more benefices in such a way that after they are united, neither become subordinate to each other—Canon 1419 n. 2; a *minus principalis* union is had *per subjectionem*, or *per accessionem*, with the result that the several benefices remain distinct, but one is made subordintae or accessory to the other—canon 1419 n. 3.

[143] Canon 1487 § 1.

have made their resignation into the hands of a proper superior with the understanding that after resignation each obtains the benefice of the other. Hence, when the superior permits such an exchange his act is tantamount to conferring a new benefice on each of the clerics. Here it might be asked whether the Administrator can permit the exchange of benefices after the first year of vacancy has elapsed, since after that time he is permitted to confer parochial benefices of free appointment. Golden[144] rightly observes that the canon governing the exchange of benefices makes no exception in favor of the Administrator, and hence, even after the see has been vacant for one year, he is not permitted to exercize this prerogative of the bishop.

10. The right of the Administrator to alienate ecclesiastical property is circumscribed by certain limitations in view of canons 435 § 3 and 436. It has been noted before that these canons restate the law of the decretals by prescribing that during vacancy of see nothing shall be undertaken which will result in an innovation of the status of the diocese, or prove prejudicial to the rights of the succeeeding bishop. Since certain acts of alienation bring about this effect, the prohibitory force of the present Code in this regard must be measured by former law.

In general, the Administrator enjoys the same powers as the bishop himself with respect to alienating church property, and consequently must follow the prescription of the Code in such matters.[145] The general principle found in canons 435 § 3 and 436, however, must govern each act of alienation. Hence, the general prohibition is that the Administrator may not alienate when such an act would result in a change in the status of the diocese, or be detrimental to the rights of the see or of the succeeding bishop.[146] In particular, however, the Administrator is forbidden to alienate the goods of the *mensa episcopalis* or of any parish or benefice which is

144 *Parochial Benefices in the New Code*, p. 81.

145 Canons 1529-1543; cf. Raus, *Institutiones*, p. 225.

146 Cf. Cocchi, *Commentarium*, II, 344.

vacant during the vacancy of the see. This was the law prior to the Code,[147] and since no change was made in this regard, the principle of canon 6 number 2 requires that the old prescriptions remain in full force.[148]

But even in this instance, the Administrator can alienate when there is a case of grave necessity, or evident utility to the Church, and the alienation itself cannot be postponed until the arrival of the new bishop, and no time remains at hand to petition the Holy See for the proper facilities.[149] Augustine[150] maintains that the Administrator (Vicar Capitular) is permitted to conclude a favorable financial transaction such as getting money at a lower rate of interest, or converting bonds into more profitable ones since this would not be prejudicial to the diocese. The opinion appears to be in keeping with the spirit of the law and permissible, yet it would probably be better if the Administrator petitioned for faculties even in such cases. It must be remembered, however, that the Administrator must comply with all canonical provisions governing alienation in the same manner as the bishop himself.

Canon 2347 gives the penal sanction for those transgressing the law in regard to alienation. It is here stated that if ecclesiastical property is alienated contrary to the prescriptions of canon 1532, the violator must be fittingly punished by the proper ecclesiastical superior in proportion to the amount alienated. If the alienation furthermore, were *knowingly* [151]

147 "Hanc facultatem competere Episcopis . . . quoque, Sede Vacante, vicariis Capitularibus, qui tamen his facultatibus uti nequeunt circa bona mensae episcopalis vacantis, ac vacantium Ecclesiarum et beneficiorum vacantium, quia ex *cap. Novit. Ne Sede vacante aliquid innovetur,* non possunt haec bona, tempore votationis beneficii alienari, ut optime advertit S. Congregatio Episcoporum et Regularium Vicario Capitulari Pontiscurvi sub die 14 Junii 1788."—De Angelis, *Praelectiones Juris Canonici,* lib. III, tit. XIII, n. 5; cf. *Fontes,* n. 1882; Wernz, *Jus Decretalium,* II, n. 795, (p. 610); Schmalzgrueber, *Jus Eccl. Univ.,* lib. III, tit. IX, nn. 48-52; Raus, *loc. cit.*

148 Cf. Augustine, *Commentary,* II, 489.

149 Schmalzgrueber, *op. cit.,* lib. III, tit. IX, n. 52.

150 *Op. cit.,* II, 489-90.

151 Cf. Canon 2229 § 2.

effected without the permission of the Holy See when this is demanded by law, all who participated in the transaction, as well as those who gave their consent (Board of Diocesan Consultors and the Board of Administration) incur excommunication, *latae senteniae* reserved to no one. The terms *praesumpserit* and *scienter praetermissum* must be understood in the light of canon 2229 § 2.

A word may be added here in regard to the term *mensa episcopalis.* This legal usage signifies all the revenues which contribute to the support of the bishop. In many countries, the *mensa* takes the form of an endowment, while in other regions it is a pension provided by the civil government. "In the United States," writes Augustine,[152] "the Church had no other revenues than the free donations or oblations of the faithful. Therefore a means was resorted to, which is certainly not in keeping with Canon Law, *viz.,* the *cathedraticum* which appears to take the place of the *mensa* or episcopal revenues. Although this is not a canonical means of supporting the bishop, yet it is at present the only one available. Therefore, we may as well call the *mensa episcopalis* the *cathedraticum* which is paid by all those who are obliged thereto (see can. 1505)." Since the *cathedraticum* is a revenue arising from a tax, and cannot, therefore, be called stable capital, and since, furthermore, money which is not stable capital is not alienated in the canonical sense when used in purchasing and paying of debts,[153] it might be asked as to how it is possible for the Administrator in the United States to alienate the goods of the *mensa episcopalis.* Alienation of the *mensa episcopalis* in this country is certainly possible, for in many dioceses the Church has property holdings from which the accruing revenues partially contribute to the support of the bishop. Then, too, in some dioceses the surplus of the *cathedraticum* of each year is invested in order to build up a foundation or endowment which will in time be a true *mensa episcopalis.*

152 *Rights and Duties of Ordinaries,* pp. 47-48; cf. Woywod, *A Practical Commentary,* I, 154.

513 Vromant, *De Bonis Ecclesiae Temporalibus,* p. 295.

CHAPTER XII

The Honorary Rights, Salary, and Obligations of the Administrator

The honorary rights of the Administrator are identical to those of the vicar-general.[1] He is privileged, therefore, with the right of precedence, within the diocese, over all the clergy, including the pastor of the cathedral Church,[2] and all dignitaries and members of the Board of Diocesan Consultors, on all occasions both public and private. The only ones who precede him are those who possess the episcopal character when he lacks the same himself.[3] If the Administrator be a bishop,[4] is conceded all the honorary privileges of titular bishops,[5] while on the other hand, if he lacks the episcopal character, he is given right to all the privileges and insignia of Titular Prothonotaries Apostolic.[6]

The college of Prothonotaries Apostolic was remodeled by Pope Pius X in his motu proprio *Inter Multiplices* on February 21, 1905,[7] and is comprised of four distinct classes of Prothonotaries: the *participantes* (seven in number), the *supranumerarii,* the *ad instar participantium,* and the *titulares aut honorarii.* The last named dignity, therefore is possessed

[1] Canons 439, 370.

[2] S.C.C., 17 Maii 1919—AAS, XI (1919), 349.

[3] Canon 370 § 1.

[4] During the interval a transferred bishop administers his see *a qua,* he enjoys all the honorary privileges of a residential bishop: Canon 430 § 3, n. 2. An Administrator Apostolic who is permanently appointed possess the same privileges (canon 315 § 1), while an Administrator Apostolic who is commissioned for a limited period of time possesses the same privileges as the diocesan Administrator spoken of in the text: canon 315 § 2, n. 2, 308.

[5] Canons 439, 349 § 1, 370 § 2; cf. Sipos, *Juris Canonici,* p. 243.

[6] Canons 370 § 2, 439.

[7] Cf. *American Ecclesiastical Review,* XXXII (1905), 612-628; *Il Monitore Ecclesiastico,* XVII (1905-06), pp. 133 ss.

by the Administrator who is not a bishop. He retains the honors and privileges of this dignity during his entire tenure of office, and may use them only within the limits of the diocese.[8]

The Administrator who is thus endowed with the dignity of a titular Prothonotary Apostolic enjoys the title of "Monsignor,"[9] and possesses the following privileges.[10] His dress is a black cassock with a folded train (*cauda nunquam tamen explicanda*), a silken sash and two pendants on the left and each pendant may have a tassel. He may wear a rochet, mantelet, and a biretta, but all must be in black, nor is he permitted to add ornaments of any other color. He does not genuflect to the cross or to a bishop and is incensed *duplici ductu.* He officiates at sacred functions in the same manner as a simple priest, but he may use the bugia or hand-light (*palmatoria*), although not the Canon and other *pontificali supellectili.* On solemn occasions, including audiences with the Holy Father, he may wear over his habitual dress a silken sash with a tassel, and also a hat with a band and two tassels, but all must be of black color. Should he have a coat-of-arms, he may insert in it a hat with ribbons and six tassels on each side. This also must be in black.

The present Code does not enter into the delicate question of the salaries of the Administrator and the Econome. Canon 441 simply states that these officers have a right to a decent support and that unless other norms have legitimately been made, the salaries shall be determined either by the provincial council or by accepted custom, and are to be taken from the episcopal revenues or other sources. All other revenues of the diocese, the same canon continues, shall be reserved to the future bishop for the needs of the see, provided, however, such incomes belonged to the bishop during occupancy of see.

[8] S.C. Rit., declar., 14 Martii 1906—*Analecta Ecclesiastica,* XIV (1906), 166; cf. De Meester, *Compendium,* II, n. 656, (p. 128).

[9] *Il Monitore Ecclesiastico,* s², VII (1905), 133-34; *Periodica,* VI-VII, (1912-13), 46; Augustine, *Commentary,* II, 404.

[10] Pius X, motu proprio, *Inter Multiplices,* 21 Feb. 1905, nn. 62, 64, 66-68, 70, 76—*American Ecclesiastical Review,* XXXII (1905), pp. 625-26; *op. cit.,* XXXIII (1905), 77; cf. Augustine, *loc. cit.*

The salary of the Administrator and of the Econome, therefore, is determined by one of three ways. The reference made in the canon with respect to norms legitimately made concerns chiefly those countries where the salary of the Vicar Capitular is determined by way of a concordat between the Holy See and the civil government,[11] and consequently has no bearing upon the discipline in the United States. In this country, therefore, the salary must be regulated either by custom, or by provincial council. Since the present law demands that all ecclesiastical provinces hold a provincial council only once in every twenty years,[12] there have been but few provinces in the church where such councils have been held since the promulgation of the Code. In this country it appears that no province has as yet held a council. The salary of the Administrator in the United States depends entirely, therefore, upon custom.

It is believed that custom, generally speaking, has established the amount of the Administrator's salary for the individual provinces in the United States. But if there are provinces in which this matter is regarded as being indefinite or uncertain, it would probably be advisable to discuss the question at the conference of bishops [13] in order to establish a temporary provision which may serve until particular legislation is forthcoming from a provincial council. It cannot be denied that grave misunderstandings and embarrassing situations may arise when it is not definitely known just how much salary the Administrator is to receive.

The present Code does not specify the amount of salary the Administrator and the Econome should receive. Canon 441 n. 1 provides that the salaries be fitting (*congruam retributionem*). In the past the Sacred Congregations have assigned to the Vicar Capitular, in particular instances, a salary equal to that of the vicar-general, or to one-fourth of the

[11] Cf. S.C.C., 8 Feb. 1913—AAS, VII (1915), 46; Ferreres, *Institutiones,* I, n. 725.

[12] Canon 283.

[13] These conferences must be held every five years in each province: canon 292.

bishop's income.[14] This may be a guide for the hierarchy of this country, as well as of others, for setting the rate of salary, when such a duty is incumbent upon them. It is the opinion, however, of many bishops in the United States, that owing to the particular conditions prevailing here, the Administrators should receive more income than the vicar-general. The final decision in this matter, however, must be arrived at in the provincial councils.

It is interesting to note the opinion of Augustine in regard to the salary of the Administrator. "The vicar-capitular or administrator," he writes,[15] "is entitled to the *cathedraticum pro rata temporis* as well as to the income received from dispensations." This opinion is, indeed, a generous concession to the Administrators in the United States, but is not substantiated by either former or present legislation. It is true that in many dioceses in this country, the income of the bishop is so meagre that it is scarcely sufficient for his support. In such instances, of course, Augustine's opinion is applicable. But in a good many other dioceses the *cathedraticum* is no small figure, and if the Administrator were entitled to the whole amount *pro rata temporis* his office would indeed be lucrative, and this might lead to very undesired consequences which would possibly result from the action of those who would unduly seek this office.

A suitable salary, therefore, is deducted from the *mensa episcopalis,* or from other revenues. The second section of the same canon 441 continues to state that all other revenues accruing during the vacancy of see must be reserved for the future bishop to be expended for the needs of the diocese, provided, however, such revenues belonged to the bishop during the occupancy of see.

The disposition of the present Code in this matter is taken from the law of the decretals,[16] and consequently the former legal provision, together with the pronouncements of the sacred

[14] Cf. Wernz, *Jus Decretalium,* II, n. 795, (pp. 610-11).

[15] *Commentary,* II, 493.

[16] C. 7, *de electione et electi potestate,* I, 3, in Clem.

Congregation of the Council will serve as the interpretation of the true significance of the prevailing discipline. The law of the decretals specified that all the income which the bishop received *ex jurisdictione et sigillo curiae ecclesiasticae* (chancery fees), and from other sources during the occupancy of see, must be reserved for the future bishop, with the exception of that portion which must be deducted from the total in order to meet all reasonable expenses during vacancy.[17] This prescription was further explained and its meaning clarified by a response of the Sacred Congregation of the Council on February 8, 1913.[18] According to this response, the goods and revenues which must be reserved for the future prelate comprise only that, which, during the occupancy of see, belong to the bishop. If any goods and income belong to the vicar-general by force of his proper right, the Congregation continued to state, such belong to the Vicar Capitular (Administrator) during the vacancy of see. The revenues of the *mensa episcopalis* furthermore, are not understood as such, unless all reasonable expenses are deducted from the total. Hence, a reasonable salary for the Vicar Capitular must first of all be estimated and deducted from these incomes. The same Congregation declared also [19] that all pecuniary fines which accumulate during vacancy from ecclesiastical penalties may not be converted by the Chapter or the Vicar Capitular to their own uses, but must be contributed to pious places and causes.[20]

The obligations in general which are incumbent upon the bishop, apply equally as well to the Administrator. This follows naturally from the fact that the Administrator possesses the jurisdiction of the bishop, and succeeds him as the ruler of the diocese and the custodian of its spiritual and temporal

[17] Cf. S.C.C., *Agrigentina,* 17 Nov. 1594, *Cephaluden,* 17 Nov. 1594, *Nullius,* II Jul. 1626—*Fontes,* nn. 2275, 2276, 2470; Monacelli, *Formularium Legale,* t. I, tit. I, form. 2, n. 15; De Angelis, *Praelectiones,* lib. I, tit. XXVIII, n. 22.

[18] AAS, XI (1915), 45-47.

[19] *Resp.,* 6 Dec. 1642—*Fontes,* n. 2639; rescr., 28 Mart. 1648—*op. cit.,* n. 2681.

[20] Cf. Canon 2297.

interests. But owing to the transitory character of the office of the Administrator and the very nature of certain legal requirements, there are several duties which need not be complied with by the Administrator. Thus, the duties of visiting *ad limina Apostolorum* [21], of the canonical visitation of the diocese [22], and of reporting the status of the diocese to the Holy See,[23] certainly are not incumbent upon the Administrator, especially since it is the policy of the Holy See in modern times to avoid long periods of vacancy. The Code explicitly mentions, however, certain duties which must be complied with by the Administrator. Several of these duties have already been referred to. Thus, the duty of the Administrator to report his election or appointment to the Holy See when the diocese has become vacant by the death of the bishop [24]; he is obliged to make the profession of faith before the Board of Consultors before exercising jurisdiction [25]; and since he possesses legislative power he must be present at plenary and provincial councils and is endowed by law with a decisive vote *(deliberative)* in all considerations of the conclave.[26] Besides these obligations, the Code explicitly mentions the duties of the Administrator with reference to residence, the *Missa pro populo* and the final account of his administration to be rendered to the new bishop. The latter duty will be considered in the subsequent chapter in connection with the cessation of the administrative office.

Canon 440 imposes upon the Administrator the duty of saying the "Mass for the people" and of residing in the diocese in

[21] Cf. Canon 341.

[22] Cf. Canon 343. Attention may be called to the right of the Administrator to make the canonical visitation of the diocese. He may not proceed with this measure until one full year has elapsed from the time the Ordinary had made the last visitation. Cf. S.C.C., 13 Sept. 1721—*Fontes,* n. 3232; Benedict XIV, *De Synodo Diocesana,* lib. II, c. 9, n. 6; lib. X, c. 10, n. 6.

[23] Cf. Canon 340 § 3; cf. Blat, *Commentarium,* II, 409.

[24] Canon 432 § 4; also when an Administrator is appointed to govern a quasi-vacant see; cf. canon 429 § 4.

[25] Canon 438.

[26] Canons 282 § 1, 286 § 1.

the same manner as the law obliges residential bishops. The former obligation is an innovation in this particular discipline, for in times prior to the present Code, the Vicar Capitular was not obliged to say the *Missa pro populo.*[27] As soon as the Administrator accepts the office, therefore, his obligation of saying the Mass for the people begins, and he must comply with this duty on all Sundays of the year, on the ten Holydays mentioned in canon 1247, on all suppressed Holydays, including those suppressed feasts which are of precept by particular law.[28] If the Administrator is at the same time a pastor, or otherwise obliged to say the Mass for the people, both obligations will be satisfied by saying but one Mass. This fact is not expressly stated in the Code, but appears certain by analogy with canon 399 § 5

The law of residence obliges Administrators in identically the same manner as it does residential bishops, for canon 440 applies the norm of canon 338 to the office of the Administrator without further comment. In consequence of this fact, the Administrator must reside personally in the diocese. This legal provision is a distinct departure from former discipline, since formerly the Vicar Capitular was strictly obliged to reside in the episcopal city, and even in the episcopal palace.[29] According to the present law, there is no strict obligation incumbent upon the bishop, and consequently upon the Administrator, to reside in the episcopal city, for the Code prescribes

[27] S.R.C., decret., *Marsorum*, 12 Nov. 1831 ad 23—*Decreta Authentica S.C. Rit.*, n. 2682.

[28] Canons 440, 339 § 1; S.C.C., 28 Dec. 1919—AAS, XII (1919), 42; S.C.C., resol., 19-31 Julii, 1930—AAS, XXII (1930), 521; cf. *Periodica*, XX (1931), 86-88. There are no suppressed feasts which are of precept by particular law in the United States. A list of these days on which the *Missa pro populo* must be said may be found in the Acta (1919) cited above, in Woywod *(A Practical Commentary*, I, 122), and in the *Ordo* published by B. Herder, St. Louis, Mo.

[29] "Iste tenetur habitari in episcopio, ut, ex mente Sacrae Congregationis super Episcopis, resolvit Riccius (resol. 116, n. 1 et 2); ubi advertit nihil obstare quod Episcopus in quacumque parte suae dioecesis sibi benevisa possit pro tribunali sedere; quia in his et similibus vicarius non aequiparatur Episcopo, cui major et liberior facultas concessa est."—Pignatellus, *Consultationes Canonicae*, t. IV, consult. 4, n. 6; cf. Bouix, *De Capitulis*, p. 576.

residence *in the diocese.* Canon 339 § 3 requires that the bishop should not be absent from the cathedral church in Advent, Lent, or Christmas, Easter, Pentecost, Corpus Christi, except for grave and urgent reasons. This provision, of course, demands that the bishop be present in the episcopal city at least on specified occasions. But in the case of Administrators, the law does not make even this requirement, for the Sacred Congregation of the Council in a response on the ninth of May, 1931,[30] clearly specified that the Vicar Capitular (Administrator) is not obliged to supply the bishop in this respect. According to the strict wording of the law, therefore, the Administrator need not reside in the episcopal city, but the general character of his office would, of course, necessitate his frequent presence there, since the office of the diocesan curia is the center of diocesan activity.

The second paragraph of canon 338 provides the legitimate causes of absence from the diocese. These also apply to both bishops and Administrators. Hence, when the Administrator is attending provincial or plenary councils, or when other official, not personal, obligations mentioned in the canon necessitate his absence, his leave from the diocese is legitimate. The same canon states, moreover, that except for these reasons, bishops must not be absent more than two or at most three months, continuous or interrupted, each year, and that they must see to it that their absence does not injure the interests of their dioceses. Since the law makes no distinction between bishops and Administrators in this regard, the Administrator is fully entitled to the same privilege. But since the periods of vacancy of see in the present day are relatively brief, it appears that an Administrator could not take two or three successive months leave from the diocese shortly after his appointment, or even during the period of vacancy, without injuring the interests of the diocese to some extent. But according to the letter of the law, he may do so as long as he makes provisions which will ward off possible injury to the interests

[30] Ad III—AAS, XXIII (1931), 235; cf. *Jus Pontificum,* XI (1931), 192; canon 397 n. 1.

of the see. When all is considered, however, it seems that an Administrator who would take advantage of this prescription of the Code, would more or less be defeating the purposes of his appointment to the administrative office.

The sanction of the law of residence is found in canon 2381. Any ecclesiastic, accordingly, who violates the law of residence forfeits his right to the income of his office or benefice, in proportion to the duration of his illegitimate absence. There is no reason for doubt but that this norm applies also to the Administrator.

CHAPTER XIII

Cessation of the Administrative Office and the Final Account

The moment the office of the Administrator or the Econome ceases, the incumbents lose all powers and rights which they acquired by force of the office. The immediately return, consequently, to the status which they possessed previous to their appointment. Although the general law of the Code governing the loss of ecclesiastical offices finds its proportionate application with respect to the loss of the administrative office, there are certain provisions prescribed by canon 443 which have particular reference to this office.

Canon 443 § 1 states that the Holy See alone is the competent superior who may remove the Administrator or the Econome from office. This provision precludes any right on the part of the Board of Diocesan Consultors, or the metropolitan or senior suffragan bishop to interfere in this regard, even though the appointment had been made by the metropolitan or senior suffragan. The removal does not become effective, however, until the fact is intimated to the Administrator or the Econome by the Holy See.[1]

The same is true in case the Apostolic See places the incumbents under censure; but if the Board of Diocesan Consultors incurs this penalty, it has no effect upon the Administrator or Econome.[2]

The Administrator or Econome may lose their office also by resignation. Canon 443 § 1 prescribes that the resignation be presented in authentic form to the Board of Consultors, and that it is not necessary for its validity that the Board

[1] Canon 192 § 3.

[2] Wernz-Vidal, *Jus Canonicum*, II, n. 713, (p. 764); Coronata, *Institutiones*, I, 539.

accept it. The authentic form of resignations from ecclesiastical offices is regulated by canon 186. Hence, the resignation of the Administrator or the Econome, must be made in writing, or orally before two witness, or by proxy appointed by a special mandate. This presupposes, moreover, that the act of resignation be in full accord with canon 184-185 which specify that, in order that a resignation be valid, the one resigning must be in full possession of his mental faculties and capable of performing an human act; furthermore, the act must be free, unhampered by unjust and grave fear, substantial error, or deceit, and entirely disassociated from any simoniacal agreement connected with the resignation. As soon as the Administrator or Econome presents his authentic resignation to the Board of Consultors, it becomes effective immediately, for, as it has previously been mentioned, the validity of this resignation is not dependent upon its acceptance by the Board.[3]

When the office of the Administrator or Econome is made vacant by the death, removal, or resignation of its incumbent, canon 443 § 1 specifies that the Board of Diocesan Consultors must proceed with a new election according to the norms of canon 432. This signifies that the Board of Consultors must hold the election in the same manner as it had done in the first instance, unless, of course, the Holy See appoints an Administrator Apostolic.

Coronata [4] takes into account the possibility of the Administrator becoming hindered from exercising of his power, in the same manner as the bishop is during quasi-vacancy of see. Coronata holds that in such instances, the Administrator himself would have to have recourse to the Holy See if it is at all possible for him to do so; otherwise this must be done by the Board of Consultors. In the meanwhile the author believes that, by analogy with canon 429, the governance of the see would pass to the Board, unless the Administrator is able to delegate some one to administer the see in his stead. In the

[3] Canons 443 § 1, 187 § 1; it must be remembered that the Administrator and the Econome may lose office also by tacit resignation, according to the prescriptions of canon 188.

[4] *Op. cit.*, I, 539.

latter instance, the delegate, and not the Board, has the right to govern the diocese until the Holy See has otherwise provided. This analogous application of canon 429 appears entirely acceptable and in complete accord with the spirit of the law.

Canon 443 § 2 gives the most common cause for the cessation of the administrative office of the Administrator and the Econome. This has reference to the new bishop taking canonical possession of the diocese. According to this prescription, when the newly appointed bishop, even though he is not as yet consecrated, presents, either personally or by proxy, his Apostolic Letters of appointment to the Board of Diocesan Consultors in the presence of the secretary of the Board, or the chancellor of the curia, the office of the Administrator and the Econome *ipso jure* ceases.[5] And if it should happen that the Administrator or Econome should be promoted to the see which they are administering, they would continue in the administrative office until they have taken canonical possession of the diocese.[6]

When the new Bishop has taken canonical possession of the diocese, he must demand an account of the Board of Diocesan Consultors, the Administrator, the Econome, and other officials who were appointed during the period of vacancy, concerning their office, jurisdiction, administration, and charges; and he must proceed against those who have been delinquent in the discharge of their duties and offices, even though these individuals had given an account to the Board of Consultors, or had been absolved or acquitted by the same. The same officials, furthermore, shall also render account to the new bishop of whatever documents of the Church have come into their hands.[7]

The law is clear in its statement, and hence no further explanation as to the extent of the account to be given is necessary. It must be remembered, however, that all who in

[5] Canons 443 § 2, 334 § 3.

[6] Canon 334 § 2.

[7] Canon 444.

any way have shared in the administrative government during vacancy must be asked to report on their office. Thus, if an Administrator had resigned and was replaced by another, both must give account of their office.

Here it may be asked: what obligation has the new bishop to exact or demand this account? The canon uses the phrase *exigere debet officiorum,* which carries with it the same obligatory force as the phrase *Episcopus . . . rationem exigat* found in the law of the Council of Trent.[8]

The new bishop, therefore, may not arbitrarily neglect this duty, for the law imposes this obligation as binding *sub grave,* and according to the older canonists,[9] a culpable omission would constitute a grievous sin.

The law leaves the infliction of punishment upon the delinquents to the good judgment of the new bishop, unless crimes had been committed, or the negligence were of such a nature that, according to the penal Code,[10] certain penalties would have to be imposed. But if one compares the law of the Council of Trent with that found in the present Code with respect to punishments to be inflicted upon delinquents by the new bishop,[11] it will be observed that the present law has supplied the term *punire* by the milder expression *animadvertere.* The latter term, however, does not remove the idea of punishments, but signifies rather a mitigated form of the same, for in law especially this term has the meaning of proceeding against, or punishing in a less severe manner.[12]

[8] Cf. Canon 444; Council of Trent, sess. XXIV, *de ref.* c. 16—*Canones et Decreta,* p. 196.

[9] Bouix (*De Capitulis,* pp. 592-93), quotes Leurenius and Monacelli as holding this opinion; cf. Coronata, *op. cit.,* I, 539, footnote 1; Augustine, *Commentary,* II, 496.

[10] Cf. canons 2405-2406; Sipos, *Juris Canonici,* p. 289.

[11] Cf. footnote 8 supra.

[12] Cf. Coronata, *loc. cit.;* Augustine, *loc. cit.*

CHAPTER XIV

Quasi-vacant Sees

The present Code has made a wholesome change in the previous discipline with respect to the nature, causes and effects of quasi-vacancy. According to former practice based on the decree of Pope Boniface VIII, quasi-vacancy strictly speaking was realized only when a bishop was held captive by pagans and schismatics and was unable to communicate with his diocese. In this instance the jurisdiction of the bishop was regarded as suspended. This carried with it the result that the bishop was unable to govern his see through his vicar-general, for the latter's jurisdiction was suspended with that of the bishop. So also was the bishop unable to delegate anyone to assume the governance in his name. The law provided, therefore, that the administration of the diocese pass into the hands of the Cathedral Chapter and be retained by them until the Holy See made other arrangements.[1]

According to the present law quasi-vacancy *(sedes episcopalis impedita)* may result from any one of several causes, physical and canonical. The effects which follow from physical impediments differ from those of the canonical. Each, therefore, shall receive distinct consideration.

Art. 1. *Physical Impediments*

Canon 429 § 1 prescribes that when a bishop, through captivity, relegation, exile, inability or incapacity, is hindered from discharging the functions of his office to such an extent that he is unable to communicate, even by letter, with his diocese, the governance of the see shall devolve upon specified individuals. Since the law in no way modifies these causes with circumscriptions they are to be understood as encompassing all possible cases. Hence, captivity or imprisonment of the bishop may result from the action of pagans, heretics,

[1] Cf. Historical Synopsis, pp. 27-28, 41-43.

or schismatics or one's own civil government, or of a foreign power, or even of fellow citizens. Relegation signifies confinement to a given place outside the diocese, while exile refers to expulsion from one's own country. Since quasi-vacancy becomes a reality only when the bishop is unable to communicate, even by letter, with his diocese, the fourth cause—inability, or incapacity—may be identified with mental affliction which would render the bishop unable to perform an human act.[2]

When a bishop is thus hindered from administering his diocese and unable even by letter to communicate with the people of his see, the governance of the diocese rests with the vicar-general or another priest delegated by the bishop, unless the Holy See has already made other provisions.[3]

The phrase *nisi Sancta Sedes aliter providerit,* found in canon 429 § 1, undoubtedly has reference to an Apostolic Administrator, for, according to canon 312, the Holy See is wont to make such appointments when grave and special circumstances arise. The bishop may even for a grave cause appoint several delegates, not to govern the diocese together, but to succeed one another if circumstances demand it.[4] Hence, if one would die or be imprisoned, the other would take his place.

It may be opportune to observe here before proceeding with complimentary legislation, the special character of the power of the vicar-general during the time he administers a quasi-vacant see. According to canon 455 § 3, the vicar-general, during quasi-vacancy of see, does not need a special mandate to appoint parochial vicars, to confirm the election or accept the presentation to a vacant parish and grant the elected or presented priest the canonical institution as pastor, and finally to confer parishes of free collation.[5]

[2] Cf. Wernz-Vidal, *Jus Canonicum,* II, n. 705 (p. 756); Coronata, *Institutiones Juris Canonici,* I, 528; Chelodi, *Jus De Personis,* p. 358.

[3] Canon 429 § 1.

[4] Canon 429 § 2.

[5] Coronata, *op. cit.,* I, 554, footnote 9; Augustine, *Commentary,* II, 525.

These rights are enjoyed by the Administrator during quasi-vacancy and vacancy of see, who is permitted, however, to confer parishes of free collation only after one year has elapsed from the time of vacancy.[6]

When the vicar-general administers a quasi-vacant see, he may, according to a convincing opinion of canonists, confer parishes of free collation even within the first year of quasi-vacancy, nor is there any necessity that he wait a year before exercising his power as is incumbent upon the Administrator.[7]

The Code makes further provision for the administration of quasi-vacant sees. It has already been stated that the quasi-vacant see is governed by the Apostolic Administrator if one be appointed, otherwise by the vicar-general or the delegate of the bishop. It may happen that no Apostolic Administrator was appointed and that the bishop had left the diocese without a vicar-general or his delegates. On the other hand, these administrators may themselves become hindered from exercising their power because of some physical impediment. Under these circumstances the law prescribes that the Board of Diocesan Consultors shall appoint an Administrator, who shall assume the governance of the see with the powers of the Administrator appointed during vacancy.[8]

The appointment of the Administrator must be performed in accordance with the prescriptions of canon 433 § 2, where a true canonical election is demanded.[9]

In all cases of quasi-vacancy caused by a physical impediment, the one who assumes the governance of the see, whether he be the vicar-general, the delegate of the bishop, or the

[6] Canon 455, § 2.

[7] "Ob erst, wenn die Behinderung ein Jahr lang gedauert hat? Nach dem Wortlaut des can. 455 § 2 und 3 müsste man das annehman. Jedoch der Grundsatz des can. 436, dass sede vacante nihil innovetur, und die Ausnahme davon, die bisher nach Jahresfrist oder nach längerer Dauer der Stuklerledigung auf Grund ausserordentlicher päpstlicher Vollmachten entrat, in Zukunft aber von Gesetzes wegen eintreten soll, kommet bei behindertem Stuhl nicht in Betracht."—Stutz, *Der Greist des Codex Juris Canonici*, p. 311, footnote 5; Cf. Sipos, *Juris Canonici*, p. 285.

[8] Canon 429 § 3.

[9] De Meester, *Compendium*, II, n. 784 (p. 227).

Administrator elected by the Board of Diocesan Consultors, is strictly obliged to inform the Holy See (Sacred Consistorial Congregation) as soon as possible of the state of affairs and of his having taken over the governance of the see.[10]

The text of canon 429 § 3 [11] does not expressly state that the governance of the quasi-vacant see passes to the Board of Diocesan Consultors, but rather prescribed that the Board shall elect an Administrator who shall assume the duty of governing the diocese. The canon omits also to specify the time within which the election must be performed. This appears to be an implication that the Board of Consultors is obliged to do so as soon as possible. Coronata [12] regards the silence of the law in these matters as indicative of the intention of the legislator that the governance of a quasi-vacant see does not pass into the hands of the Board. This opinion, however, is contrary to the common interpretation which canonists [13] place upon this canon. According to the latter opinion, the governance of the see devolves upon the Board of Consultors as soon as the circumstances described in canon 429 § 3 become a reality, and the Board is then obliged to elect the Administrator. The second opinion seems to be in keeping more with the intention of the legislator, for the general tenure of canon 429 clearly demonstrates the desire of the Church that a diocese, when quasi-vacant, should not be left without governing authority, even though the interval be brief.

The present Code does not take into account a circumstance which would place a diocese in a state very much akin to quasi-vacancy. Such circumstances would be present in case a bishop is detained in remote regions, e.g., on a vacation,

[10] Canon 429 § 4.

[11] "His deficientibus, vel, uti supra dictum est, impeditis, capitulum ecclesiae cathedralis suum Vicarium constituat, qui regimen assumat cum potestate Vicarii Capitularis."

[12] *Institutiones,* I, 529.

[13] Wernz-Vidal, *Jus Canonicum,* II, n. 705, (p. 756); Vermeersch-Creusen, *Epitome,* I, n. 477 (p. 304); Chelodi, *Jus De Personis,* n. 216 (p. 358); Cappello, *Summa Juris Canonici,* I, n. 399 (p. 410); Ayrinhac, *Constitutiones of the Church,* p. 269.

visit *ad limina*, etc., and the vicar-general, in the meantime, either dies or becomes physically or canonically hindered from fulfilling the duties of his office. If the bishop would provide a new vicar-general, there would, of course, be no difficulty. But in case the bishop were unable to appoint a vicar-general, or a delegate to govern the see, some provision would then have to be made. Vermeersch-Creusen [14] is of the opinion that since this case is not expressly mentioned in the Code, the Board of Diocesan Consultors is not permitted to assume the governance of the see, and the only measure remaining is that the matter be placed before the Holy See. Other canonists,[15] however, who give this problem consideration apply the prescriptions of canon 429, and hold that in such instances the Board of Diocesan Consultors must inform the Holy See and the bishop of the situation immediately, and until provisions are forthcoming, shall assume the governance of the diocese. Former practice in this regard offers little assistance to commentators on the present law, for the Holy See has never been called upon to decide the question, and canonists in the past have taken both sides of the issue.[16]

In practice it appears that the second opinion may safely be followed until the Holy See decides to the contrary, for the application of canon 429 to such circumstances seems entirely justifiable on the strength of canon 20, which states that if there is no definite rule of law, neither in general nor in the particular law, concerning some affair, a norm of action may be taken from laws given in similar cases, and from the general principles of law applied with the mildness proper to Canon Law.

14 *Op. cit.*, I, n. 477, (p. 304).

15 Wernz-Vidal, *op. cit.*, n. 706, footnote 7 (p. 757); Coronata, *op. cit.*, I, 529; Chelodi, *op. cit.*, n. 216, footnote 1, (p. 358); cf. Blat, *Commentarium*, II, 399-400.

16 Cf. Historical Conspectus, p. 42.

Art. 2. *Canonical Impediments*

Quasi-vacancy has been considered thus far from the viewpoint of physical causes which render it impossible for the bishop to discharge the functions of his office. In all of physical impediments cases, it has been observed, the bishop retains his jurisdiction and the right to exercise it. This is clearly seen in the fact that he can always delegate his power to others. Canon 429 § 5, however, considers quasi-vacancy from the aspect of canonical impediments. In this case the nature and effect of quasi-vacancy differs greatly from quasi-vacancy which is due to physical impediments.

A canonical penalty hinders a bishop from discharging the functions of his office insofar as it consists in an ecclesiastical penalty which suspends his jurisdiction. A concomitant result of the suspension of the jurisdiction of the bishop is that the jurisdiction of the vicar-general is also suspended.[17]

Hence, when a bishop incurs the penalty of excommunication, interdict or suspension, neither he, nor the vicar-general may exercise their powers of jurisdiction, nor may they delegate others to act in their name.[18]

Thus, if a bishop would consecrate another bishop without special permission from the Apostolic See, the penalty of suspension would be incurred *ipso jure* and reserved to the Holy See.[19]

In all cases of quasi-vacancy arising from a canonical impediment the governance of the see does not pass to any individual, nor is the bishop, in view of his suspended jurisdiction, able to delegate others for this purpose. Neither does the governance of the diocese devolve upon the Board of Consultors. The Code prescribes only one course of action to be taken in such instances, and that is that the metropolitan, or if he be himself under canonical penalty, the senior suffragan bishop, make swift recurrence to the Holy See. The supreme authority of the Church will then take the difficulty into con-

[17] Canon 371.

[18] Cf. Canons 2259 § 2; 2261; 2265; 2275; 2283; 2284.

[19] Canon 2370; cf. Cocchi, *Commentarium*, V, 348-49.

sideration and make proper provisions.[20] The senior suffragan bishop referred to in this canon is, according to the unanimous teaching of canonists,[21] the one who was first promoted to one of the suffragan sees.[22] In the case of bishops who are not subject to any metropolitan, or of abbots or prelates *nullius* and of archbishops who are without suffragans, the report to the Holy See should be made by the metropolitan who has been chosen by the respective prelate once for all as the one at whose provincial council they must assist.[23] The abbey *nullius* situated at Belmont, North Carolina, provides the one possible occasion for this latter prescription of canon 429 § 5 to be applied in this country. Although canon 327 § 2 specifies that all quasi-vacant abbeys and prelatures *nullius* are governed by the norms of canon 429, an analysis of the common law and the particular constitutions concerned will disclose that this canon has reference only to quasi-vacancy arising from a canonical impediment with respect to the Belmont Abbey *nullius* in North Carolina. The constitutions of the American-Cassinese Benedictine Congregation—which congregation is in possession of the abbey *nullius*—provide that "when the Abbot is absent . . . let the Prior govern the monastery with prudence and moderation, and not dare to change what the Abbot has appointed. When the Prior is hindered or absent the Subprior takes his place." [24] This constitutional provision covers the situation of quasi-vacancy arising from physical impediments affecting the abbot Ordinary, and serves as the norm for action even though canon 327 § 2 does not explicitly recognize particular constitutions in this regard. This appears beyond question from the very fact that the Code recognizes the constitutions of Orders which have charge of abbeys and prelatures *nullius* with re-

[20] Canon 429 § 5.

[21] Augustine *(Commentary* II, 483) is the only canonist who considers the senior suffragan Bishop to be the one whose diocese was first erected.

[22] Cf. Canons 284, 292.

[23] Canon 429 § 5, 285.

[24] *Declarationes in Regulam S.P.N. Benedicti et Statuta Congregationis Americano-Cassinensis,* caput LXV, p. 38.

spect to vacancy;[25] and since the jurisdiction of the abbot Ordinary is not suspended when he is physically hindered from exercising his power, there appears no reason why the constitutions should not be followed when they amply provide for the circumstances. But in the case of quasi-vacancy resulting from a canonical impediment, the jurisdiction of the Ordinary is suspended, and consequently the prescriptions of canon 429 must be followed. If this should occur, the metropolitan who has been chosen once for all as the one at whose provincial council the abbot must assist is obliged to report the matter to the Holy See as soon as possible.[26] The Code does not provide for an instance in which this metropolitan is not at hand to make the report. Blat [27] is of the opinion that in such circumstances, the senior suffragan bishop, who is senior according to canons 284 and 292, must then make the report; and this opinion he bases on the strength of canon 20. The opinion appears valid and in accord with the spirit of the law in this regard.

In all cases of quasi-vacancy arising from a canonical impediment, therefore, the regular affairs of the episcopal curia cease until the Holy See has made provision. Little delay would result in this regard, however, since the means of communication in modern times is very efficient, thereby enabling the situation to be remedied promptly. It may safely be said, however, in conclusion to this discussion on canonical impediments, that circumstances of this nature will scarcely be confronted in practice. In the first place, if the bishop is censured by a declaratory or condemnatory sentence, this can be inflicted only by the Holy See, for, according to canons 2227 and 1557, the Roman pontiff alone is competent to inflict punishments upon bishops. Should the Holy See find such action necessary, it might rightly be expected that provision for the administration of the see would accompany the sentence. If,

[25] Cf. Canon 327 § 1, 432 § 3; Wernz-Vidal, *Jus Canonicum,* II, n. 570, (p. 603); Vermeersch-Creusen, *Epitome,* I, n. 395, (p. 265).

[26] Canons 429 § 5, 327 § 2.

[27] *Commentarium,* II, 401.

on the other hand, a bishop would commit an act to which the law attaches a penalty *ipso facto* incurred, there would scarcely be an instance where this would efficaciously impede a bishop from exercising his jurisdiction. This will readily be seen if one gives consideration to canons 2264, 2232, 2227 § 2, 349 § 1, no. 1 and 239 § 1, n. 2.[28]

[28] Cf. Coronata, *op. cit.*, 528; Wernz-Vidal, *op. cit.*, n. 706, (p. 757).

BIBLIOGRAPHY

1. Source

Acta Apostolicae Sedis, Rome, 1909.

Acta Sanctae Sedis, 41 vols., Rome, 1865-1908.

Acta et Decreta Sacrorum Conciliorum recentiorum; Collectio Lacensis, 7 vols., Friburgi, Brisgoviae, 1870-1890.

Canones et Decreta Sacrosancti Oecomenici Tridentini, Editio Novissima ad Fidem Oprimorum Exemplarium castigatae Impressa, 19 ed., Taurini, 1913.

Codex Juris Canonici Pii X Pontificis Maximi jussu digestus Benedicti Papae XV auctoritate promulgatus, Romae, 1917.

Codicis Juris Canonicis Fontes, cura Emi. Petri Card. Gasparri editi, 5 vols., Romae, 1923-1930.

Collectanea S. Congregationis de Propaganda Fide, 2 vols., Romae, 1907.

Concilii Plenarii Baltimorensis I (1852), *Acta et Decreta,* Baltimorae, 1853.

Concilii Plenarii Baltimorensis II (1866), *Acta et Decreta,* Baltimorae, 1880.

Concilii Plenarii Baltimorensis III (1884), *Acta et Decreta,* Baltimorae, 1886.

Concilii Provincialis Baltimorensis (1869), *Acta et Decreta,* Baltimorae, 1870.

Corpus Juris Canonici, Editio Lipsiensis II (Richter-Friedberg), 2 vols., Lipsiae, 1922.

Declarationes in Regulam S.P.N. Benedicti et Statuta Congregationis Americano-Cassinensis, Typis Mandata Jussu Reverendissimi et Amplissimi Domini Domini Ernesti Helmstetter, O.S.B., Abbatis, Praesidis Congregationis, Atchison, 1925.

Decreta Authentica Congregationis Sacrorum Rituum ex actis ejusdem collecta ejusque auctoritate promulgata sub auspiciis SS. D.N. Leonis XIII, 6 vols., Rome, 1898-1912.

Decretales Liber Sextus decretalium D. Bonifacii Papae VIII suae integritati una cum Clementinis extravagantibus, eorumque glossis restitutus. Cum privilegio Gregorii XIII, Romae, 1582.

Hardouin, Jean, *Acta Conciliorum et Epistolae Decretales ac Constitutiones Summorum Pontificum,* 12 vols., Parisiis, 1715.

Mansi, Joannes Dominicus, *Sacrorum Conciliorum Nova et Amplissima Collectio,* 53 vols., Paris-Arnhem-Leipzig, 1901-1927.

Thesaurus Resolutionum Sacrae Congregationis Concilii, 167 vols., Romae, 1718-1908.

2. Works of Reference

Alteserra, Antonius Dadinus, *Opera Omnia,* 10 vols., Neapolitana, 1777.

Alzog, *Universal Church History,* 3 vols., Cincinnati, 1878.

Augustine, Charles [Bachofen], O.S.B., *A Commentary on the New Code of Canon Law,* 8 vols., St. Louis, 1921-1925.

———————, *The Canonical and Civil Status of Catholic Parishes in the United States,* St. Louis, 1926.

———————, *Rights and Duties of Ordinaries according to the Code and Apostolic Faculties,* St. Louis, 1924.

———————, *The Pastor according to the New Code of Canon Law,* St. Louis, 1924.

Ayrinhac, H. A., *Constitution of the Church in the New Code of Canon Law,* New York, 1925.

———————, *General Legislation in the New Code of Canon Law,* New York, 1923.

Baart, Peter, *Legal Formulary,* New York, 1898.

Badii, Caesar, *Institutiones Juris Canonici,* 3 ed., 2 vols., Florence, 1921-1922.

Barbosa, Agostino, *Pastoralis Solicitudinis, seu, De Officio et Potestate Episcopi,* 2 vols., Lugduni, 1656.

———————, *Tractatus de Canonicis et Dignitatibus,* Lugduni, 1679.

———————, *De Jure Ecclesiastico,* 2 vols., Lugduni, 1650.

Bargilliat, M., *Praelectiones Juris Canonici,* 37 ed., 2 vols., Parisiis, 1923.

Baronius, Caesar, *Annales Ecclesiastici, denuo exet ad nostra usque tempora perducti ab Augustino Theiner,* 37 vols., Barri-Ducis, 1864-1883.

Bastnagel, C., *The Appointment of Parochial Adjutants and Assistants,* Washington, 1930.

Benedict XIV, *De Synodo Dioecesana,* 2 vols., Parma, 1764.

Berardi, Carolus Sebastianus, *Gratiani Canones Genuini ab Apocryphis Discreti, Corrupti ad emendatiorum Codicum Fidem, Difficiliores Commoda interpretatione illustrati,* 3 vols in 4, Venetiis, 1777.

Bernardi de Battone, *Gregorius IX, Decretales cum glossa ordinaria,* (Speyer, Peter Drach, 1486) (Hain 8019).

Bevilacqua, Americo, *De Episcopi seu Ordinarii ex novo Codice Canonico Juribus ac Obligationibus,* Romae, 1921.

Bingham, J., *Antiquities of the Christian Church,* 6 vols., London, 1856.

Bizzarri, Andreas, *Collectanea in usum Secretariae Sacrae Congregationis Episcoporum et Regularium edita,* Romae, 1885.

Blat, Albertus, O. P., *Commentarium Textus Codicis Juris Canonici,* 6 vols., Romae, 1921-1927; liber II, *De Personis,* Romae, 1919.

Bonal, A., *Institutiones Canonici ad usum Seminariorum,* 4 ed., 2 vols., Paris, 1898.

Borkowski, Aurelius, *De Confraternitatibus Ecclesiasticis,* Washington, 1918.

Bouix, D., *Tractatus de Capitulis,* Parisiis, 1882.

Brueck, Heinrich, *History of the Catholic Church,* 2 vols., New York, 1885.

Cappello, Felix, *Summa Juris Canonici in usum scholarum concinnata,* 2 vols., Romae, 1928-1930.

———————, *Tractatus Canonico-Moralis de Censuris juxta Codicem Juris Canonici,* 2 ed., Taurinorum Augustae, 1925.

Castillo, Cayo, *Disertacion Historico-Canonica Sobre La Potestad Del Cabildo en Sede Vacante o Impedida Del Vicario Capitular,* Washington, 1918.

Catholic Encyclopedia, 15 vols., New York, 1907-1912.

Chelodi, Joannes, *Jus de Personis,* 2 ed., Tridenti, 1927.

Cicognani, Hamletus, *Jus Canonicum Primo Studii Anno in Usum Auditorum Excerpta,* 2 vols., Romae, 1925.

Coady, John, *The Appointment of Pastors,* Washington, 1929.

Coronata, Matthaeus Conte A., *Institutiones Juris Canonici ad Usum Utrinsque Cleri et Scholarum,* Taurini, 1928.

————————, *De Locis et Temporibus Sacris,* Augustae Taurinorum, 1922.

Cocchi, Guidus, *Commentarium in Codicem Juris Canonici ad usum Scholarum,* 3 ed., 8 vols., Taurinorum Augustae, 1925-1927; lib. II, *De Personis,* 1922.

D'Annibale, Josephus, *Summula Theologiae Moralis,* 5 ed., 3 vols., Romae, 1908.

De Angelis, Philippus, *Praelectiones Juris Canonici,* 6 vols., Romae, 1878.

De Labriolle, Pierre, *History and Literature of Christianity, from Tertullian to Boethius,* translated from the French by Herbert Wilson, New York, 1925.

De Meester, A., *Juris Canonici et Juris Canonico-Civilis Compendium,* 3 vols., Brugis, 1921-1928.

Dictionary of Christian Antiquities, William Smith and Samuel Cheetham, 2 vols., Harford, 1880.

Du Cange, Carolus Du Fresne, *Glossarium ad Scriptores Mediae et Infimae Latinitatis,* 6 vols., Parisiis, 1734.

Fagnanus, Prosperi, *Commentaria in Quinque Libros Decretalium,* 4 vols., Venetiis, 1696.

Fanfani, Ludovicus, O.P., *De Jure Religiosorum ad Norman Codicis Juris Canonici,* 2 ed., Taurini-Romae, 1925.

Ferraris, Lucius, *Prompta Bibliotheca Canonica, Juridica, Moralis, Theologica, necnon Ascetica, Polemica, Rubricistica, Historica,* 9 vols., Romae, 1885-1899.

Ferreres, J., *Institutiones Canonicae,* 2 ed., 2 vols., Barcinone, 1920.

Funk, F. X., *Lehrbuch der Kirchengeschichte,* 2 vols., increased and revised by Karl Bihlmeyer, Paderborn, 1921.

Garcia, Nicolaus, *De Beneficiis Ecclesiasticis,* 2 vols., Venetiis, 1618.

Gardellini, Aloysius, *Decreta Authentica Congregationis Sacrorum Rituum,* 7 vols., Romae, 1824-1826.

Giraldi, Ubanldo, *Expositio Juris Pontificii,* 3 vols., Romae, 1829.

Golden, Henry, *Parochial Beneficis in the New Code,* Washington, 1925.

Gottlob, Theodor, *Der abendländische Chorepiskopat,* Bonn, 1928.

Guilday, Peter, *The Life and Times of John Carroll,* 2 vols., New York, 1922.

————————, *A History of the Councils of Baltimore (1791-1884),* New York, 1932.

Gutierrez, Joannes, *Canonicarum Questionum,* 3 vols., Lugduni, 1661.

Hefele, Carl Joseph von, *Conciliengeschichte,* 2 ed., 9 vols., Freiburg, 1873-1890.

Hermes, Henricus Josephus, *Dissertatio Historico-Canonica De Capitulo Sede Vacante Vel Impedita et De Vicario Capitulari,* Lovanii, 1873.

Hostiensis, (Henricus, Card. de Segusio), *Summa Aurea,* Lugduni, 1568.

Hinschius, P., *System des Katholischen Kirchenrechts*, 4 vols., Berlin, 1869-1888.

Joannes de Imola, *In Clementinas, Hrsg. v. Franciscus Breviares. Venedig. Johannes de Colonia et Hohann. Manthen* VI *Kal. Maii.* 1480. (Hain, 9144.)

Kearney, Raymond, *The Principles of Delegation*, Washington, 1929.

Klekotka, Peter, *Diocesan Consultors*, Washington, 1920.

Leurenius, Petrus, *Forum Beneficiale sive Questiones et Responsa canonica Materiam de Beneficiis Universam*, 4 vols., Venetiis, 1742.

Maroto, Philippo, *Institutiones Juris Canonici*, 3 ed., 2 vols., Romae, 1921.

Martin, Conrad, *Omnium Concilii Vaticani quae de doctrinam et disciplinam pertinent documentorum collectio*, Paderbornae, 1873.

Melo, Antonius, *De Exemptione Regularium*, Washingtonii, 1921.

Michiels, Gommarus, *Normae Generales Juris Canonici Commentarius Libri I Codicis Juris Canonici*, 2 vols., Lublin, 1929.

Migne, Jacques Paul, *Patrologiae Cursus Completus—Series Graeca*, (MPG), 161 vols., Parisiis, 1858-1864.

——————, *Patrologiae Cursus Completus Series Latina* (MPL), 221 vols., Parisiis, 1844-1855.

Monacelli, Franciscus, *Formularium Legale Practicum fori Ecclesiasticum*, 4 vols., Venetiis, 1706.

Monumenta Germaniae Historica, Legum Sectio, 2, *Capitularia Regum Francorum*. Tom. I, ed. Ed. A. Boretius, Hannoverae, 1883.

Noval, Josephus, *De Judiciis*, Augustae Taurinorum, 1920.

Oesterle, Gerardus, *Praelectiones Juris Canonici*, tom, I, Romae, 1931.

Ojetti, B., *Commentarium, In Codicem Juris Canonici*, 2 vols., Romae, 1927-1930.

Pallottini, Salvator, *Collectio Omnium Conclusionum et Resolutionum quae in causis propositis apud S. Cong. Cardinalium S. Concilii Tridentini Interpretum prodierunt ab anno 1564 ad annum 1860*, 17 vols., Romae, 1868-1893.

Panormitanus Abbas, (Tudeschis, Nicolaus de), *Super Libros Decretalium*, Venice, Nicolaus Jenson, 1477, vol., I, 2 parts. (Hain, 12310.)

Pellegrinus, Carolus, *Praxis Vicariorum*, Venetiis, 1706.

Phillips, Georg, *Kirchenrecht*, 7 vols., Regensburg, 1885-1889.

Pignatelli, J., *Consultationes Canonicae*, 11 vols., Coloniae Allobrogum, 1700.

Pirhing, Enric, *Jus Canonicum in V Libros Decretalium Distributum*, 2 vols., Dillingae, 1674.

Prümmer, Dominicus M., *Manuale Juris Canonici In Usum Scholarum*, 4 et 5 ed., Friburgi Brisgoviae, 1927.

Quaranta, Stephanus, *Summa Bullarii earumque summorum pontificium*, Venetiis, 1622.

Raus, P., *Institutiones Canonicae in Forma Compendii Juxta Methodum Faciliorem, Novi Codicis Juris*, Parisiis, 1923.

Rebuff, Petrus, (Joannes Nicolaus Gimont), *Praxis Beneficiorum*, Venetiis, 1554.

Reiffenstuel, A., *Jus Canonicum Universum*, 4 vols., Romae, 1833.

Richter, A. L., *Canones et Decreta Concilii Tridentini*, Lipsiae, 1853.

Roberti, Franciscus, *De Processibus,* 2 vols., Romae, 1926.

Roberts, A., & Donaldson, J., *Translation of the writings of the Fathers down to* A.D. 325, *American ed.* by A. C. Coxe, 10 vols., New York, 1903.

Ryder, Raymond, *Simony,* Washington, 1931.

Sägmüller, Johannes Baptist, *Lehrbuch des katholischen Kirchenrechts,* 4 ed., Freiburg im Breisgau, 1925-1930.

Scarfantoni, Joannes, *Animadversiones ad lucubrationes canonicales,* 2 vols., Lucae, 1723.

Schäfer, P. Timotheus, *De Religiosis ad Norman Codicis Juris Canonici,* Münster, 1927.

Schmalzgrueber, F., *Jus Ecclesiasticum Universum,* 12 vols., Romae, 1843-1845.

Schmier, Franciscus, *Jurisprudentia canonico-civilis, seu, Jus Canonicum Universum,* 2 vols., Venetiis, 1754.

Schneider, Philipp, *Die Entwicklung der Bischöflichen Domkapitel bis zum vierzehnten Jahrhundert,* Mainz, 1882.

Shea, John, *History of the Catholic Church in the United States,* 4 vols., New York, 1886-1892.

——————, *The Life and Times of Archbishop Carroll,* New York, 1888.

Sipos, Stephanus, *Enchiridion Juris Canonici,* Pécs, 1926.

Smith, S.B., *Elements of Ecclesiastical Law,* New York, 1877.

Smith, S., *Notes on The Second Plenary Council of Baltimore,* New York, 1874.

Soglia, Joannes, *Institutiones Juris Publici et Privati Ecclesiastici ad usum Seminarium, opera et studio S. M. Vecchiotti,* 2 vols., Boscocici, 1842.

Stebbing, George, *The Story of the Catholic Church,* St. Louis, 1924.

Stutz, Ulrich, *Der Geist des Codex juris canonici,* Stuttgart, 1918.

Theiner, Aug., *Histoire des Institutions d'Education Ecclesiastique,* Translated from the German by Jean Cohen, 2 vols., Paris, 1841.

Thomassinus, L., *Nova et Vetus Disciplina Ecclesiae,* 10 vols., Moguntiaci, 1787.

Tixeront, J., *A Handbook of Patrology,* authorized translation based upon the fourth French Edition, 2 ed., St. Louis, 1923.

Van-Espen, Z., *Jus Ecclesiasticum Universum,* 4 vols., Louvain, 1753.

Van Hove, *De Legibus Ecclesiasticis,* Romae, 1930.

Vecchiotti, S. M., *Institutiones Canonicae ad usum Seminariorum accomadatae,* 16 ed., Augustae Taurinorum, 1875.

Vermeersch, A., *De Religiosis Institutis et Personis Tractatus Canonico-moralis,* 2 vols., Brugi, 1909.

Vermeersch, A.—Creusen, J., *Epitome Juris Canonici Cum Commentariis ad Scholas et ad Usum Privatum,* 3 vols.; I-II, 4 ed.; III, 3 ed., Romae, 1928-1930.

Villien, A., Magnin, E., *Dictionnaire de Droit Canonique,* Paris, 1924.

Vromant, G., *De Bonis Ecclesiae Temporalibus,* Louvain, 1927.

Walter, Ferdinand, *Lehrbuch des Kirchenrechts,* 11 ed., Bonn, 1854.

Waterworth, J., *The Canons and Decrees of the Sacred and Oecumenical Council of Trent,* London, 1848.

Wernz, Franciscus, *Jus Decretalium,* vol. II, Romae, 1906.
Wernz, F. X.—Vidal, P., *Jus Canonicum ad Codicis norman exactum,* 3 vols., Romae, 1925-1928.
Woywod, S., *A Practical Commentary on the Code of Canon Law,* 2 vols., New York, 1925.
———, *The New Canon Law, A Commentary and Summary of the New Code of Canon Law,* New York, 1929.
Zallwein, Gregorius, *Principia Juris Ecclesiasticae,* 4 vols., Augustae, 1763.
Zaplotnik, John, *De Vicariis Foraneis,* Washington, 1927.

Periodicals

American Ecclesiastical Review, The, Philadelphia, 1889.
Analecta Ecclesiastica, Romae, 1893-1911.
Apollinaris, Romae, 1928-
Archiv für katholisches Kirchenrecht, Mainz, 1862-
Homiletic and Pastoral Review, The, New York, 1900-
Il Monitore Ecclesiastico, Romae, 1888-
Irish Ecclesiastical Record, The, Dublin, 1864-
Jus Pontificium, Romae, 1921-
Nouvelle Revue Theoligique, Tournai, 1869-
Periodica de re canonica et morali utili praesertim Religiosis et Missionariis, Brugis, 1905-

UNIVERSITAS CATHOLICA AMERICAE

WASHINGTON, D. C.

FACULTAS JURIS CANONICI

1932

No. 81

DEUS LUX MEA

TITULI

QUOS

AD DOCTORATUS GRADUM

IN

JURE CANONICO

Apud Universitatem Catholicam Americae

CONSEQUENDUM

PUBLICE PROPUGNABIT

LEO ARNOLDUS JAEGER

SACERDOS ARCHIDIOECESIS DUBUQUENSIS

JURIS CANONICI LICENTIATUS

HORA XI A. M. DIE XX MAII MCMXXXII

TITULI

In Jure Canonico

I. De Dissertatione.
II. De Historia Juris Canonici.
III. Canones 1-7 De Ambitus Codicis.
IV. Canones 8-24 De Legibus Ecclesiasticis.
V. Canones 25-30 De Consuetudine.
VI. Canones 31-35 De Temporis Supputatione.
VII. Canones 36-62 De Rescriptis.
VIII. Canones 124-144 De Obligationibus Clericorum.
IX. Canones 160-178 De Electione.
X. Canones 423-428 De Consultoribus Dioecesanis.
XI. Canones 492-498 De Erectione et Suppresione Religionis, Provinciae, domus.
XII. Canones 499-517 De Superioribus et de Capitulis.
XIII. Canones 518-530 De Confessariis et Cappellanis.
XIV. Canones 531-537 De Bonis Temporalibus eorumque Administratione.
XV. Canones 539-541 De Postulatu.
XVI. Canones 542-552 De Requisitis us quis in Novitiatum Admittatur.
XVII. Canones 553-571 De Novitorum Institutione.
XVIII. Canones 572-586 De Professione Religiosa.
XIX. Canones 587-591 De Ratione Studiorum in Religionibus Clericalibus.
XX. Canones 592-612 De Obligationibus Religiosorum.
XXI. Canones 613-625 De Privilegiis Religiosorum.
XXII. Canones 1094-1103 De Forma Celebrationis Matrimonii.
XXIII. Canones 1104-1107 De Matrimonio Conscientiae.
XXIV. Canones 1108-1109 De Tempore et Loco Celebrationis Matrimonii.
XXV. Canones 1110-1117 De Matrimonii Effectibus.
XXVI. Canones 1406-1408 De Fidei Professione.
XXVII. Canones 1552-1556 De Notione Judicii et de Foro Competenti.
XXVIII. Canones 1569-1607 De Variis Tribunalium Gradibus et Speciebus.
XXIX. Canones 1608-1645 De Disciplina in Tribunalibus servanda.
XXX. Canones 1646-1666 De Partibus in Causa.
XXXI. Canones 1667-1705 De Actionibus et Exceptionibus.
XXXII. Canones 1706-1725 De Causae Introductione.
XXXIII. Canones 1726-1746 De Litis Contestatione, de Litis Instantia, et de Interrogationibus Partibus in Judicio Faciendis.
XXXIV. Canones 1747-1836 De Probationibus.
XXXV. Canones 1837-1857 De Causis Incidentibus.

XXXVI. Canones 1865-1877 De Processus Publicatione, de Conclusione in Causa, de Causae Discussione, et de Sententia.
XXXVII. Canones 2147-2161 De Modo Procedendi in Remotione Parochorum Inamovibilium et Amovibilium.
XXXVIII. Canones 2195-2198 De Natura Delicti ejusque Divisione.
XXXIX. Canones 2199-2211 De Imputabilitate Delicti, de Causis illam aggravantibus, vel minuentibus, et de Juridicis effectibus.
XL. Canones 2212-2213 De Conatu Delicti.
XLI. Cannoes 2214-2240 De Poenis in Genere.
XLII. Canones 2241-2305 De Poenis Medicinalibus seu de Censuris et De Poenis Vindicativis.

In Jure Romano

XLIII. The Sources of Roman Law.
XLIV. Personality.
XLV. Citizenship.
XLVI. Slavery.
XLVII. Patria Potestas.
XLVIII. Personae in Manu.
XLIX. Personae in Mancipio.
L. Ownership.
LI. Delictal Obligations.
LII. Contractual Obligations.
LIII. Contracts, Innominate Contracts, *Pacta vestita.*
LIV. The Modalities of Contracts.
LV. The Transmission and Extinction of Obligations.

In Jure Americano

LVI. The Title to Church Property.
LVII. Tax Exemption.
LVIII. Family Law.
LIX. Christian Burial.
LX. Religious Liberty.

Vidit Facultas:

Valentinus T. Schaaf, O.F.M., J.C.D., Vice-Decanus.

Ludovicus H. Motry, S.T.D., J.C.D., a Secretis.

Franciscus J. Lardone, S.T.D., J.U.D.

Johannes McDill Fox, A.B., LL.B.

Vidit Rector Magnificus Universitatis:

Jacobus Hugo Ryan, S.T.D., Ph.D., LL.D., Litt.D.

BIOGRAPHICAL NOTE

Leo A. Jaeger was born on August 12, 1903. He received his early education at St. Francis Academy and Xavier High School in Dyersville, Iowa. He attended Columbia Academy and College in Dubuque, and in 1924 received the degree of Bachelor of Arts from this institution. He prepared for the priesthood at St. Paul Seminary, St. Paul, Minnesota, and was ordained on June 2, 1928. During the next two years he was engaged in the service of his diocese in the capacity of parochial assistant. In the fall of 1930 he was sent by his archbishop to the Catholic University of America to pursue a graduate course of studies in the School of Canon Law.

CATHOLIC UNIVERSITY OF AMERICA

Canon Law Studies

1. Freriks, Rev. Celestine A., C.PP.S., J.C.D., Religious Congregations in Their External Relations, 121 pp., 1916.
2. Galliher, Rev. Daniel M., O.P., J.C.D., Canonical Elections, 117 pp., 1917.
3. Borkowski, Rev. Aurelius L., O.F.M., J.C.D., De Confraternitatibus Ecclesiasticis, 136 pp., 1918.
4. Castillo, Rev. Cayo, J.C.D., Disertacion Historico-canonica sobre la Potestad del Cabildo en Sede Vacante o Impedida del Vicario Capitular, 99 pp., 1919 (1918).
5. Kubelbeck, Rev. William J., S.T.B., J.C.D., The Sacred Penitentiaria and Its Relations to Faculties of Ordinaries and Priests, 129 pp., 1918.
6. Petrovits, Rev. Joseph J. C., S.T.D., J.C.D., The New Church Law on Matrimony, X-461 pp., 1919.
7. Hickey, Rev. John J., S.T.B., J.C.D., Irregularities and Simple Impediments in the New Code of Canon Law, 100 pp., 1920.
8. Klekotka, Rev. Peter J., S.T.B., J.C.D., Diocesan Concultors, 179 pp., 1920.
9. Wannenmacher, Rev. Francis, J.C.D., The Evidence in Ecclesiastical Procedure Affecting the Marriage Bond, 1920. (Not Printed.)
10. Golden, Rev. Henry Francis, J.C.D., Parochial Benefices in the New Code, IV-119 pp., 1921. (Printed 1925.)
11. Koudelka, Rev. Charles J., J.C.D., Pastors, Their Rights and Duties According to the New Code of Canon Law, 211 pp., 1921.
12. Melo, Rev. Antonius, O.F.M., J.C.D., De Exemptione Regularium, X-188 pp., 1921.
13. Schaaf, Rev. Valentine Theodore, O.F.M., S.T.B., J.C.D., The Cloister, X-180 pp., 1921.
14. Burke, Rev. Thomas Joseph, S.T.B., J.C.D., Competence in Ecclesiastical Tribunals, IV-117 pp., 1922.
15. Leech, Rev. George Leo, J.C.D., A Comparative Study of the Constitution "Apostolicæ Sedis" and the "Codex Juris Canonici," 179 pp., 1922.
16. Motry, Rev. Hubert Louis, S.T.D., J.C.D., Diocesan Faculties According to the Code of Canon Law, II-167 pp., 1922.
17. Murphy, Rev. George Lawrence, J.C.D., Delinquencies and Penalties in the Administration and Reception of the Sacraments, IV-121 pp., 1923.
18. O'Reilly, Rev. John Anthony, S.T.B., J.C.D., Ecclesiastical Sepulture in the New Code of Canon Law, II-129 pp., 1923.
19. Michalicka, Rev. Wenceslas Cyrill, O.S.B., J.C.D., Judicial Procedure in Dismissal of Clerical Exempt Religious, 107 pp., 1923.
20. Dargin, Rev. Edward Vincent, S.T.B., J.C.D., Reserved Cases According to the Code of Canon Law, IV-103 pp., 1924.

21. GODFREY, REV. JOHN A., S.T.B., J.C.D., The Right of Patronage According to the Code of Canon Law, 153 pp., 1924.
22. HAGEDORN, REV. FRANCIS EDWARD, J.C.D., General Legislation on Indulgences, II-154 pp., 1924.
23. KING, REV. JAMES IGNATIUS, J.C.D., The Administration of the Sacraments to Dying Non-Catholics, V-141 pp., 1924.
24. WINSLOW, REV. FRANCIS JOSEPH, A.F.M., J.C.D., Vicars and Prefects Apostolic, IV-149 pp., 1924.
25. CORREA, REV. JOSE SERVELION, S.T.L., J.C.D., La Potesdad Legislativa de la Iglesia Catolica, IV-127 pp., 1925.
26. DUGAN, REV. HENRY FRANCIS, A.M., J.C.D., The Judiciary Department of the Diocesan Curia, 87 pp., 1925.
27. KELLER, REV. CHARLES FREDERICK, S.T.B., J.C.D., Mass Stipends, 167 pp., 1925.
28. PASCHANG, REV. JOHN LINUS, J.C.D., The Sacramentals According to the Code of Canon Law, 129 pp., 1925.
29. PIONTEK, REV. CYRILLUS, O.F.M., S.T.B., J.C.D., De Indulto Exclaustrationis necnon Sæcularizationis, XIII-289 pp., 1929.
30. KEARNEY, REV. RICHARD JOSEPH, S.T.B., J.C.D., Sponsors at Baptism According to the Code of Canon Law, IV-127 pp., 1925.
31. BARTLETT, REV. CHESTER JOSEPH, A.M., LL.B., J.C.D., The Tenure of Parochial Property in the United States of America, V-108 pp., 1926.
32. KILKER, REV. ADRIAN JEROME, J.C.D., Extreme Unction, V-425 pp., 1926.
33. MCCORMICK, REV. ROBERT EMMET, J.C.D., Confessors of Religious, VIII-266 pp., 1926.
34. MILLER, REV. NEWTON THOMAS, J.C.D., Founded Masses According to the Code of Canon Law, VII-93 pp., 1926.
35. ROELKER, REV. EDWARD G., S.T.D., J.C.D., Principles of Privilege According to the Code of Canon Law, XI-166 pp., 1926.
36. BAKALARCZYK, REV. RICHARDUS, M.I.C., J.U.D., De Novitiatu, VIII-208 pp., 1927.
37. PIZZUTI, REV. LAWRENCE, O.F.M., J.U.L., De Parochis Religiosis, 1929.
38. BLILEY, REV. NICHOLAS MARTIN, O.S.B., J.C.D., Altars According to the Code of Canon Law, XIX-132 pp., 1927.
39. BROWN, BRENDAN FRANCIS, A.B., LL.M., J.U.D., The Canonical Juristic Personality with Special Reference to Its Status in the United States of America, V-212 pp, 1927.
40. CAVANAUGH, REV. WILLIAM THOMAS, C.P., J.U.D., The Reservation of the Blessed Sacrament, VIII-101 pp., 1927.
41. DOHENY, REV. WILLIAM J., C.S.C., A.B., J.U.D., Church Property; Modes of Acquisition, X-118 pp., 1927.
42. FELDHAUS, REV. ALOYSIUS H., C.PP.S., J.C.D., Oratories, IX-141 pp., 1927.
43. KELLY, REV. JAMES PATRICK, A.B., J.C.D., The Jurisdiction of the Simple Confessor, X-208 pp., 1927.
44. NEUBERGER, REV. NICHOLAS J., J.C.D., Canon 6, or the Relation of the Codex Juris Canonici to the Preceding Legislation, V-95 pp., 1927.
45. O'KEEFFE, REV. GERALD MICHAEL, J.C.D., Matrimonial Dispensations, Powers of Bishops, Priests, and Confessors, VIII-232 pp., 1927.

46. QUIGLEY, REV. JOSEPH, A.M., A.B., J.C.D., Condemned Societies, 139 pp., 1927.
47. ZAPLOTNIK, REV. IOANNES LEO, J.C.D., De Vicariis Foraneis, X-142, 1927.
48. DUSKIE, REV. JOHN ALOYSIUS, A.B., J.C.D., The Canonical Status of the Orientals in the United States, VIII-196 pp., 1928.
49. HYLAND, REV. FRANCIS EDWARD, J.C.D., Excommunication, Its Nature, Historical Development and Effects, VIII-181 pp., 1928.
50. REINMANN, REV. GERALD JOSEPH, O.M.C., J.C.D., The Third Order Secular of Saint Francis, 201 pp., 1928.
51. SCHENK, REV. FRANCIS J., J.C.D., The Matrimonial Impediments of Mixed Religion and Disparity of Cult, XVI-318 pp., 1929.
52. COADY, REV. JOHN JOSEPH, S.T.D., J.U.D., A.M., The Appointment of Pastors, VIII-150 pp., 1929.
53. KAY, REV. THOMAS HENRY, J.C.D., Competence in Matrimonial Procedure, VIII-164 pp., 1929.
54. TURNER, REV. SIDNEY JOSEPH, C.P., J.U.D., The Vow of Poverty, XLIX-217 pp., 1929.
55. KEARNEY, REV. RAYMOND A., A.B., S.T.D., J.C.D., The Principles of Delegation, VII-149 pp., 1929.
56. CONRAN, REV. EDWARD JAMES, A.B., J.C.D., The Interdict, V-163 pp., 1930.
57. O'NEILL, REV. WILLIAM H., J.C.D., Papal Rescripts of Favor, VII-218 pp., 1930.
58. BASTNAGEL, REV. CLEMENT VINCENT, J.U.D., The Appointment of Parochial Adjutants and Assistants, XV-257 pp., 1930.
59. FERRY, REV. WILLIAM A., A.B., J.C.D., Stole Fees, X-107 pp., 1930.
60. COSTELLO, REV. JOHN MICHAEL, A.B., J.C.D., Domicile and Quasi-Domicile, VII-201 pp., 1930.
61. KREMER, REV. MICHAEL NICHOLAS, A.B., S.T.B., J.C.D., Church Support in the United States, VI-136 pp., 1930.
62. ANGULO, REV. LUIS MARTINEZ, C.M., J.C.D., Legislacion de la Iglesia Catholica sobre la intencion en la aplicacion de la Misa, VII-104 pp., 1931.
63. FREY, REV. WOLFGANG NORBERT, O.S.B., A.B., J.C.D., The Act of Religious Profession, VIII-174 pp., 1931.
64. ROBERTS, REV. JAMES BRENDAN, A.B., J.C.D., The Banns of Matrimony, XIV-140 pp., 1931.
65. RYDER, REV. RAYMOND ALOYSIUS, A.B., J.C.D., Simony, IX-151 pp., 1931.
66. CAMPAGNA, MICHAEL ANGELO, Ph.B., J.U.D., Il Vacario Generale del Vescovo, VII-205 pp., 1931.
67. COX, REV. JOSEPH GODFREY, A.B., J.C.D., The Administration of Seminaries, VI-124 pp., 1931.
68. GREGORY, REV. DONALD JOSEPH, S.T.B., J.U.D., The Pauline Privilege, XV-165 pp., 1931.
69. DONOHUE, REV. JOHN FRANCIS, M.A., J.C.D., The Impediment of Crime, VIII-110 pp., 1931.
70. DOOLEY, REV. EUGENE ALOYSIUS, O.M.I., J.C.D., Church Law on Sacred Relics, IX-143 pp., 1931.

71. Orth, Rev. Clement Raymond, O.M.C., J.C.D., The Approbation of Religious Institutes, 171 pp., 1931.
72. Pernicone, Rev. Joseph M., A.B., J.C.D., The Ecclesiastical Prohibition of Books, XII-267 pp., 1932.
73. Clinton, Rev. Connell, A.B., J.C.L., The Paschal Precept, 1932.
74. Donnelly, Rev. Francis B., A.M., S.T.L., J.C.L., The Diocesan Synod, 1932.
75. Torrente, Rev. Camilo, C.M.F., J.C.L., Las Processiones Sagradas, 1932.
76. Murphy, Rev. Edwin J., C.PP.S., J.C.L., Suspension Ex Informata Conscientia, 1932.
77. MacKenzie, Rev. Eric F., A.M., S.T.L., J.C.L., The Delict of Heresy in its Commission, Penalization, Absolution, 1932.
78. Lyons, Rev. Avitus E., S.T.B., J.C.L., The Collegiate Tribunal of First Instance, 1932.
79. Connolly, Rev. Thomas A., J.C.L., Appeals, 1932.
80. Sangmeister, Rev. Joseph V., A.B., J.C.L., Force and Fear as Precluding Matrimonial Consent, 1932.
81. Jaeger, Rev. Leo A., A.B., J.C.L., The Administration of Vacant and Quasi-Vacant Dioceses in the United States, 1932.
82. Rimlinger, Rev. Herbert T., J.C.L., Error Invalidating Matrimonial Consent, 1932.
83. Barrett, Rev. John D. M., S.S., J.C.L., Comparative Study of the Third Plenary Council and the Code, 1932.

www.ingramcontent.com/pod-product-compliance
Lightning Source LLC
LaVergne TN
LVHW050250080826
844660LV00012B/618

* 9 7 8 0 8 1 3 2 2 2 7 0 7 *